The Incarnality of Being

SUNY series in Environmental Philosophy and Ethics
J. Baird Callicott and John van Buren, editors

The Incarnality of Being

The Earth, Animals, and the Body in Heidegger's Thought

Frank Schalow

State University of New York Press

Published by
State University of New York Press, Albany

Printed in the United States of America

For information, address State University of New York Press,
194 Washington Avenue, Suite 305, Albany, NY 12210–2384

Production by Michael Haggett
Marketing by Michael Campochiaro

Library of Congress Cataloging in Publication Data

Schalow, Frank, 1956–
The incarnality of being : the earth, animals, and the body in Heidegger's thought / Frank Schalow.
p. cm. — (SUNY series in environmental philosophy and ethics)
Includes bibliographical references and index.
ISBN 0-7914-6735-X (hardcover : alk. paper)
ISBN 978-0-7914-6736-7 (pbk. : alk. paper)
1. Heidegger, Martin, 1889–1976. 2. Incarnation. I. Title. II. Series.

B3279.H4S3365 2006
193—dc22

2005014017

ISBN-13: 978-0-7914-6735-0 (hardcover : alk. paper)

10 9 8 7 6 5 4 3 2 1

To Michael E. Zimmerman

Contents

Acknowledgments

I wish to credit John van Buren for giving me the guidance and encouragement to bring this project to fruition. I also wish to thank J. Baird Callicott, the coeditor of this series, along with Jane Bunker and her staff at the State University of New York Press. I must also include Parvis Emad for his continual support of my efforts to develop new possibilities for interpreting Heidegger's thought.

During the years of composing my book, I have received direction from Daniel Dahlstrom, Todd Furman, Charles Guignon, Donald Hanks, Lawrence Hatab, Edward Johnson, George Kovacs, Susan Krantz, Michael Langlais, Eric Nelson, Gerald Nosich, Richard Polt, Dennis J. Schmidt, and Alan Soble.

I would also like to express my appreciation to those who have unselfishly given of their friendship over the years: Julie Bates, Shawn Finney, Kenneth Kahn, Brittany Tucker, and Michael Verderame.

Thanks also goes to the following editors for first publishing earlier versions of portions of chapters 1, 3, and 4 as the following articles:

"Decision, Dilemma, and Disposition: The Incarnatedness of Ethical Action," *Existentia* 22:3–4 (2002): 241–51. Gábor Ferge, ed. (ch. 3)

"Everydayness and the Problem of Human Addiction," *Southwest Philosophy Review* 19:2 (July 2003): 91–106. Jim Swindler, ed. (ch. 1)

"Repeating Heidegger's Analysis of Everydayness," *Philosophy Today* 46:3 (Fall 2002): 275–84. David Pelleauer, ed. (ch. 1)

"Who Speaks for the Animals? Heidegger and the Question of Animal Welfare," *Environmental Ethics* 22 (Fall 2000): 259–72. Eugene Hargrove, ed. (ch. 4).

Introduction

In recent years, contemporary continental philosophy has increasingly come to appreciate the importance of the problem of embodiment. And yet among those thinkers who have had the greatest influence on shaping this tradition, Martin Heidegger stands out as having neglected this problematic, even though he devotes considerable attention to the importance of humanity's "dwelling" upon the *earth* and develops a *radical* concept thereof.[1] This tension between emphasizing the earth and downplaying the body becomes never more evident than when we reflect upon a single parenthetical statement from the first division of Heidegger's magnum opus, *Being and Time* (1927). Upon addressing the lived character of our spatial comportment, directionality, and orientation, he remarks: "This 'bodily nature' hides a whole problematic of its own, though we shall not treat it here."[2] Can we, by drawing upon the entirety of Heidegger's thought, recover the body as an explicit concern of his phenomenology? In this book, I will attempt to answer this question affirmatively, and, in the process, show the environmental, ecological, and ethical implications of transposing the issue of embodiment into the forefront of Heidegger's thinking.

To develop this problematic, it will be necessary to address the omissions in Heidegger's earlier thought, which his discussion of the earth in the "Origin of the Work of Art" (1935) begins to make apparent.[3] Specifically we must counter a trend in *Being and Time* that he attempts to rectify in *Contributions to Philosophy* (1938), namely, the tendency to overplay the importance of temporality at the expense of addressing the corollary occurrence of spatiality.[4] While in the late 1920s Heidegger appeals to time as the key to uncovering the meaning of being, in *Contributions* he more concretely addresses the dynamic of temporality by considering its occurrence in conjunction with spatiality, that is, as the interdependence of "time-space" (*Zeit-Raum*). Space reemerges as the place (Ort) where being discloses itself within the scope of human existence's (Dasein's) historical sojourn on the earth. In his 1962 lecture, "Time and Being," Heidegger reflects upon the importance of addressing his earlier omission: "The attempt in *Being and Time*, section 70, to derive spatiality from temporality is untenable."[5]

In the following, I will observe Heidegger's self-testimonials and develop the clues that he leaves, by his hermeneutics of facticity, that embodiment constitutes an important permutation in how being becomes manifest to us. By developing this theme of the *incarnality of being*, I will open up a range of pivotal topics whose exploration will bring Heidegger's thinking to bear on various provocative questions of contemporary philosophy: sexuality, the intersection of human and animal life, the precarious future of the earth we inhabit,[6] and the implications that reclaiming our embodiment has upon an ethics and a politics that take into consideration the current ecological crisis. Because sexuality is among those issues that Heidegger seems to have neglected, my appeal to our embodiment and tie to nature (*physis*) assumes a provocative character.

In chapter 1, I undertake the task of "repeating" Heidegger's analysis of everydayness within the context provided by the facticity of our contemporary existence. I expand this analysis to include the way that the computer age has altered the concept of the everyday work world, as well as the ubiquitous problems that bring our own "embodied" condition into question (e.g., the plight of addiction from "substance abuse" to Internet gambling). In chapter 2, I bring the issue of embodiment into the foreground by addressing that aspect of human existence that perhaps most epitomizes it—but that Heidegger ignores—the predisposition toward sex. I thereby take the initial steps to confront objections to Heidegger's tendency to discount the problem of embodiment, as advanced by such critics as Hans Jonas and David Krell.[7] In chapter 3, I raise the question of what ethics means for Heidegger at the historical crossroads where we balance the prospect of the earth's destruction with the possibility of safeguarding it for future generations. In the oblique form of a series of questions from *Contributions*, Heidegger expresses concern about the problem of exploiting nature for the purpose of our leisure and diversion. As a prelude to his influential critique of technology in the early 1950s, he emphasizes for the first time the *danger* of machination and the corollary prospect of destroying the earth:

> And finally what was left [of nature] was only "scenery" and recreational opportunity and even this still calculated into the gigantic and arranged [through machination] for the masses? And then? Is this the end?
>
> Why does earth keep silent in this destruction?[8]

In this ominous way, Heidegger provides an occasion to address the incarnality of our being-in-the-world, the manner of our dwelling on the earth, as well as our kinship with all organic life. Given this emphasis on incarnality, the *ethos* of our being-in-the-world broadens to include our stewardship of the earth and our conservatorship of animals, as well as our concern for the welfare of other human beings.

In chapter 4, I consider the possibility of extending ethics to include a concern for the welfare of animals, the translation of Heidegger's "original ethics" from his "Letter on 'Humanism'" (1947)[9] into a "*transhuman ethics*."[10] In chapter 5, I explore the multifaceted character of Heidegger's concept of freedom, which is presupposed in his formulation of an original ethics. In this way, I will extend his vision of an original ethics so it can address the problems arising from the *contemporary ecological crisis* and thereby provide the cornerstone for any forum of political exchange, the "body politic." In chapter 6, I show how the entire sweep of Heidegger's thinking, or what can be construed as the "turning" (*die Kehre*), points to "incarnality" as a distinct permutation of being's manifestness, as exemplifying the diversity of its appearances. The incarnality of being, then, becomes a gathering point for the development of language that is sufficiently nuanced and concrete to address the most provocative issues of our era, including the impact that our *stewardship of the earth may have upon future generations*.

Does Heidegger's critique of technology provide the prototype for today's ecological awareness?[11] As this book demonstrates, how we answer this question depends to a large extent on how radically we develop the problem of embodiment as a central focus of his phenomenology. Ultimately, my thesis about the incarnality of being proves compelling, because it enables us to enter the debate about Heidegger *as* a protoecologist precisely at the juncture where concerns about today's ecological crisis intersect with the expanding frontiers of ethics and ontology.

Chapter 1

The Materiality of the World

What do we mean by "embodiment," by the "human body," by "physicality?" Can the body become for Heidegger, as it was for Maurice Merleau-Ponty, a "cardinal *ontological* problem?"[1] Could this question provide another avenue for raising a perennial question, which due to its historical forgottenness Heidegger sought to re-ask, the question of the meaning of being? Following in Heidegger's footsteps, any concern for "meaning" must, after all, take a hermeneutical form. The "hermes" of interpretation is the intermediary that guides us in rendering the indeterminate determinate, in addressing something *as* something, in this case in allowing being to become manifest in terms of physicality. But the formulation of any such meaning-question must assume a historical character, because human understanding is historically situated and is *always concretely enacted through one mode or another*, for example, "everydayness." Thus when we ask the preceding, we are asking what is distinctive about our historical circumstances that could allow us to translate the perennial question of being into an enigma pertaining to the fact of embodiment? Indeed, we are seeking the "between" (*Zwischen*) that would enable us to address the manifestation of being in terms of the permutations of physicality and materiality.

In this chapter, I will take the initial steps to mark the crossover between the historical presuppositions that govern Heidegger's selection of a point of departure for re-asking the question of being and the chasm, the *chiasmus*, that separates us, emerging on the cusp of the twenty-first century to criticize his thought. Only by marking the historical variables that shape the relevancy of our point of departure can we, as inquirers, take up Heidegger's task and pursue it through the opening provided by our era.[2] I will begin by identifying the common thread interweaving our lives into a "global" culture, the engine propelling technology in all of its facets, whose impact Heidegger never foresaw despite condemning its Americanized expression, namely, the economic system of capitalism. More specifically, I will show how the emergence of capitalism as the center of the dominant contemporary "lifestyle" provides a historical backdrop against which to recast Heidegger's *analysis of everydayness* and retrospectively confirm his account of the everyday "they-self" as prevalent in various cultural forms. Specifically, the downward plunge into the cycle of production/consumption, which occurs under the technological rule of capitalism, epitomizes the tendency of falling inherent in human existence. This manner of falling into the grips of technology makes explicit a latent concern for materiality, which is determined less by the physical processes of production as by their global linchpin, namely, the medium of exchange (e.g., currency and money). As this medium makes explicit, humanity's experience of materiality is always "translinguistic" or linguistically mediated, if only at a prearticulated level of a gesture (e.g., a wink).

After addressing the issue of materiality, I will identify an "aberration" of mass society that both has its roots in falling and illustrates a predicament to which the fact of our embodiment makes us vulnerable, namely, addiction. Heidegger provides the key to exploring the unique dynamic of this phenomenon, in its manifold dimensions, in such a way that addiction appears as a basic "modification" of Dasein's being as care, or an existential tendency inherent in everydayness.[3] Why should we turn to a phenomenon such as addiction in order to address our manner of embodiment? The answer lies in how human existence always discloses (or conceals) itself from the side of one modality or another, including that shaped by the distinctive historical-cultural-environmental climate in which we already find ourselves. By undertaking these concrete analyses, we will "repeat" the account of everydayness that Heidegger undertakes in the first division of *Being and Time*, and, indeed, according to the dictates and design of his own hermeneutical methodology. The outcome of this repetition will be to raise the problem of rethinking spatiality in conjunction with, rather than in subordination to, temporality, which correlates with the precedent set by Western philosophy to privilege the soul over the body, spirit over materiality.

Work, Exchange, and Technology

Rilke once exhorted us to "resolve always to be a beginner."[4] In executing his hermeneutical method, Heidegger follows this mandate in setting an example for future philosophical inquiry. No matter how far we progress in such inquiry, we never abandon the beginning but instead recover it and reaffirm its possibility. In selecting everydayness as his point of departure, Heidegger emphasizes that his inquiry into being must always return to this starting place, in order that its "presuppositions" can be further clarified by the questioning already undertaken. By clarifying the totality of these presuppositions, or what Heidegger calls the "hermeneutical situation," the inquiry yields to the openness that all along has provided it guidance. The opportunity then arises to "repeat" the beginning through its inception within this openness. As we reenact this beginning, the inquiry's pattern of development—of an advance predicated on the counter-movement of return—can appear as an instance of temporalizing itself whose historical concretion provides the backdrop for re-asking the question of being. The circular movement of this return—the hallmark of the hermenuetical circle—stems from the historical character of human understanding and thereby testifies to its finitude.

Heidegger does not dictate the terms of the hermeneutical circle, however, as does the circular character of understanding, whose potential for disclosedness originates from the ecstases of temporality. The more diligently we employ the hermeneutical method, the more we come to appreciate our place within a concrete historical situation. If as inquirers we adhere to his mandate of "repetition," then the reinception of everydayness as the point of departure for inquiry must incorporate the changes in the historical situation in which the inquirer finds himself or herself. We must reconcile the analysis of everydayness with the specific facticity of the inquirer, in such a way that the contingencies of our historical situation in the twenty-first century reinform our experience of the everyday use of tools, and so on. In this regard, the insights of Heidegger's subsequent inquiry into technology can be redirected to illuminate the everyday realm of work, because it is only by anticipating the era of "globalization" in which we reside that his discussions acquire the contemporary relevance they do. Accordingly, the analysis of everydayness must bring to light how the modus operandi of work comes to be redefined by these contemporary forces of globalization. In this regard, we would follow the example set by Heidegger's own hermeneutics, in which the insights of later discussions serve to illuminate the presuppositions of earlier ones to permit the continual widening of the circumference of the hermeneutical circle.

While philosophy, unlike other disciplines, is distinguished by its preoccupation with beginnings, Heidegger differentiates his interest in the same from other philosophers—whether Plato or Aristotle, Descartes or Kant, Hegel or Husserl—by his desire to arrive at the least presumptuous of all beginnings. That is, Heidegger seeks a point of departure that is most removed from a concern for the perennial topic of philosophy, being itself. Indeed, he selects everydayness as his point of departure in order to identify the basic tendency of human existence to neglect the question of being. By beginning at this prephilosophical level of indifference, Heidegger proceeds from the most innocuous presupposition of what each of us, as Dasein, already understands about himself or herself. Given this orientation, hermeneutics can avoid prejudging the inquiry with the introduction of prefabricated concepts about "being," which may be derivative and thereby allow Dasein's pre-understanding to point the way to the emergence of a primordial understanding of its being, and, correlatively, of being itself. By entering the inquiry at the juncture where a consideration of being remains most withdrawn, hermeneutics can then allow the dislocations and omissions in everyday existence to indicate, by contrast, the origin of ontological understanding, and, thereby, of the manifestation proper to being itself. But, most importantly, by tracing the emergence of the question of being from a prephilosophical level, Heidegger establishes the wider significance of this question, the scope of its relevance; he thereby marks the experience of "wonder" that summons each individual to engage in philosophical inquiry and to make that endeavor the foremost consideration of all.

We seem to state the obvious in saying that philosophy must begin where we already are, with the pre-understanding of everyday existence. But is the concept of "everydayness," which Heidegger outlines in the first division of *Being and Time,* set in granite, or, instead, is it open to revision as the historical circumstances of the inquirer change?[5] Before attempting to answer this question, we must recall that part of what is involved in the self's facticity is its embeddedness in a culture oriented toward change and development. In light of this observation, I will attempt to show that a revision of Heidegger's analysis of everydayness is not only possible, indeed, it is necessary, for this revision fulfills an explicit hermeneutical mandate of retrieving the point of departure for ontological inquiry, that is, of "repeating" the earlier analysis in order to uncover its presuppositions within a wider historical context. As Heidegger states at the conclusion of *Being and Time*—quoting an earlier passage—"philosophy is 'universal phenomenological ontology,' and takes it departure from the hermeneutic of Dasein, which, as an analytic of *existence*," has made fast the guiding line for all philosophical inquiry at the point where it *arises* and to which it *returns*.[6]

A.

The fact that we are immersed in history means that the variables that govern our consideration of the equipmental whole of everydayness may be much different than those that first led Heidegger to undertake such a phenomenological analysis in the 1920s. The facticity that distinguishes those who live in the "information age" of computers and e-commerce is different from that which defined our predecessors who inhabited the industrialized realm of typewriters and corner markets. If everydayness is simply the routine by which we adapt to changes in *technē*, then awareness of the global character of this change defines modern technology as such. Thus the *technē* of technology and everydayness become two sides of the same coin, insofar as the latter maps on a global scale the practical dealings that preoccupy us in the immediate proximity of our everyday environment. For Heidegger, then, the question of technology springs from the soil of everydayness; conversely, a change in our experience of technology—the historical unfolding of its possibilities—requires altering our concept of the everyday world of equipment. Insofar as Heidegger equates the *technē* of technology with production, which in turn comes to light in its nascent form in the everyday work world, a change in the face of contemporary technology implies another axis along which the significance of equipmental relations unfolds. Given this new axis of the work world, the basic modus operandi of everydayness is no longer production but exchange.

In this section, I will show how the issue of exchange remains latent in Heidegger's critique of "productionist metaphysics" as providing the *Gestalt* for proliferating technology on a global scale.[7] Then I will establish how "exchange" has an ontological meaning, which in turn can be interpreted in light of the dynamics of the disclosure of being itself. Finally, I will argue that reintroducing economic issues compensates for Heidegger's neglect of them, *insofar as it interweaves the concern for our condition as embodied beings into the composition of everydayness.* For this reintroduction yields the key to retrieving his earlier analysis of the everyday work world—where embodiment becomes as much a dimension of "world" as it is of the "there"—albeit now recast in light of his insight into technology. Thus a new hermeneutic circle emerges in which a reexamination of Heidegger's critique of technology returns us to his analysis of everydayness, and, conversely, the repetition of this analysis (with an emphasis on exchange versus production) both sharpens and expands his portrait of technology.

When Heidegger developed his analysis of everydayness in the mid-1920s, he was undoubtedly influenced by the cultural milieu of his time. His examples from the first division of *Being and Time* bear this out: the appeal to the hammer and nail to distinguish the matrix of instrumentality, or the car, turn signal, and road sign to outline the totality of signifying relations which makes explicit the disclosure of world.[8] By the same token, Heidegger undertakes a phenomenological description of everydayness in order to delineate a structure intrinsic to any culture. He establishes a common thread in how we face the regimentation of daily life or the fact that in any cultural context human beings become embroiled in certain routines and succumb to the pressures of social conformity. In any event, the work-a-day-world arises in conjunction with a nexus of social relationships, in such a way that world admits different variations to accommodate a diversity of cultural dealings and pursuits (even within a single culture).

For Heidegger, "everydayness" is first and foremost an existential-ontological structure. While his own vision of instrumentalism includes components of twentieth-century industrialized society, he also acknowledges from the opposite pole how the routine concerns of everydayness pervade even "primitive" mentality. In chapter 6 of the first division of *Being and Time*, Heidegger recounts the "fable" of care that exemplifies the concernful awareness that so-called "mythic" Dasein displays about its "thrownness" into a situation, its relation to others, and the purposiveness of all activities. While the thread of everydayness traverses both the worlds of industrialized and mythic Dasein, its texture of composition changes from culture to culture and historical epoch to historical epoch. And since philosophy is essentially a historical enterprise, it is equally necessary to reopen the question of the composition of everydayness, as it occurs, so to speak, "today." Through the exercise of hermeneutic phenomenology in *Being and Time*, Heidegger unfolds the minimal set of presuppositions that governs the development of philosophical understanding from its origin in everyday life. Conversely, upon entering a new millennium, we must reconsider how the routine of everydayness as displayed in twenty-first-century America both extends Heidegger's analysis and incorporates nuances that reflect contemporary society.

When placed within its wider context, Heidegger's discussion of instrumentality coincides with his attempt to address the being of "intraworldly" things. In *Being and Time*, he coins the term "ready-to-hand" (*zuhanden*) to describe the being of equipment. When immersed in everydayness, the self's preoccupation with the ready-to-hand leads it to forsake larger concerns about the "meaning" of human existence. The familiarity of routine has the indirect effect of rendering human existence as unproblematic as possible. Thus only through the interruption of this "security" does Dasein take the initiative to question itself, to defer its interest in "mastering" things in favor of addressing the larger concern for who it is.

By contrast, the self's preoccupation with instrumentality goes hand in hand with its tendency to become absorbed in the concerns of the impersonal "they-self," the ubiquitous crowd.[9] An indifference to the meaning of human existence and ultimately to being itself follows from Dasein's identification with the "they-self." What remains ambiguous for Heidegger, however, is whether the importance of instrumental dealings stems from the inordinate importance that the "they" places on them, or instead whether a preoccupation with the things of instrumentality is already inherent in Dasein's tendency to "fall." While this ambiguity may not have been problematic for Heidegger, it nevertheless may be symptomatic of specific limitations in his analysis of everydayness, namely, an emphasis on "production" to the detriment of the "exchange" side of the equation.

In addressing equipmentality in *Being and Time*, Heidegger incorporates Aristotle's portrait of the ends-means continuum that culminates in the project of "that for the sake of which," of some possibility of human existence as care. To a large extent, this Aristotelian vision remains intact more than 2,000 years later, even as industrialization replaces an agrarian society, and the "information age" replaces industrialization. Yet the succession of paradigm shifts that have transpired over the centuries may make the Aristotelian view inadequate to address the different axis on which the world turns today. Among Heidegger's students, Herbert Marcuse was among the first to relocate the roots of everyday instrumentality—whether approached economically (Marx) or even phenomenologically—in the "technological work-world."[10] Yet even Marcuse's understanding of technology lagged dramatically behind the advances of the information/digital age.

If there is one aspect of technology that Heidegger underestimated, it is the exponential rate of change that occurs once technology provides the spring for its own innovation. This self-propelling character of technology means that the immediacy of what was originally classified as "ready-to-hand" is now refracted through the optic lens of an artificial system of computer icons and graphics, for example, the mentality of "having the 'world' at your fingertips." Thus your hammer may be broken, but the possibility of its replacement hinges on the presence of an inventory that is registered through a computer at some centralized place of distribution. In chapter 2 of the first division of *Being and Time*, Heidegger points to the breakdown of the nexus of equipmental relations as offering a phenomenological clue to the appearance of world; the unready-to-hand points back to the completeness of the equipmental totality that is presupposed in everyday praxis. But with the advent of information technology, such dislocations exceed the confines of any specific environment and instead interface on many different fronts—like a matrix—cutting across multiple environments simultaneously. Moreover, it is not just the ensemble of equipment that is relevant; instead, what proves pivotal is the anonymous character of the process in which these various items are linked together within a global network—a "transactional" interreality, of which "cyberspace" is the hyperbole. In the spirit of Heidegger's famous description of the "they" (*das Man*), the impersonalization of everyday praxis, lies as much in this transactional dimension (i.e., in exchange, as it does in production). In this process of impersonalization, the production/use of things (e.g., the ready-to-hand) takes a backseat to the strategies for their marketing and selling as commodities, what Marcuse calls "total commerialization."[11]

While we may debate to what extent the paradigm of the ready-to-hand has changed, what becomes significant is how this change has made the physical aspect of working depend upon an *artificial mechanism for the mobilization of work itself*—the medium of exchange that connects workers together from every quadrant of the globe. Through his interpretation of Ernst Jünger's writings, Heidegger was familiar with the concept of the "mobilization of the worker."[12] But for the most part, work remains an extension of a human being's use of technological devices in proximity to him or her rather than hinging upon a communicative network of exchange relations. This network creates new synergies that redefine the nature of work itself, transposing the importance of what we do and what we own into a global nexus of transactions on which we all depend for our livelihoods. By the same token, money assumes an ambiguous role both as a way to satisfy material needs and as a token or cipher to communicate the complex synergies and partnerships to which we all belong as members of this "exchange" economy.

As such, money is not merely a numerical measure but is also an "insignia" by which human beings express "concern" about their own welfare as natural and social beings. In this regard, Heidegger's view of the "mobilization of the worker" seems to suffer from underestimating Karl Marx's insight into the unique status of money as "capital." That is, qua capital money is not only a "bartering" tool (having a "use-value"),[13] but is also a vehicle for expressing the confluence of interests among different members of society, a formula for simplifying diverse interests (e.g., of both need and desire) into a common language. As Marx emphasizes, money is more than just the physical currency that we circulate, or, even, as in the case of gold, a representation of the value of that currency. Instead, money as capital is the "declension" of worth that *bespeaks* society's interest (in the value) of the commodities we exchange—the entire circuit of buying and selling; money thereby "stands for" the process of circulation itself, its social as well as fiscal dynamics.[14]

If we take Marx's clue about the importance of capital, and transpose it within the macro-context of Heidegger's critique of technology—rather than utilize that analysis for the purpose of advancing one ideology over another (e.g., communism over capitalism)—another portrait emerges: *exchange becomes part of the composition of the existentiale of everydayness*. To the extent that we emphasize the priority of exchange over production, and shift the focus of Heidegger's discussion of everydayness accordingly, we must then address how this change occurs in ontological terms. No matter in which cultural milieu we may exist, and however everydayness in turn comes to be expressed, in one way or another, care (*Sorge*) continues to define the constitution of human being. And if exchange is to define a mode of interaction made possible by care, then the importance of money must depend on how it contributes to the self's potentiality or ability to be (*Seinkönnen*). Indeed, money is not only something with which we are passively concerned (e.g., as in whether the New York Yankees win another World Series); money instead pertains to the capability we have, or, more specifically, to facilitating the development of that potential.

In a free-market economy, to be of "means" is an inescapable aspect of having opportunity. Insofar as the potentiality to be, and, concomitantly, specific possibilities, define the self, money derives its importance through the creation of opportunity, for example, travel or a college education. But does not the allusion to "being of means" suggest that the value of money resides in its instrumentality? On the contrary, the "of means" is as much a suggestion of an ability that poses a challenge to the self, as an instrument of use (i.e., use-value) in acquiring things to possess. Once again, money exhibits an ambivalent character because we associate its value with the material goods that can be bought with it. Yet when construed as having an affiliation as much with care as with things ready-to-hand, the "ability to be" assigns to money its importance as the key to unlocking the self's opportunities within the exchange economy of capitalism. In support of this contrast, we can point to Heidegger's distinction in *Being and Time* between "not genuine" and "genuine," by which the development of any possibility implies a tension between the self's pursuit of instrumentality and its choice of individuality.[15]

But did not Heidegger reject capitalism particularly as epitomized in the American way of life? Indeed, he did. But I am not suggesting that capitalism is a self-sustaining system, as much as indicating how information technology relocates the axis of everyday commerce on a global plane, thereby integrating the capitalist medium of exchange into the fabric of everydayness. This view is still consistent with Heidegger's claim that technology unfolds as a historical possibility, which exacts special social and economic changes. Conversely, the medium of exchange exemplified in capitalism assumes its unique dynamism precisely because of information technology. When seen in this light, capitalism becomes the preferred economic system less through accident than through the constellation of historical circumstances within the frame (*Gestell*) of technology.[16]

Are we not going far afield from Heidegger's thinking, even if a new questioning of technology allows us to mark the convergence between the milieu of everydayness and the ubiquity of the exchange medium within postindustrialized society? After all, Heidegger was primarily concerned with the question of being. Is there any warrant in believing that being in Heidegger's sense exhibits a dynamism that enables us to reinterpret the "exchange medium" in ontological terms? To this question we will now turn.

B.

If we take Heidegger's ontology seriously, then we must look to being, to the diversity of its manifestations, to discover the wellspring for our social and worldly possibilities. And if we are to include material concerns among these possibilities, then the same must be true in the case of economics. Thus the sense we ascribe to economics arises from the side of our experience of being. Conversely, an inquiry into economics would cast light, to paraphrase a famous line from *Introduction to Metaphysics*, "on how matters stand with being." Since we are finite, the conditions, whereby being invites a response from us or, reciprocally, what allows us to participate in its disclosure, will define the most primordial sense of economics. Among these conditions of finitude, of course, is time, and space as well, whose interdependence (in clearing the "there") demarcates the scope of human inhabitation.

Because time and space are intrinsic to being's manifestation, together they (*Zeit-Raum*) condition our earthly sojourn and allow for the acquisition of "roots" or a sense of belonging to the wider expanse of things.[17] For Heidegger, this momentum of "bringing into one's own" (*Ereignis* as appropriation or "enowning"), of gaining a sense of rootedness, predetermines all other senses of "having," "possessing," or "owning." The transitoriness of time and the restriction of space determine the relevance of whatever material benefits we may attain, the money we may accumulate, or the things we may possess. Indeed, the value of whatever we possess is a function of these other dimensions—of the conjunction of time-space. For example, it is only due to a certain temporal allocation that we describe as "leisure" that having an expensive yacht becomes important, not to mention the spatial proximity of living by a coastline. Heidegger underscores this point in a lecture course from 1931–32:

> The genuine comportmental character of having becomes a self-losing of he who has. The autonomy of the self gives way to the contingency and arbitrariness of needs and desires to be immediately satisfied. Although this kind of having has the appearance of fulfilled possession, it is not an *authentic having in the strict sense of authenticity. What we understand by authenticity [Eignentlichkeit] is that mode of human existence wherein man (authentically) appropriates himself, i.e., wherein he comes to himself and can be himself. The having which we have just described is inauthentic, because its apparent freedom of disposition fundamentally amounts to servitude under the arbitrary rule of needs.*[18]

In this regard, the temporalizing of time and the spatializing of space are the "protoeconomic" dimensions that condition all other economies.

We often refer to nature as operating according to an "economy" uniquely its own. For example, the cycle of birth and death, the regeneration of life, is itself an economic process in committing everything within nature to the dynamism of emerging into presence and withdrawing into absence: witness the blossoming and withering of a rose. Of course, Heidegger emphasizes the parallels between his own conception of being and the Greek sense of nature as *physis* or self-emerging presence.[19] Through his analysis of technology, he shows how the historical manifestation of being conditions our preoccupation with the network of everyday involvements and economic concerns. Following the example of the pre-Socratics, Heidegger also suggests that being displays its own unique economy. Indeed, the manner of historical appropriation commits the plurality of manifestations comprising "being" to an economy of its own. This special economy becomes evident in the way that the "negation" proper to being does not diminish its efficacy, but, on the contrary, serves as a "conservatorship" and preservation of the luminosity of its truth.[20] As Heidegger illustrates in *The Principle of Reason*, the withdrawal and concealment of being provide an "incubation period" (*Incubationszeit*) during which their meanings remain shielded (albeit dormant) until the occasion of their subsequent recollection.[21] Once again, we discover that even on this highest ontological plane, time and space remain vital to coordinating the "economy" into which the dynamic "exchange" between being's withdrawal and emergence, concealment and unconcealment is gathered, distributed, and preserved in all of its variations. Being's historical manifestation is not a linear progress in the Hegelian sense but is, as Michael Heim suggests, the "trade-offs" of "gains and losses" in the "historical drift" of culture.[22]

A famous remark from Heraclitus reinforces my attempt to unfold the ontological implications of Heidegger's thought and to bring it into dialogue with economics proper: "All things are an exchange for fire, and fire for all things; as goods are for gold, and gold for goods."[23] For Heraclitus, change is not absolute gain or absolute loss but instead is a continuum of exchange wherein the diversity of nature's appearances converts from one thing to another. There seems to be a compelling link between a more esoteric sense of "economy" ascribed to being and a more mundane sense exhibited in the material transactions of everyday life. If the Heideggerian allusion to "economy" is not to be merely metaphorical, then we must show how fiscal issues exhibit concerns so all-encompassing that their relevance can only be understood in ontological terms.

C.

While capitalism has triumphed as the major fiscal system of our day—in a way that would have shocked Heidegger—it may not have a monopoly on all forms of exchange. Based on the spirit of competition in a free-market arena, capitalism is a system that separates its participants according to alliances of self-interest—Microsoft™ versus American Online™, Coca-Cola™ versus Pepsi™. But perhaps there is another form of exchange that brings together individuals of diverse interests and joins them despite their competitive desires. The mode of exchange embodies on a cultural level the finitude that animates the cyclical movement of being's disclosure: repetition. This exchange is a mode of reciprocation, the kind that Heidegger first identifies as the dynamic whereby the self pays homage to the cultural tradition of which it is an heir. The appropriation of tradition is a form of exchange as "reciprocal rejoinder" (*Erwiderung*) by which the self receives the bequest of the past only through the reciprocity of a promise of safeguarding that legacy and then "handing it down" (*Überliefern*) to successive generations. The cyclical movement of repetition shapes the contours of Dasein's understanding—its confinement to finitude—and thereby mandates that any ontological inquiry returns to its point of departure, the hallmark of the hermeneutical circle.

While an appeal to this kind of "exchange" may be enlightening, does Heidegger at any point employ concrete economic locutions to provide a clue for correlating the fiscal and ontological sense of "economy?" Indeed, the German word *Schuld,* or guilt, betrays a vestige of economic meaning in conveying a sense of indebtedness to the past. When we allude to someone's having to pay his or her "dues" in order to reach a certain station of life, for example, the literal connotation of *Schuld* still shines through. Although in its everyday usage *Schuld* assumes a negative connotation, when reenacted as a key to authentic existence "guilt" defines the self's way of taking over its capability for commitment and thereby renewing its ties to the past. When conceived positively, the "payback" of guilt is the exchange between accepting the gift of existence and exercising responsibility for one's having been endowed with the power to choose. Even in the most formal senses of authenticity and freedom, we discover a dynamic of exchange. But how is that dynamic different from other forms?

For Heidegger, freedom constitutes a "power" that is preserved precisely through its distribution, for example, in clearing the way for a spirited exchange between participants of a dialogue. This form of economy differs from that which is involved in the accumulation of prestige, money, and social status with which the "they" is preoccupied. In these instances, power is only attained given the corollary risk of its dissipation, as occurs in the case of the faded luster of a retired university president, for "economizing" in a more primordial sense is a mode of replenishment that stems from sharing and safeguarding rather than from monopolizing and exploiting. In this regard, temporality stands out as a cyclical movement that incubates possibilities of the past so that they can be recovered in the future, and, likewise, space unfolds human existence from its roots, from its place of dwelling. Together space and time comprise an "economy" that adheres to definite limits rather than annulling them in the totalizing drive of technology that "rations" earth's resources only when their depletion—witness today's energy crisis—poses the threat of scarcity (e.g., oil and gasoline).[24] The fact that we can distinguish between these two senses of economy suggests that it is relevant to formulate ontological questions to cast light on everyday economic matters.

But is not this appeal to ontology just another standard refrain that states that there are other things more important than money and prestige, a disclaimer that primarily makes sense within a Christian worldview? On the contrary, I am suggesting that if "exchange" can be understood in ontological terms, then we can appreciate the broader relevance of the fiscal processes that preoccupy us in our everyday lives. In other words, money is not simply a numerical measure. It is also a communicative vehicle for conveying the significance of our worldly activities, namely, the concern expressed for the self's condition as an "embodied" being, its embeddedness within a complex tapestry of relations to which nature and culture both contribute.

The capitalist may believe that financial assets compound in a vacuum, but the truth is, the synergies of prosperity within capitalism become important only through the maximization of opportunity by which the individual takes over the decision-making power of his or her life. Of course, there are different ideologies within capitalism that address how this end of "maximizing opportunity" can best be achieved. We need not concern ourselves with them here. What is important to see, however, is that no matter how prominent financial matters may become, they are still bound by ancillary concerns that merit ontological investigation: the distribution of freedom as a power with which human beings are endowed and its cultivation as a possibility for each individual to safeguard. The "letting be" of the other, the inviting of the voice of the other and the possibility of dissent, defines the heart of reciprocity that we must uphold as beneficiaries of the fruits of "autonomous" decision making, including that involved in the pursuit of wealth. These more primordial exchange relationships bound those that facilitate our ability to benefit from the economic processes of buying and selling.

And what about this pursuit of wealth? Is it not primarily an individual matter? Perhaps. But even here there is a finality to the amount of wealth that one can achieve in one's life, an economy in the distribution of time that bounds such fortunes from the period of their attainment to their bequest to one's descendants. The old adage "you can't take it with you" rings true in indexing time as the dimension that "economizes" all other economies, from the compounding of financial assets, to the enjoyment of the opportunity for leisure that it creates, to its ultimate divestiture through inheritance. And what role does space have? Without its corollary allocation, there can be no tangible benefits for the leisure we seek, no land on which to build a mansion, no fairways on which to hit a golf ball, no clear water in which to boat or swim.

Indeed, without the conservatorship of the earth, as well *as its bequest to future generations*—the greatest "inheritance" of all—all of the benefits that we associate with being wealthy add up to very little in the end. In a subsequent discussion (chapter 3), we will return to consider the importance of this inheritance, along with the question of whether we have an "*obligation to future generations*."

Would not it be ironic if what today falls under the heading of "ecology" actually receives its importance in connection with "economics"? Indeed, this may be true when we consider that each term shares a common root ("eco" as the "house," "residence" or "place of dwelling") *in such a way that the possibilities we ascribe to the stewardship of one's quest (i.e., ecology as caring for one's habitat) will inevitably hinge upon retrieving the ancestral meaning of "economics" as the "nomos" or "management" of this abode.* While on the surface ecology and economics seem to diverge sharply, historical destiny forms an uneasy alliance between them, just as it juxtaposes the greatest critic and innovator of technology in the twentieth century: Martin Heidegger and Bill Gates. Despite the historical gulf that separates them, the innovations of the latter have actually confirmed the prophecies of the former.

In heeding this destiny in his monumental essay "The Question Concerning Technology" in 1953, Heidegger displayed a foresight into the future globalization of *technē* (far surpassing the vision of most of his contemporaries), including the catastrophic danger inherent in weapons of mass destruction of which *today* we are more acutely aware than ever. This is why Heidegger remains a giant in twentieth-century philosophy, despite the shadow cast by his involvement in National Socialism. Yet because of these political leanings, on the one hand (including his disinterest in Karl Marx's economic analysis), and his limited grasp of the exponential growth of technology, on the other hand, Heidegger never envisioned how the advances of the "information age" would clear the way for the development of capitalism on a global scale. Indeed, in criticizing the "productionist" side of technology, he neglected to consider the other side of the equation—latent in his treatment of the "mobilization of the worker"—in which the processes of exchange become integral to understanding both the scope and limits of technological innovation today. As a result, he did not foresee how the tendency toward concealment inherent in (the routine of) the everyday work world becomes reenacted even more extensively in the ubiquity of our fiscal system. This occlusion creates an illusion of material comfort as witnessed, for example, in the promise of great wealth that lies at the other end of the "day trader's" click of a computer mouse. Like any illusion, this one has its importance, because in pointing to the concealment of being, it also indirectly points to the unfolding of its truth.

To decipher this clue, we must consider the implications that the *technē* of economic exchange has for redefining the workaday world, and, conversely, how the insight thereby achieved can both sharpen and expand Heidegger's critique of technology. The opening forth of the expanse of Dasein's finitude through temporality (the "there") finds its renewal in the reenactment of our thrown condition as embodied beings beset by economic concerns (the physicality of "world").

Whether developed from the side of the hermeneutics of facticity or from the side of the question concerning technology, the discussion of everydayness provides equal access to Heidegger's thinking. Thus the division between "early" and "later" Heidegger becomes irrelevant, because a new hermeneutical circle emerges that grants entrance to his thought at any point. By undertaking a repetition of Heidegger's analysis of everydayness, thinking can confront a "brave new world" in which the circuit of everyday involvements is interwoven into a global economy, and "money" becomes a language more universal than any single dialect.[25]

Indeed, the more we reinscribe economic issues into the composition of the *existentiale* of everydayness, the more we will discover that embodiment and materiality are parallel concerns that contribute to reshaping the landscape of the question of being. Embodiment cannot be reduced to the activities that are associated with the appendages of our physical beings, for example, the hands involved in the sensuality of touch.[26] Instead, such physicality includes a capacity to signify whose parameters are set by the disclosedness of the world itself, the nexus of reference relationships. The wink of an eye constitutes a gesture conveying a shared intimacy between friends. For Heidegger, such a gesture is an example of the prediscursive origin of language, prior to the articulation of words, which acquires its meaning through the way that the "winker" coinhabits a world with others. Rather than something static, materiality is an adjustment within the tension of our facticity to how we occupy a world. The case in point is the material character of an exchange medium of which money or currency is an instance. That is, the act of "handing over" money, whether physically or electronically, illustrates the translinguistic character of materiality, the double way in which the linguistic, as prediscursive, is tied to the physical (e.g., a handshake that signifies closing a deal), but, equally as important, the way in which materiality is always linguistically mediated through the context of being-in-the-world. From a Heideggerian standpoint, everydayness is the dynamic field of this translinguistic materiality.

We cannot fully appreciate the materiality of everydayness, however, without also considering the downside of having a body, namely, the potential to become addicted by certain substances of either an artificial or a natural origin. The elements that define addiction will be seen to arise from the structures defining Dasein's being as care, including the "intensification" of its tendency to fall. As Heidegger says in his essay "On the Essence of Truth," Dasein is a turning into misery, a turning into need.[27] Few phenomena illustrate this better than that of addiction, yet we cannot fully appreciate the material aspect of addiction without considering the unique mode of its transformation within the historical crucible of technology. Indeed, the ubiquity of the problem of addiction in today's society has its roots in the technological mechanisms of production and distribution, which allow drugs and alcohol (think of the scope of Internet sex sites) to be used on a global scale. *In the phenomenon of addiction, the physicality of the hand of the ready-to-hand, the "within-reach" of satiating desire, shines forth* in its worldly setting.

Problems Arising from Having a Body—Addiction

A.

In this section, I will employ Heidegger's fundamental ontology in order to provide a phenomenological account of an affliction of the self that is commonly called "addiction." The varieties and forms of addiction, as well as the so-called root causes—special topics of consideration for psychologists and physiologists alike—need not concern us here. Instead, the simple question that guides us is what is it about the constitution of human beings that makes them vulnerable to the aforementioned affliction, of which "substance abuse" would be the most frequent example, albeit not the only one. Conversely, the problem of human addiction offers an important and a unique perspective on the problem of human embodiment and what is distinctive to our experience of it as thrown into the world. *Here we need to cite a rare instance from Seminar in Le Thor (1968) where Heidegger, perhaps echoing Merleau-Ponty, differentiates between the "lived-body," as emerging within the meaningful context of the world, and the "body," as distinguishing only physiological processes.*[28] On the one hand, addiction is not simply a physical-physiological problem, as testified by the fact that in their natural habitat animals show no tendency to become addicted. Indeed, the propensity to become addicted, as will discover in the next chapter on sexuality, is interwoven into the fabric of the possibility of being-a-self, the capability of selfhood as such. On the other hand, the curious symptoms that psychologists associate with addiction, for example, in the case of substance abuse, withdrawal symptoms, and "mood alteration," provide evidence in a negative form that the capacity for selfhood cannot be divorced from the fact of embodiment, for without a body one could not fall prey to substance abuse, much less to the thrill and euphoria created by gambling or indulging in Internet pornography. Though much could be said on this topic, we must acknowledge the role played by dispositions—a chaotic vacillation between relief and discomfort, euphoria and fear—with the entire matrix of addiction, for these moods, which distinguish the character of the self's thrownness (*Geworfenheit*) into the world, *underlie the addict's experience of being placed at the mercy of a "bipolar" vacillation between extremes of emotion (e.g., of "highs" and "lows")*. The craving for "mood-altering" substances and the counter-problem of withdrawal symptoms hinge on the fact that dispositions are more than just "mental" states. Instead, moods indicate the way in which the individual already discovers himself or herself to be "thrown" into the world without the capability of ever completely mastering his or her circumstances, that is, as a being who is inherently temporal and finite. By finding relief in mood-altering substances and activities, the addict seeks to escape from the inescapable condition of thrownness. Etymologically speaking, addiction (from the Latin, *addictus*) is a way of "giving oneself over to," which has similar connotations to Heidegger's description of inauthenticity or disownedness.

In a technological age that seeks to maximize comfort at all costs, there is a backlash of emotion that reminds us of our thrownness. Indeed, the emotion that people in contemporary society complain about most and from which they continuously seek relief—as illustrated by those who use addictive substances—arises in conjunction with our character as embodied beings, namely, stress. As Heidegger remarks in *Zollikon Seminars*:

> The diverse ways of a claim made on one (i.e., "stress") show up in these ways of stimulation. Stress is always oriented toward a particular situation, that is, toward the particular, factical [*faktish*] being-in-the-world where the human being, as existing, does not step into occasionally from time to time, but, on the contrary, *where he essentially and constantly and always already is*.[29]

Given Heidegger's insights into the finite constitution of human being (i.e., Dasein) as care, one might suppose that his existential analytic in *Being and Time* yields important clues as to the origin(s) of addiction or its special occurrence as a phenomenon as such. To be sure, other existentialist philosophies, as seen in Sartre's analysis of "bad faith," might also identify important characteristics of that phenomenon, for example, a tendency toward "self-deception," which would explain much of the behavior of the so-called "addict." What sets the Heideggerian account apart, however, is not the prospect of isolating existential structures that can more or less satisfactorily explain certain kinds of behavior. Even of less interest would be an effort to distinguish general character traits such as those prominent in "obsessive-compulsive" disorders, as if they were the root causes of a specific kind of aberration or "disease" such as addiction. On the contrary, what makes Heidegger's phenomenology a fruitful point of departure is the ontological removal of the Cartesian bifurcation of inside/outside.[30] Thus the analysis of specific kinds of behavior remains inseparable from the prevailing dispositions through which the self discovers its entanglement in a situation, and, conversely, the self's vulnerability to affective states remains interwoven with the development and interpretation of its possibilities by which each of us carves out the "meaning" of his or her existence in the world. While addiction has a physical locus, it is not reducible to strictly physical elements such as brain chemistry or mental elements such as weak volition, for human beings also *experience* that problem as a *crisis of meaning*. This experiential dimension, insofar as it is linked to the embodied, "fleshly" character of human existence as "thrown" into the world, becomes the focus of our phenomenological inquiry into addiction. The inherent ambivalence of this phenomenon, which cannot be reduced either to mental or physical states, accounts for why the malady of addiction so stubbornly resists both psychological and medical treatments.

This section will be divided into two parts. First, I will lay bare the phenomenon of addiction in terms of the self's relation to a mode of being most simply described as the "within-reach," which may best be characterized as a kind of variation on "readiness-to-hand." Second, I will delineate finitude (temporality) as the heart of freedom, the capacity for which is significantly diminished in the addictive state. Then we will be able to answer the question of the "who" of addiction, namely, the individual's misidentification of himself or herself (i.e., of having its being "to be") with the "within-reach" of a "substance," which offers the illusion of a kind of stability beyond the transitoriness of human existence.[31]

The traditional, if not commonsense way of addressing addiction is to assume the perspective of the addict, and then, as if by a method of regression, seek the root causes or conditions for that affliction. Once having circumscribed the life situation of the addict, the attempt is then made to delineate the effects that affliction has on others, including family and friends, as well as their part in denying (and thereby indirectly contributing to the problem) the so-called cycle of "codependency." At any rate, there is a decided tendency to treat addiction as a kind of aberration, which is reflected in the continual debate as to whether alcoholism is a "disease," a "moral weakness," or some combination thereof. But what if we take the opposite approach, the "road less traveled," and assume instead the understanding that is common to us all, addict and nonaddict alike? Hermeneutically speaking, that perspective would correspond to the unarticulated "pre-understanding" that is embedded in what Heidegger calls "everydayness," or the self's absorption in its daily routine.

As the example of Heidegger's own hermeneutics illustrates, everydayness provides the backdrop from which to develop philosophical understanding. Indeed, everydayness offers such a point of departure because it harbors all of the confusions and misconceptions whose unraveling yields the counterpoint from which to bring into relief, into a full "self-showing," a more differentiated and complete understanding of our being-in-the-world. As we will discover, Dasein's absorption into the routine of everydayness (i.e., "falling") fosters the development of the "they-self," the face of convention. Since we are all to a certain extent products of convention, we find that the "they-self" dictates many of the attitudes we uncritically accept as members of society. We might then consider everydayness as that thread of commonality that the addict shares with the nonaddict, insofar as both are equally shaped by the factors that enable us to "fit into" society. Due to a passivity in which the desire for acceptance becomes acute, a climate of uncritical tolerance toward other people's actions often results. Then we have a situation in which the en masse participation in an activity (e.g., "drinking") becomes so "common" as to legitimate widespread acceptance of it, with the tactic legitimization of a norm condoning the consumption of alcohol as such, albeit with a curious twist of concealing its potential danger. Thus in social gatherings we tend to minimize or overlook the deleterious effects of excessive drinking because of the prelegitimization of the activity among those who practice it in moderation. Of course, this is not to advocate banning alcohol, because it is not the substance that is "bad" (as the ineffectiveness of the 1930s' Prohibition shows) nor even the degree of its use. Where the problem arises is in the attempt to blur the lines between acceptable and unacceptable use, so that "everyone" can have equal opportunity to indulge without fear of reprisal or condemnation.

In turning from this perspective offered in everydayness, we undergo a dislocation of focus in which an emphasis on the self's existence "preceding its addiction" takes priority over its subsequent falling "into addiction." The climate of passive acceptance then means that, prior to addiction, any so-called decisions to indulge or not to indulge are made in behalf of one's undifferentiated membership in a group and thereby reflect a will to "fit in" or "belong" from the standpoint of the "they-self,"[32] (e.g., what is "cool," "daring," or even just "customary," as in the locution "what everyone else does"). The scope of the "they-self," however, is not restricted to white-collar professionals who endorse the "two-martini lunch," much less to the children of these suburbanites. On the contrary, the sphere of its influence can also be found at the margins of "average" society, where the antisocial attitude of nonconformity, as epitomized by illegal drug users, harbors a curious side of conformity to it, insofar as that culture still upholds its own unusual mannerisms of dress, speech, and so on—rites of passage, so to speak—as prerequisites for the individual's inclusion therein. Wherever people congregate, in any social setting, the "they's" influence already extends; and the ubiquity of this influence, insofar as it gives the individual a license to indulge, takes the popular form of what we commonly call "peer pressure." As Twerski points out, it is difficult to get addicts to establish "goals in life other than sense gratification," since "our culture [already] embraces addictive thinking."[33]

If we take Heidegger at his word that the they-self is an *existentiale* of Dasein, then we should not be surprised that peer pressure should be so pervasive and its effects so far reaching. By the same token, we might view addiction, insofar as it flourishes in this climate of peer pressure, less as an anomaly and more as a regular or an "expected" adjustment or mode of adaption to the inherently problematic, painful, and, most of all, enigmatic character of human existence. But if this is the case, can we identify specific structures, and "modifications" of these, within the essential constitution of Dasein as care, in existence, in facticity, but most notably in the structure linked to the emergence of the they-self, to its absorption in everydayness, namely, falling? According to Heidegger, falling belongs to the basic momentum of human existence, insofar as Dasein is thrown into a situation, and, in its facticity, it already confronts a limited range of possibilities in relation to which it exists. Within the structure of falling, Heidegger in turn distinguishes different elements: "tempting," "tranquilizing," "entangling," and "alienating,"[34] the interplay of which distinguishes the "downward plunge" of that momentum into a kind of apathy or, almost paradoxically, an inertia.[35] Even in the most apathetic state of not caring—which we might equate with an extreme state of addiction—the self still expresses some kind of concern.

Dasein exercises care in falling, as seen in the self's administering to its basic life task, making a living, or in its involvement with the instrumental concerns of its environment. In the downward plunge or the intensification of falling, Dasein still "cares," but in such a way that the tension distinctive thereof,[36] that its being is always an issue, becomes diminished or slackened. One is now adrift, going along with the flow, albeit now seeking a substitute for that tension of existence, an alternative source of stimulation that simultaneously relieves the "difficulty," if not the challenge of having to take up one's existence in new and manifold ways.[37] The necessity of taking up one's existence anew is displaced by the relinquishment thereof, the disownedness of the self or its inauthenticity. In this disownedness of the self, addiction can take hold, for the self relocates its identity in something unself-like, an alien mode of being that promises to restore the unity otherwise lost to the self in its falling: the illusion of wholeness that indulgence in a specific "substance" or pursuit (e.g., gambling) holds out.[38]

It is almost cliché to suggest that the addict yields to misunderstanding or falls prey to self-dissemblance. The fact of "denial" testifies all too clearly to this tendency toward dissimulation. What is more important, however, is that the possibility of such confusion is foretold in the structure of falling itself, as it were, "preontologically," in a slippage back and forth between two divergent ways of being, that distinctive of the self and that proper to entities we utilize or the "ready-to-hand." It is not literally the entity itself (e.g., this or that potential source of addiction) that proves decisive but rather how its "being" epitomizes "availability," as already lying within-reach, that distinguishes the dynamic of becoming addicted. To be sure, many vehicles of addiction have a "natural" origin. Yet from the standpoint of everydayness, they require a system of *distribution*, and thereby a prior mechanism of production, which "proximally and for the most part" relegates them (e.g., drugs, Internet sex, cigarettes, slot machines, beer) to the instrumental context of the ready-to-hand. Because Dasein as being-in-the-world discloses the ready-to-hand in its everyday pursuits, it can fall under the spell of the "within-reach" (of a "substance") in ways animals cannot. Animals become "addicted" only under human influence, as laboratory tests show, because they lack the "handiness" to smoke (except when connected to machines) and they also are "world poor" in lacking a network of instrumental involvements.[39] Ironically, the potential to become addicted seems to be reserved primarily to human beings who are capable of disclosedness or care. Perhaps a reason for this is that Dasein discloses its being-in-the-world through "moods" or "dispositions" (e.g., anxiety), that are inherently fluid. By the same token, a certain vulnerability to these dispositions, a sense of frailty at one's inability to master them, seems to impel the individual to seek solace in various "substances" that promise "relaxation," "excitement," or some other hope of "mood alteration." This desire for mood alteration, however, is still a symptom of the addict's overall tendency to "flee" existence and the accompanying difficulty of enduring the tension of its "openness."

When a person becomes addicted, it is as if the individual restricts his or her attention to the narrow reach of availability, thereby closing himself or herself off to the expanse of possibilities that can alone promise a course of development. Conversely, whatever fits the bill of this "(immediately) within-reach"—a beer, a joint, a call to the sex hotline—has the effect of diminishing the self's initiative to undertake the struggle of existence and defer its own fulfillment in favor of a journey of maturation and discovery. The addict's well-documented desire for immediate gratification thereby appears to have ontological roots in the movement of disownedness in which Dasein forsakes the self-concern of "having its being to be" in favor of the mode of "within-reach" more properly reserved to entities ready-to-hand. This ontological transposition, as it were, creates the "space" in which addiction can occur. In *Being and Time*, Heidegger describes this way of allocating space as "deserving," or the impetus to bring close, make available, or place within-reach. To quote Heidegger: "'De-severing' amounts to making the farness vanish—that is, making the remoteness of something disappear, bringing it close. Dasein is essentially de-severant: it lets any entity be encountered close by as the entity which it is."[40] We cannot underestimate the importance of Heidegger's early discussion of space, as incomplete as it is, for the allusion to Dasein's spatiality provides a direct inroad to the issue of embodiment, as the locutions that describe the phenomenon of addiction attest: the "within-reach," "availability," and "ready-to-hand." In *Zollikon Seminars*, Heidegger refers back to his earlier discussion of spatiality in a way that explicitly takes up the question of embodiment:

> Therefore, the following statement concerning the "spatiality of being-in-the-world" appearing in *Being and Time*, section 23: "Da-sein constantly takes these directions [e.g., below, above, right and left, in front, and behind] along with it, just as it does its de-serverances. Da-sein's spatilaization in its bodiliness is similarly marked out in accordance with these directions. (This bodiliness hides a whole problematic of its own, though we will not deal with it here.)"
>
> *The Da-sein of the human being is spatial* in itself in the sense of making room [in space] [*Einraümen von Raum*] and in the sense of *the spatialization of Da-sein in its bodily nature*. Da-sein is not spatial because it is embodied. But its bodiliness is possible only because Da-sein is spatial in the sense of making room.[41]

Precisely because Dasein is capable of making room, it is also capable of focusing its attention, its circumspective concern, on the source of immediate gratification that lies "within-reach." In addiction, however, falling determines the compass and directedness of the fixating tendency at work. Correlatively, the "spacing" that occurs when the addict focuses on the "within-reach" is really an enclosure that narrows and narrows, trapping him or her in a nowhere realm bereft of any "openness" to himself or herself, others, and the world as such. In view of this fixating tendency, we might call the addict's obsessive urge to get the thing or "substance" that provides satisfaction—insofar as his or her field of attention shifts to entities rather than to being (*Sein*)—an "*ontical craving*" for "power, security, and pleasure."[42]

Heidegger offers an interesting account of this experience of being "closed off" under the auspices of "hankering after," which he links to the phenomenon of addiction. "Such hankering *closes off* the possibilities. . . . Dasein's hankering as it falls makes manifest its *addiction* to becoming 'lived' by whatever word it is in. . . . What one is addicted 'towards' [*Das 'Hinzu' des Hanges*] is to let oneself be drawn by the sort of thing for which the addiction hankers."[43] The greater the addict's wish to regain control over an aspect of his or her life, the greater the "contraction" of the self's original "ontological openness."[44] Within this realm of indeterminacy, all of the addict's priorities become skewed in favor of acquiring whatever environmentally satisfies the condition of "within-reach," whether drugs, alcohol, gambling, or gratuitous sex, just to name the "garden variety" vices. To be sure, unlike legal substances such as alcohol, narcotics may not literally be "within-reach," yet they are passionately sought with the intent of making them so (e.g., addicts commit crimes to acquire the cash to purchase drugs). As Seeburger emphasizes, the hallmark of addiction is that the addict is always "thinking about" the next opportunity to indulge, in such a way that this "preoccupation" displaces all other concerns.[45] As Heidegger remarks: "If Dasein, as it were, sinks into an addiction then there is not merely an addiction present-at-hand, but the entire structure of care has been modified. Dasein has become blind, and puts all possibilities into the service of the addiction."[46]

This contrast between the addict's desire for immediate gratification, on the one hand, and the longevity of the path of self-development, on the other hand, implies that the difference between inauthenticity and authenticity hinges on a *temporal distinction*. We should not be surprised at this revelation, since in *Being and Time* Heidegger reinterprets the analysis of care undertaken in division I in light of the account of temporality provided in division II. The analysis of temporality proves vital, because it brings into the foreground the ontological element in the dynamic of making room, as indicated by the spatiality of being-in-the-world, the clearing or openness as such. As the emphasis on the problem of embodiment suggests, the importance of spatiality needs to be retrieved from its omission throughout the tradition. At least within the confines of *Being and Time*, Heidegger tends to follow suit, by privileging time over space, although the thrust of retrieving the question of being anticipates a further stage of inquiry that will necessitate reexamining the intimacy between temporality and spatiality. In making the problem of addiction an occasion for reopening the concern for the body, and its corollary, spatiality, we actively take this further step of anticipating the radicalization of hermeneutics. Beginning from the hermeneutical outline of *Being and Time*, we should be able to illuminate the phenomenon of addiction by distinguishing the actual temporal coordinates that sustain it, and conversely, the precise mode of the enactment of authentic temporality that would arrest the downward plunge of addictive behavior.

B.

Having initiated an inquiry into the phenomenon of addiction, we might ask what interest there may be, much less payoff, for those whose mission it is to extend the frontiers of Heidegger's thought. At this stage, perhaps the simplest answer lies in discovering that the same conditions that delineate human finitude are also what allow us to address a problem, that is, addiction, which seems to be interwoven with the fact of our embodiment. How we become addicted is not reducible to physiological elements, but, instead, the reference to embodiment serves as a "formal indicator" to the larger question of human finitude.[47] By analyzing the phenomenon of addiction, we thereby supply a concrete example to confirm the hermeneutic premise that the analysis of everydayness undertaken in division I of *Being and Time* must be repeated in light of the account of temporality provided in division II. The hermeneutic circle can be unfolded at a deeper level, insofar as the fragmentation of the self occurring in inauthentic temporality yields a point of contrast to delineate more sharply the dynamic of the self's reunification in authentic temporality. If addiction is like a downward plunge [*Absturz*] into chaos, then how must human existence be capable of the opposite, or how can the self harbor the potential to recover its uniqueness?

Paradoxically, we will discover that the key to the self's reunification lies in relinquishing the pretense of complete control over its situation, in a way consistent with its finitude. Conversely, the "within-reach" constitutes a fabricated way of imposing that control, albeit over an increasingly narrower range of the environment, rather than accepting the invitation of a greater possibility of openness. This openness, however, is not a simple given. Instead, it springs from a tension that Dasein endures, a double relation in which it acquires the potential to project possibilities only as "thrown" into a situation, and hence its uniqueness can be "won" only through a counter-concession of admitting its limitations. Heidegger describes the vector of this "doubling" in terms of the trajectory of ecstatic temporality (i.e., transcendence). In transcendence, Dasein enters a temporal horizon or expanse in which its identity can be achieved only by maintaining a relation to otherness, of confronting both the terror and wonder of what lies "beyond" the reach of simple mastery—the awe of the fact of existing. The transcendence of "beyond reach" occurs in stark contrast, as we will see, to the concave vector of closure of "within-reach," whereby the addict seeks to absolve the encounter with otherness and artificially "solve" the problematic character of human existence.

If Buddhism may offer an "eightfold path" to redemption,[48] then Heidegger's authentic self travels along a "twofold" path whose borders are demarcated by the grammar of middle voice: the balance between passivity and activity. As van Buren and Kisiel have documented, Heidegger examined "primal Christianity," which is embodied in St. Paul's Epistles and later reinterpreted by Luther and Kierkegaard, in order to distinguish an instance of middle voice in the facticity of the faithful who must first lose his or her life in order to win it.[49] Yet perhaps the easiest link can be made to the Greek notion of temperance or moderation, most notably to that of Aristotle.[50] Aristotle's notion of moderation implies that the enjoyment of any benefit occurs in proportion to the acceptance of a condition of self-restraint or limitation. In the grammar of middle voice, one can be liberated for the abundance of life's possibilities only through the parallel concession of admitting one's own finitude.[51] The twofold path dictates that one wins one's life back only by confronting, in Jaspers's terms, the "limit situation" of existence.[52] And only in conjunction with its finitude does Dasein, paradoxically, first acquire the power to choose (i.e., freedom).

For Heidegger, freedom does not simply involve making choices in a voluntaristic sense of the will. As an extension of human finitude, freedom corresponds to an openness in which the self entertains its unique possibilities, albeit always within a limited temporal horizon. From the standpoint of the self, the inevitability of death demarcates that limited horizon, as the end of all of my possibilities. As such, authentic Dasein approaches death as an ultimate limitation, so the self can be catapulted into openness only by the counter-concession of admitting the withdrawal and concealment signified by the end of death. Once again, the finitude mandated by Dasein, and, indeed, of the unconcealing-concealing power of being, entails that the self can welcome the light of the clearing (*Lichtung*) only by confronting the shadow of concealment. Though the "self-destructive" behavior of the addict may suggest an attraction toward the "nothing," the actual facts (i.e, the "factictity" of the falling, inauthentic self) demonstrate quite the reverse. That is, the addict "denies" death first and foremost, to employ Becker's terminology,[53] or, more precisely, the finitude associated with it. The addict does not have so much a "death-instinct" in Freud's sense as a longing to compensate for what he or she seems most deprived by the double admission that the transitoriness of temporality spawns the wellspring of "meaning." Indeed, the addict seeks in the "within-which" a refuge of "permanency," something that offers an easy path of return to it through the "recurrence" of use, something that appears constant and self-sustaining (i.e., in the worst case, what we commonly call a "substance"). Perhaps the "everyday" use of that lexicon should not go unnoticed, since metaphysically "substance" has connotations both in Latin and Greek of a "permanency" (ascribed to "being") that arises in tandem with a mounting indifference to the temporality constitutive of human finitude. If we then define addiction as an enslavement to a specific "substance" (which could also be a recurrent activity such as gambling), we then see this activity as a deprivation of freedom that seeks solace in the illusion of "permanency" and denies the pulse of temporality.[54] The addict's bondage to such an illusion defies the prerequisite of any true eternity, to quote Rosenzweig, so "life . . . must first become wholly temporal, wholly alive, before it can become eternal life."[55]

The self's retreat into the illusion of permanency displays a distinct mode of fallen, inauthentic temporality in which denies the priority of the future as the harbinger of death and finitude. By foregoing the reaching ahead of anticipating death, the inauthentic self temporalizes by substituting one present instance for another, so novelty is not developed directly from the future but instead is vicariously relived, as it were, by seeking to recapture through a throwback to the past what the present yields in a restricted form. The present is not actively lived but is sacrificed for its discomfort, pain, and inadequacy for an alternative of comfort, pleasure, and fulfillment that a retreat toward the past supposedly offers. Thus this fugitive affinity for the past, developed out of intensified falling, is constantly in service of it to the point of fixation, because the past alone can offer the illusion of transposing the self into a refuge of solace. And it is this search for a refuge of solace that lies at the basis of the commonsense belief that addicts are seeking an escape. But the escape is not only indexed by a "where" (i.e., what is defined environmentally by the set of circumstances yielding the "within-reach") but, just as fundamentally, by a "when," a fleeing toward the past. *And this fugitive relation to the past, as it were, yields a portal of escape in the direction of what, in the guise of the within-reach, emerges as a fixation to which one keeps returning (e.g., the bottle, the joint, Internet pornography).*

Yet what role does the future play in this fugitive process, insofar as the past provides the handle of fixation? The future become a hankering for the constellation of the set of circumstances, for esample, the end of the workday, which affords the opportunity to "kick back" and retreat vis-à-vis the past, into the refuge of solace. In *Being and Time*, Heidegger designates such a future as inauthentic, insofar as the self passively "awaits" something to occur by assuming a stance of "expectation."[56] He contrasts the authentic future, in which the self is actively involved in transforming its situation by "anticipating" or reaching ahead to meet its possibilities.[57] As the temporal corollary of addiction, expectation is waiting for something better to come along, a momentary release from one's circumstances, which only the immediate gratification of the "within-reach" can provide. Although addiction provides the avenue of escape, the future serves to reinforce the passivity by which the self becomes repeatedly vulnerable to its temptations in the guise of a "patient" rather than an "agent." When the addict is not literally "escaping into the bottle," the bondage of addiction still holds in the individual a futural preoccupation with drinking even while he or she is at work and is prohibited from drinking. As Seeburger properly summarizes this aspect: "as members of Alcoholics Anonymous often remark, regardless of how much time they actually spent drinking, back in their drinking days, their concern with alcohol was pervasive. As they like to put, even when they were not actually, they were still always 'thinking drinking.' That is, they were planning how they were going to get their next drink."[58]

When occurring either authentically or inauthentically, temporality always includes three dimensions: future, past, and present. In its inauthentic occurrence pertaining to addiction, we can distinguish the schemata for the interplay of the three temporal dimensions or ecstases. Adopting an originally

Kantian term, which Heidegger does in chapter 4 of the second division of *Being and Time*,[59] we can identify the schema of the future as the prospect or "plan" (as referred to by Seeburger previously) of seeking in what awaits one something better, a passive condition of wishing for a change, no matter how transitory or superficial, for example, an alteration of mood (relaxation, euphoria). The schema of the present involves the logistics of desevering and making available the expectancy held by the promise of the "within-reach." Within that schema of *making present*, the self, through the fixity of its addiction, seeks to ensure a sense of *stability and continuity*—otherwise lost in the dispersion of its falling—in short, a measure of *control,* over a life that appears directionless and futile. The commonsense belief that addiction is a form of immediate gratification holds, but only to the extent that this immediacy is a way of reclaiming control "here and now" (e.g., the "rush" of feeling better), and hence it implies the past. The schema of the past is the postponing of, or allowing to pass by, the challenge of existence, in exchange for retreating into a comfort zone of security and solace. Within the addictive experience, each of these three temporal ecstases is already in play and related to one another. Nevertheless, because the mark of addiction lies in its fixating tendency, the past dominates in the sense of falsely subordinating to it the expectancy of the future. Two key points arise. First, the future remains closed off, because in its expectancy, it is already dominated by a previous standard of satisfaction supplied by some past experience (e.g., the euphoria of Internet gambling). Second, without the fugitive, escapist character of the past, the obsessive-compulsiveness inherent in addiction would be lacking. Indeed, addiction is like a faulty reconstruction of the routine of everyday life, in which its regimen is not defined by the entire course of one's day but instead by a singular activity—drinking or gambling. In pointing to the similar addictive effects that both stimulants and depressants may have, despite their contrary medical aims, Seeburger remarks: "Both provide a way of regulating the organism's level of excitation, keeping it constant. It is precisely such sameness, such routine repeatability, that the addict seeks in the object of addiction."[60] In this exaggerated routine of obsessive-compulsiveness, the self "plunges" to the *bottom of everyday existence*.

Addiction closes off the future, restricts it to the next opportunity to fixate on a source of immediate gratification, in short, to "get a fix." According to Heidegger, the temporalizing of the future yields an expanse of possibilities and spawns the fundamental openness of existence. Conversely, by closing off the future, the fixity of addiction constricts the original "ontological openness." Herein lies the ontological "fact" as to why it is so difficult for the addict to break the cycle of addiction and start on the path of recovery. Because deception and denial fuel addiction, the addict can overcome these tendencies only by cultivating the openness of existence which, however, remains most foreign to him/her. Put another way, the impetus toward responsibility, to be answerable, is what the addict possesses least, but requires most, if recovery is to be possible. But if enslavement takes this form in the inauthentic self's mode of temporalizing, then how can we understand the restoration of "freedom," which ostensibly pertains to the temporality of the authentic self?

In chapter 2 of division II of *Being and Time*, Heidegger states: "Freedom, however, *is* only in the choice of one possibility—that is, in tolerating one's not having chosen the others and one's not being able to choose them."[61] That is, the factical exercise of freedom entails that the self forego certain possibilities in order to select those that prove most viable and best signify the course of its unique development. Once again, death stands as the ultimate arbiter of this finitude, because as the possibility of no longer having possibilities it brings the self before its origins in an openness over which it is essentially powerless. As a result, the necessary counterpart of death is "guilt" as embodying the nullity of one's thrownness into the world, the irreducible fact of always having one's being as an issue.[62] Arising with this potential for "being guilty" is a sense of responsibility, that is, Dasein's way of cultivating those responses that exact maximum concern over its existence as care and thereby hold forth the uniqueness of individuality that equally allows for an appreciation of the differences of others. Indeed, being guilty entails that the first order of responsibility is to oneself, or self-responsibility. But such responsibility should not be construed narrowly as excluding concern for the welfare of others, or putting "me" ahead of them. On the contrary, self-responsibility allows me to stand forth within that openness where the other can become manifest in his or her singularity, that is, *as* other, and thereby elicit from me a co-responding mode of concern or "solicitude." When understood in this way, self-responsibility means that Dasein no longer "gives in" to those compromises that make it vulnerable to the influences (e.g., "peer pressure" of the "they"). Conversely, when making these compromises, the self construes others as mere "instruments" to aid it in the pursuit of its "indulgences," which licenses the tacit "victimization" of others (e.g, family, friends) in whatever form the pursuit of the "within-reach" takes. To be sure, Heidegger could have explained more clearly how the scope of my freedom includes (a concern for) others. Yet at least he saw that the renewed vow of commitment to oneself, or "resoluteness" (*Entschlossenheit*), can alone circumvent the compromising mentality of the "they-self" and hence hold forth the possibility of interacting with others in a climate of friendship and community.

Levinas was among the first to criticize Heidegger for not adequately taking into consideration the singularity of the other as the key fulcrum from which to understand human existence.[63] Yet the dilemma posed by the problem of addiction seems to confirm Heidegger's point of departure. On the one hand, by only having attained a sense of self and the accompanying responsibility can an individual benefit other people. On the other hand, a narcissistic independence cannot be any more viable if its outcome lies in excluding any commitment to the welfare of others The paradox of addiction is that it is neither simply a "character" fault on an individual scale, which can be corrected by exhorting the person to greater responsibility (because it is precisely that capacity that seems to be most lacking). Indeed, this difficulty becomes prominent when the alcoholic, after experiencing a personally or professionally devastating upheaval due to his or her intoxication, "promises" never to drink again. But the promise remains empty, for the addict lacks the freedom to uphold what is promised, or, in Kantian terms, the "can" that sustains the binding character of any commitment.[64] Nor is addiction simply a biophysical malady like a disease (in any commonsense guise like "athlete's foot"), for no prescription of treatment or medicine can altogether speak to the breakdown of relationships and the crisis of meaning dominating the person's life. Given Heidegger's ontological orientation, we come to the rather awkward conclusion that addiction is indeed a problem that in some way or another pertains to the self's "being." We can define the self's being either negatively as that which resists compartmentalization in terms of the Cartesian dualism of mental and physical. We can also define Dasein's being positively as the thrownness that allows for the "instantiation" of human existence—as dispersed temporally as well as spatially—and thereby makes possible the condition of embodiment along with all of the problems that subsequently arise from that mode of being-a-self.[65] The *potential* to be addicted, which points to a distinctive way in which human beings *experience* their embodiment as interwoven into the "how" of existing, raises concerns that formally indicate the being of the self and its immersion in finitude.

Is addiction, then, a problem, as it were, inherent in human nature? To suggest as much would be to make a metaphysical claim. It would be more accurate to say that the fabric of everydayness changes historically, even from Heidegger's era, in such a way that the transformations that occur in humanity's understanding of being, as exemplified most in modern technology, give greater opportunity for addiction to occur. But have not there been addictive substances since the dawn of civilization, just as there has been tool use before the advent of modern technology? The answer is yes, and the parallel is more than accidental. According to Heidegger, tool use changes in accordance with the mode of revealing in modern technology, which allows beings to appear exclusively in terms of "standing reserve."[66] Similarly, the more "one-dimensionally" entities appear, the more easily human beings can be reduced to their use-value as producers and consumers. Karl Marx recognized that alienation is inherent in the capitalist economic system, and that "opiates," albeit of a spiritual kind (e.g., religion), were *available* to "relieve" the tedium of everyday life. The analogy still applies in the more literal sense of addiction as human beings are placed in service of the mechanized cog of production and consumption (e.g., the possibility of "shopping addiction"). The temptations of addiction become available everywhere and anywhere, because as Heidegger suggests, "Modernity begins its completion in directing itself to the complete *availability* of everything that is and can be."[67] Accordingly, humanity becomes more explicitly reliant on the instrumental complex of the ready-to-hand, insofar as technology incorporates increasingly sophisticated systems of production and consumption in order to facilitate *distributing* addictive substances to a larger percentage of the population (e.g., from "crack" to video poker). The corollary impersonalization of society that results—the "they-self" brought to its concrete realization—then creates a climate for human beings to fall prey to addiction. With the advent of modern technology, the "they's" scope becomes so extensive as to create blanket acceptance of a given "lifestyle," for example, drinking and smoking, thereby popularizing these activities in television, film, and music. What is the addict's primary motivation? Perhaps it is nothing more complex than seeking to regain a semblance of control or mastery over his or her life in the face of disillusionment about the way things "are." Yet in doing so he or she *becomes complicitous with the technological illusion that humanity has complete control over its destiny*, including whatever hardships the environment might arbitrarily impose.

As Dasein becomes the "laboring animal"[68] who is reduced to its "control-obsessed" cravings,[69] technology subordinates human beings to activities that are not only personally "harmful" but, indeed, may "endanger" precisely what is "at issue" in what it means to be human,[70] for example, the exercise of freedom as the ability to "let be." Under the sway of modern technology, human beings make decisions on the basis of what is expedient and useful according to convention, thereby neglecting a concern for how they themselves, and natural entities as well, become manifest in their singularity and uniqueness. As a result, human beings overlook the possibility of existence as an adventure or a sojourn,[71] and instead they are reduced to the struggle to survive and cope. Ironically, the conclusion that there is no simple answer to the problem of addiction—either moral or medical—recasts our attention back upon a deeper appreciation of the ineluctable dimension of human facticity, of factic-life experience. Precisely by affirming this element of facticity, we discover how restricted the knowledge, recommendations, and solutions of physical science may be to answer the "human, all too human" problems of human existence. Indeed, the question of human addiction points to an enigma that the conventional wisdom of mass culture cannot illuminate and before which the elaborate mechanisms of modern technology remain all but helpless.

Thus the potential for addiction appears to be part of the human predicament, whose *materiality* is shaped by the technological forces of the modern world. But how can we understand the world if not in a double sense, both as the horizon for the manifestation of beings and as its withdrawal in the frame of technology, that is, as un-world? In the latter case, the materiality of our embodied existence becomes evident by the laboring animal's control-obsessed cravings, which allocate space in the distinct way of making available the "within-reach." The fact that the critique of technology requires a more sympathetic treatment of space will merit further consideration in subsequent chapters. Just as the analysis of everydayness must be radicalized for the question of being to be formulated properly, so hermeneutics must undergo radicalization for the question to "turn around" and incorporate a latent concern for materiality and embodiment. This turning around marks the historical crossing where we can make explicit the nexus of presuppositions, the hermeneutical situation, which situates Heidegger's own inquiry.

We have now shown how the concern for the origins of human addiction provides an occasion to concretize further Heidegger's analysis of everydayness, to distinguish a problem unique to the human manner of incarnality vis-à-vis the physicality of the handiness of the "within-reach." Conversely, by repeating Heidegger's analysis of (inauthentic) temporality in order to uncover these origins, we have more sharply delineated how finite or primordial time demarcates the parameters within which freedom becomes possible for a self who *experiences* embodiment as a distinctive "fact" of its being-in-the-world. That repetition, however, brings to the foreground the need to rethink the importance of space in conjunction with, rather than in subordination to, temporality. Insofar as spatiality reemerges as an explicit concern, the problem of embodiment will also enter the forefront of our inquiry. And the more explicitly we focus this concern for embodiment, the easier it will be to vanquish the Cartesian portrait of the self as a disembodied soul and rediscover the self's incarnation in its manner of ecstatic "bodying-forth."[72]

In the next chapter, we will show how our repetition of Heidegger's analysis of everydayness provides a new point of departure for addressing the individuality of the self, as it is in part defined through the openness of bodily comportment in activities such as sexuality.

Chapter 2

The Erotic, Sexuality, and Diversity

The double helix is the symbol of the structure and ancestry of life on this earth, but it may also signify a crossing, the division that separates, differentiates, and individualizes. In biology, we speak of male and female principles of reproduction. In Heidegger's terminology, we seek the creative wellspring from which philosophy originates by differentiating being from beings (i.e., the ontological difference). Heidegger, however, did not show much interest in biology, and, if anything, he condemned its presumptuous attempt to address the origin of life as another "ism." Indeed, in emphasizing the "neutrality" of human existence, or Dasein, as the ground of the ontological difference, he neglects the creative opposition between male and female, the sexual difference.

Toward the end of the twentieth century, Jacques Derrida coined the terms "sexual difference" in order to criticize Heidegger's insistence on the gender-neutrality of Dasein. Derrida thereby transposes the thinking of being into a space capable of addressing a difference intrinsic to the generation of life,[1] of *physis*, as "self-emerging presence." This difference is not only at the root of sexual reproduction but also allows for the diversification of what becomes manifest in nature. In genetics, a process of the "crossing over" of chromosomes, by which the novelty of offspring arises by combining the complement of male and female, constitutes recombining genes to create greater diversity of individual and species. In this chapter, we will attempt to show how Heidegger, despite his indifference to the metaphor of biological diversity, raises the question of diversity as it pertains to the singularity of the manifestness of beings as such. He characterizes this shift in the interest in diversity, from the overarching concern of fundamental ontology to uncover the possibility of any understanding of being, as "metontology." Many of his works that define his thinking in the late 1920s and early 1930s distinguish the topography of this questioning. In his 1930 lectures on Kant, Heidegger states that he must re-think the relation of being to time in terms of the latter's power to "individualize" the uniqueness of what becomes manifests,[2] of which the foremost instance is the self's undertaking of "individuation" in authentic existence. Such "individuality" precedes the distinction between universal and particular, and, correlatively, even in the human arena, between "person and community," because it points to the dual capacity by which the self stands out and participates within the uniqueness of the manifestness of beings. This form of "ek-sistence" redefines the self as an ecstatic entryway into the openness (*Spiel-Raum*) that is equally constituted by spatiality (e.g., the occupation of a site, or *topos*) and temporality.

If the turning around of metontology points to the singularity of Dasein, then may it not also, along with the parallel to life's genesis mentioned earlier, implicate the individual's relation to the "generic" claim of sexuality? The self experiences this claim as a "thrownness" over which its power is limited, insofar as its way of "bodying forth," to employ Heidegger's apt phrase from *Zollikon Seminars*, stems from the bifurcation of gender into male and female sexes. Interestingly enough, in these seminars he addresses the enigma of body against the background provided by two statements from Nietzsche's *Will to Power*.

> Now we will leap to the problem of the body.
>
> To begin, let us consider two statements made by Nietzsche. *The Will to Power*, number 659 (originally written in 1885), reads: "The idea of body is more astonishing than the idea of the ancient 'soul.'" Number 489 (originally written in 1886) reads: "The phenomenon of the body is richer, the more distinct, the more comprehensible phenomenon. It should have methodological priority, without our deciding anything about its ultimate significance."[3]

While acknowledging the truth of the first claim, Heidegger questions the veracity of the second claim as to the "comprehensibility" of the body. Indeed, due to its ontic proximity to us, the body and its corollary, sexuality and gender, often appear quite opaque and inscrutable from a philosophical perspective. Is the body merely inscrutable in its own right? Or instead, as David Krell suggests, perhaps it is the case that "the body of Dasein will continue to elude us as a gauzy ghost of the counter-Cartesian: Heidegger will always be able to say what the body is *not*, but will have all too little to say about what it is or might become."[4] And as Hans Jonas, a student of Heidegger stresses, in its provocative linkage of Christian and Hellenistic sources, there is a *gnostic* background to hermeneutic phenomenology. Given this background, Heidegger is already predisposed to turn the potency granted to Dasein—as a "thrown project"—into a vision of human existence that relegates the problem of the embodiment to a subsidiary concern.[5] In the following, I will attempt to reduce much of the vagueness inherent in Heidegger's approach to the body and thereby offset the preceding criticisms by addressing the issues of gender and sexuality. Indeed, it is ironic that while Heidegger did not explore the phenomenon of sexuality in any detail, it is only by doing so that we, in accordance with his hermeneutic method, can address the body in its mode of concreteness.

This chapter will be divided into three parts. First, I will provide an outline of Heidegger's sketchy treatment of the issues of sexuality and gender in order to show their wider implication in light of Derrida's criticism that the former overlooks the problem of sexual differentiation. Second, I will show how the development of Heidegger's analysis of care casts light on the dynamics of sexuality, particularly as constituting a form of solicitous interaction between self and other. Third, I will establish how the erotic impulse implies its own form of *mimesis*, its imitation of the body's opening onto the world, and how this *mimetic* art develops a unique kind of fantasy, ignited by the spark of imagination, which resets the boundaries of sexual intimacy through its own graphics, its own portrayal of space, namely, the pornographic.

Sexual Differentiation

Heidegger says very little about matters concerning love, let alone sexuality. Undoubtably, Jean-Paul Sartre was among the first to criticize Heidegger for failing to address the issue of sexuality. As Sartre remarks in *Being and Nothingness*: "Heidegger, in particular, does not make the slightest allusion to [sexuality] in his existential analytic with the result that his 'Dasein' appears asexual."[6] Along with Michel Foucault, who sought to develop a discourse to express repressed sexual desires,[7] Derrida has pointed to this omission; specifically he emphasizes that Heidegger, by extolling Dasein's gender "neutrality" in a key passage from *On the Essence of Ground*,[8] ignores the importance of the "sexual difference." As Derrida argues, Heidegger develops the question of human being on a plane that is determined by an attempt to recover the ontological difference, the difference between being and beings. In a famous query from his Nietzsche lectures, Heidegger asks whether Dasein is the ground of the ontological difference or is the ontological difference, the ground of Dasein?[9] As Heidegger emphasizes, "we stand in *the differentiation of beings and being*."[10] Due to this ontological focus, Heidegger overlooks the ontic level in which the "fact" of sexual differentiation works itself out, the level where people actually experience sexual desire and the conflict in relationships arising thereby. But while the concern for sexuality may not be primary for

Heidegger, the inquiry into Dasein points to the question of individuality. And it is in terms of this question of individuality, and Dasein's way of taking it over and coming into its own, that the question of sexuality might be properly broached.

Indeed, if sexuality inevitably corresponds to some "fact" of Dasein, and, as a result, pertains to the *possibility of selfhood*, then it might be possible to identify the ontological conditions that shape its occurrence. If sexuality is an irreducible fact that is tied to our embodiment, then it is by construing Dasein within the wider compass of its origination with nature (*physis*), rather than as an isolated entity, that we can first address the phenomenon of sexuality. Insofar as we adopt this wider point of departure in order to address human sexuality, then the aforementioned ontological conditions pertain to the fact of Dasein's situatedness and bear specifically on the enactment of its finitude (i.e., as a being embodied within the natural domain).

In his 1928–1929 lectures in *Introduction to Philosophy*, Heidegger makes one of his rare allusions to the problem of gender, sexuality, and embodiment. While the essence of Dasein is essentially "neutral," according to Heidegger, that neutrality is "necessarily broken," "insofar as it in each case factically exists." To quote further from these lectures: "That is, Dasein is as factical in each case male and female, it is a gendered being (*Geschlechtswesen*)."[11] As Heidegger emphasizes, however, the differentiation of sex is always tied to the structure of "being-with," to the extent that the plurality and diversity of human existence translate into a fundamental differentiation between me and other, of which gender is a distinctive feature. "However, this sexual relation is only possible because Dasein is already determined in its metaphysical neutrality through the with-one-another. If each Dasein, which is factically in each case male or female, were not essentially with-one-another, then the sexual relation as something human would be absolutely impossible."[12] These passages make evident that Heidegger does not neglect the issue of sexuality.

Could Heidegger, on the contrary, be the phenomenologist of sex par excellence? Upon first glance, the title might fall more easily to either Merleau-Ponty or Sartre who, as if living up to the stereotype of the lascivious "Frenchman," makes the problem of embodiment the key to understanding human existence. Yet despite his devotion to the question of being, Heidegger does not dismiss the concern for embodiment, for he tangentially addresses Dasein's embodied condition as it pertains to its facticity, to the fact of its situatedness in the world. As care, Dasein's being emerges as *already* instantiated "individually," that is, as "dispersed" and differentiated in regard to its potential to be a self. Insofar as this factical dispersion takes the form of Dasein's "thrownness" into a specific set of circumstances, each individual is "differentiated" according to its unique mode of embodiment, that is, in regard to gender or sex (i.e., female or male).

On the one hand, Heidegger stresses Dasein's "neutrality" in regard to sex and gender. This view is important, because it suggests that Dasein's being as "care" makes possible sexuality rather than our ability to have sex, and the capacity for reproduction, defining human being as such. Implicitly, Heidegger makes two points: (1) he separates human sexuality from its expression in animals and the line of ancestry with them as developed by evolutionary theory, and (2) he suggests that there are modalities of concern by virtue of which the self can address its sexuality and thereby experience it as part of the openness by which we encounter the self's uniqueness as well as our relation to others. On the other hand, from this neutrality Heidegger allows for sexual difference in terms of the instantiation of care or Dasein's factical dispersion via its thrownness as a situated, embodied being. In emphasizing the shift in inquiry that addresses Dasein in the unconcealing event of its emergence in the midst of beings, and thereby posing a question of the "why" from out of the vortex of its thrownness into the world, Heidegger coins the terms *metontology*. He contrasts metontology with fundamental ontology, which emphasizes instead Dasein's ontic priority as a being distinct from other beings insofar as it has an understanding of being. In *The Metaphysical Foundations of Logic* (1928), Heidegger indicates that the "turning over" (*Umschlag*) of metontology allows for a deeper level of ontological inquiry.[13] The fulcrum of ontology shifts to address Dasein's manner of withstanding being's emergence into presence, by which the self acquires the capacity to let beings be in the singularity of their manifestation. But this shift of metontology also underscores the individuality of the self, the factical dispersion in which Dasein's being as care becomes instantiated. And it is in the emphasis on individuation, a problem that Heidegger inherits from Leibniz in making the theory of monads the focus of his 1928 lectures on Leibniz, that sexuality can be addressed within this wider topography of questioning.

Accordingly, in these 1928 lectures—the seeds for *On the Essence of Ground*—Heidegger provides one of his most explicit statements about sexuality than is to be found anywhere in the *Gesamtausgabe*:

> Dasein harbors the intrinsic possibility for being factically dispersed into bodiliness and thus into sexuality. The metaphysical neutrality of the human being, inmost isolated as Dasein, is not an empty abstraction from the ontic, a neither-nor; it is rather the authentic concreteness of the origin, the not-yet of factical dispersion [*Zerstreutheit*]. As factical, Dasein is, among other things, in each case disunited [*Zwiespältig*] in a particular sexuality.[14]

But what can we say about this particular sexuality that could be any way illuminating, given that ontological thrust of Heidegger's inquiry? Is sexuality, in stark contrast to a psychologist such as Freud, merely an accidental, tangential characteristic of human existence? The answer lies in the fact that, as indicative of Dasein's thrownness, sexuality is one of the ways in which the self must take over its existence, or have its being "to be." That is, it is in light of its sexuality that Dasein must always return, in one way or another, to address "who" it is and thereby to bring itself in question. As noted by Medard Boss, who studied with Jung for ten years before seeking in Heidegger's phenomenology (i.e., "Daseinanalytic") an alternative to psychoanalysis,[15] so-called sexual hang-ups—including fetish obsessions—narrow and fragment the expanse of openness within which the self can relate to its own and the other's sexuality. "The Daseinanalytic investigation of our patients made us realize mainly that the psychopathologic phenomenon of a sexual perversion can never be regarded as a single, isolated symptom[;] it can only be conceived as one of the many possible concrete manifestations of certain states-of-being and world concepts. . . . [In sexually perverted acts] love can only enter the human sphere of existence through small inlets and peripheral apertures."[16] Though no pathology as such may be involved, we need to look no further to the pubescent boy to discover how wholeheartedly sexuality grips the developing individual and wrecks havoc with the search for identity. Indeed, one has no choice over the gender into which one is born—male or female (and "sex reversals" only reinforce the primordiality of one's gender)—and the unique physicality distinctive of each. Hence, in referring the self back to the nullity of its origins, sexuality also poses a possibility about my disclosure and others as well with whom I may be sexually involved. In *Being and Time*, Heidegger suggests that "willing" and, by implication, "desiring" are derivative expressions of care. Can the same be said of sexuality? If we distinguish sexuality as a phenomenon, as opposed to a psychosomatic impulse, then we must say no. Insofar as the "to be" may be radically individuated through sexuality, we must say, instead, that it serves as a "formal indicator" of care itself. That is, the character of human sexuality is so pervasive that it can signify the encompassing structure of care.

Recalling once again Dasein's neutrality in regard to sex, then, we must be cautious not to suggest that care can be reduced to sexuality. On the contrary, because sexuality pertains to its origins, it is a possibility that (always) stands ahead of the self and hence provides an occasion for exercising care. Moreover, because Dasein is always being-with others, sexuality may also provide an occasion for expressing solicitude. Is human sexuality distinct because of such solicitude, while animal sexuality appears mainly as an impulse toward reproduction? Though primate behavior might suggest the contrary, Heidegger would disdain putting any such discussion of sex in this biological and anthropological vein. Indeed, the formally indicative link between care and sex becomes important insofar as sexual desire is always bound up with the existential task of seeking to be an individual. For Heidegger, even the experience of pleasure, which for hedonists constitutes the primary aim of sex, is a way of manifesting care, a way of revealing the individual to himself or herself. In discussing Kant's view of sensibility, Heidegger states: "In having a feeling *for* something, there is always present at the same time a *self*-feeling, and in this *self*-feeling a mode of becoming revealed to oneself."[17] Despite whatever other or object orientation sex may have, there is first and foremost a personal orientation or comportment toward oneself. In his lectures on Nietzsche, Heidegger makes a similar point in arguing that "rapture" is not simply a physical effect or even a spiritual state of mind but instead pertains to the self's ecstatic openness, its way of standing forth in the expanse of possibilities. "But . . . rapture . . . is not something 'in' the body and 'in' the soul, but rather a way of standing, embodied and attuned, over against being[s] as a whole, which for its part attunes the attunement."[18] And the factical way in which the self comes into its own through its openness becomes explicit in the way that the individual must cultivate new possibilities (bearing on its way of coming to terms with its sexuality), such as whether to marry or have children. By the same token, sexual aberrations and problems (e.g., impotency) can be seen as those that most directly "damage" individuality or impair the quest for personal identity. Just as the horizon of bodying forth does not end with one's fingertips, as Heidegger suggests in *Zollikon Seminars*, so sexuality extends beyond the scope of pleasurable stimuli to reach the expanding frontier of being-a-self.[19]

We cannot consider care, however, without also considering its reciprocity with disclosedness. Dasein discloses its "there," but equally there is the capacity for covering up, as the addict's tendency toward self-dissimulation illustrates. In the next section, we will discuss the relevance of disclosedness for sexuality in the more direct way of impacting relationships. But in terms of the fact of embodiment, there is an immediate tie to the dynamic of uncovering and covering up, as far as how human beings experience their sexuality within the wider mystery of life. One of the most obvious and unnoticed aspects of human embodiment, at least as far as mainstream society goes, is the fact that "proximally and for the most part" we wear clothes, and indeed, clothes that observe the difference between the male and female sexes. Ever since the story of Adam's and Eve's loss of innocence at the sight of their own nudity, which offers a preontological narrative of care, human beings have faced the curious dilemma of both clothing and unclothing their nakedness. Strictly speaking, it is not nakedness as such that produces sexual arousal, or, more properly speaking, a sense of the erotic. On the contrary, the erotic resides in the tension between the clothing and unclothing of our bodies, particularly of the opposite sex, where nudity makes an explicit sexual difference.

As a way in which we exercise concern toward our bodies and those of others, eroticism hinges on how subtly the exchange between revealing and concealing plays itself out. Indeed, precisely because my experience of myself as care, as self, as gender specific, is always mediated by the larger dynamic of uncovering or covering up, I may experience greater arousal when confronted with (the opposite sex's) less nakedness than more, for example, upon seeing a woman's legs exposed while walking in a split skirt. One of the paradoxes of male-oriented pornography, as magazines such as *Playboy* illustrate, as it made the transition to "full-frontal nudity" in the mid-1970s, is that erotic lure may be lost in proportion with the publication of ever-more graphic pictures. Even Hugh Hefner acknowledged in an A & E television interview that the loss of the mystery of sex was the price for showing a greater degree of nudity of the female body. Conversely, the beauty of the human body, as captured in sculpture, painting, and photography, lies in its exemplifying that dynamic component that is essential to art, the holding in reserve of concealment that provides the contrast for the singularity of manifestness. The beauty of the nude resides in its character as a form of imitation, its mimetic ability. The nude body, then, appears beautiful insofar as it allows the earth's materiality to enter into play with the luminosity of the disclosure of world, a vessel for the enactment of the strife between earth and world. As Heidegger states in "The Origin of the Work of Art": "The world, in resting upon the earth, strives to surmount it. As self-opening it cannot endure anything closed. The earth, however, as sheltering and concealing, tends always to draw the world into itself and keep it there. The opposition of world and earth is strife. . . . In setting up a world and setting forth the earth, the work [of art] is an instigating of this strife."[20] And the experience of beauty, whether in the nudity of an exquisite physique or the blossoming of a rose, is the dynamic of that "moment" of instigating the strife between earth and world. The beauty becomes an occasion for opening up a world, if only in the most fleeting manner. To the extent that the photography of the pornographic captures beauty, it does so by observing this law of strife and preventing one of the elements (e.g., the materiality of the earth) from losing its influence in relation to the other. Erotic magazines such as *Playboy* begin to fail at the point where they deny the influence of materiality in favor of an "idealized," airbrushed, if not computerized, version of the female body. In light of these reflections on eroticism, let us then consider the situational dimension of sexuality as an instance of the larger drama between self and other; then, in the subsequent section, we will consider the role that imagination plays in the production of pornography.

Sexuality and the Other

While sex may be a phenomenon, it is an elusive one when viewed from an ontological perspective. No doubt much of the difficulty is that Heidegger, unlike Merleau-Ponty,[21] never introduces the body as the focus of his ontology, electing instead to allude to it in only a circumspect way via such formal concepts of his ontology such as facticity and thrownness. Care as Dasein's way of exercising concern for itself, facticity, and the corollary concept of freedom also contributes to enabling us to delineate a mosaic of issues pertaining to the phenomenon of sexuality. Yet if we are not simply to reduce this phenomenon to the behavioral domain of psychology, then we might do well to look elsewhere to find the stamp of the insignia of its importance, namely, through the inscription of the story, myth, and poem. That is, we must look to the medium of culture to discover the transmission of sexuality's meaning in all of its polymorphic forms, its widest experiential spectrum. Can we find a concept in Heidegger's ontology that allows us to bridge the gap between the formal elements of ontology, including care, facticity, and freedom, and the cultural narrative in which much of our understanding of sexuality comes to be etched? The concept would bear the pathos of our self's situatedness, harboring a dual affinity with the ontological and the cultural, circumscribing the limitations that pertain to the enactment of any choice as it bears the full weight of our embodied condition. This concept, which through its double reference can carry out the play in the tension between the ontological and the cultural, is none other than "guilt."

As scholars have frequently recognized, Heidegger offers one of the oddest and even most unconventional views of guilt that departs from the traditional characterization of it as a drawback or deficiency of the human self.[22] On the contrary, guilt is a potency in its own right to prepare the self to assume its own capability for commitment. That is, in regard to sexuality, guilt defines the self's awakening to the impact that the pursuit of sexual opportunities has upon it, how the self's uniqueness hangs in the balance of the kinds of sexuality it pursues and the concomitant social relations with which it becomes involved. But Dasein's acquisition of guilt, its pronouncement of being guilty, does not carry any moral reservations about the kind of sexual involvements. Rather, the admission of guilt, the fact that Dasein is guilty, serves as a throwback to a preevaluative level in which the limitation that freedom includes in the name of finitude assigns a certain measure of fulfillment to certain sexual activities over others. For Heidegger, freedom consists in accepting the limitation that the choice of one possibility may mean the foreclosure of another possibility.[23] Because of its root in facticity and finitude, guilt helps determine the scope of human freedom as it decides on the pertinence of certain sexual matters and determines how they are interwoven into the fabric of interpersonal, erotic relations.

In postulating the link between sex and guilt, are we not simply falling back into some version of Christian, puritanical moralism that has become obsolete? This would be true if not for the fact that Heidegger has learned the lesson of Nietzsche's critique of that morality, and indeed, develops a concept of guilt (*Schuld*) that is as peculiar and even idiosyncratic as one might find. We make the aforementioned link upon recognizing that Heidegger's analysis of guilt and conscience forms part of a larger strategy to displace the bodiless, Cartesian *cogito* in favor of an ecstatic, "incarnational" self whose search for individuality is always counterbalanced by its encounter with otherness. According to Heidegger, Dasein's way of being guilty brings into play the "negativity" that interrupts irrevocably any promise of self-presence, casting Dasein forth, as "thrown," into an ocean of diversity of involvements and an intertwining of relationships, the full spectrum of the human predicament. The fact that the self is thrust forth into this diversity, and must bear the weight of it, means that it is marked by a measure of "powerlessness" over its existence, that it is "guilty" from the ground up. But the "powerlessness" to which one is most vulnerable is that facet of care that speaks specifically to the inception of one's thrownness and brings forth a recollection of it, namely, the fact of one's origination at all, or "birth," to which Heidegger briefly alludes in a lecture course from 1928–1929.[24] Implied in the act of birth, of course, is the assignment of gender, and subsequently in the development of the child into an adult, the impetus to replicate one's origin in its most primordial way, the sexual impulse of "conjunction" (whether it is inherently reproductive or not).

Only because Dasein, as the "there," already finds itself within the openness can it, in Heidegger's words, "win its individuality" or exist authentically. But is the way in which one comes to terms with one's sexuality essential to Dasein's selfhood or, conversely, does the development of one's uniqueness determine one's sexual conduct? Heidegger's answer to this question might be somewhat ambiguous. While Heidegger may not construe sexuality as "essential," the openness distinguishing the authentic self takes on a connotation that is associated with the rapture of the sexual act, namely, "ecstasy." Heidegger reserves the name "transcendence" to describe the interplay of the temporal ecstases propelling Dasein into the openness, as simultaneously standing forth toward its possibilities and rooted in its situation. The factical side of transcendence, however, is that Dasein becomes exposed to those influences that retroactively stem from its thrownness, including those that elicit concerns—directed responses—toward its own mode of embodiment, needs, and desires. As Heidegger states at the beginning of chapter 1, division I of *Being and Time*, Dasein always has its being as an issue before itself, its being "to-be." But as part of that task of being-a-self, Dasein also enacts concern toward, addresses, and perhaps even appropriates those facets of embodied life that bear most directly on its question of identity, of who it is (e.g., one's sexuality). In *Zollikon Seminars*, Heidegger casts additional light on the ontological character of our exposed incarnatedness:

> Ontological disposition founds the particular feelings of well-being and discontent yet is itself founded again in the human being's being exposed [*Ausgesetzheit*] toward beings as a whole [*das Seiende im Ganzen*]. Thereby, it is already said that the understanding of being as being belongs to this being exposed (thrownness), but in the same way, there cannot be an understanding that is not already a "thrown" understanding.[25]

The ecstasy of the flesh, then, is not simply a physical reaction, because incarnatedness, far from being an accidental condition of an entity possessing an intellect, constitutes a key dynamic of Dasein's openness. In an especially illuminating remark from *Zollikon Seminars,* Heidegger underscores this emphasis on Dasein's open exposure to beings. "The limit of bodying forth is the horizon of being within which I reside [*aufhalten*]. Therefore, the limit of bodying forth changes constantly through the change in the reach of my sojourn."[26]

The emotionally charged way in which people experience love and sex suggests the inherent complexity of their incarnatedness, indeed, as essentially pertaining to Dasein's being as care and its factical instantiation and differentiation in regard to gender. Traditionally, philosophers and theologians alike have characterized sex as a kind of "passion," as an experience we "undergo" and "suffer" because we do not have complete control over it. Moralists such as Spinoza suggest that "adequate ideas" grounded in reason could give proper direction to our desires, such that we control them, rather than they control us, in a struggle best described as "human bondage." In the *Ethics,* Spinoza describes the emotional dimension of this struggle in memorable words after which Somerset Maugham titled his famous novel: "Human infirmity in moderating and checking the emotion I name bondage: for, when a man is a prey to his emotions, he is not his own master, but lies at the mercy of fortune: so much so, that he is often compelled, while seeing that which is better for him, to follow that which is worse."[27] Yet in a post-Freudian, poststructuralist world, as Foucault has shown, it is not clear whether a more prudent exercise of rationality can insulate us from the eruption of emotion which accompanies sexual desire.[28] On the contrary, phenomenologically speaking, the impulsiveness of sexual desire seems to be predicated upon the irreducibility of Dasein's thrownness, and the corresponding dispersion and falling (into circumstances) that invariably ensue. In suggesting that emotions such as hope have a temporal direction (e.g., futurity), Spinoza indirectly acknowledges that emotions, as indicative of temporality and hence of what it preunifies, or care, can be construed as expressions thereof.[28]

Sandwiched between the rationalist tendency to control the emotions and the poststructuralist approach to depict the self as an emotional vortex stands

Max Scheler, a contemporary of Heidegger's. Scheler caught Heidegger's eye as a phenomenologist who opposes the intellectualist bent of his mentor, Husserl, to define intentionality in terms of mentalistic acts of consciousness. In contrast, Scheler argued that intentionality originates with emotions, whose meanings can in turn be made explicit only through the correlates that various values embody. A hierarchy of values or preferences—from sensual to spiritual—corresponds to a spectrum of emotions—from urges (e.g., food and sex) to moral and religious sentiments (e.g., love and reverence). Rather than locating intentionality in consciousness, as Husserl does, Scheler seeks a fulcrum whose unity is interwoven into the stream of life itself: the person. With his religious orientation, Scheler slants his concept of the person in favor of its higher enactment vis-à-vis the spirit and its ultimate correlate of its intentionality, God as absolute being and absolute value. Yet Scheler always conceives the spiritual dimension of the person in connection with that field of emotional responses and their corresponding values, a field whose concrete occurrence in life takes the form of a body. Because of its tie to emotions and the values through which they are expressed, the body also provides a locus for the emergence of the intentional acts of the person.

With Scheler, the body appears on the threshold of assuming premiere phenomenological significance. But embodiment does not become the "cardinal" problem of phenomenology, as it later does for Merleau-Ponty, because Scheler still subscribes to a Platonic ontology that privileges the spirit over the body, the intellect over the emotions, in order to maintain the religious focus of transcendence in his hierarchy of Christian-based values. As such, Scheler remains a curious anomaly. In subscribing to Christian values and the exaltation of the spirit at the expense of the body, he remains pre-Nietzschean. Yet by bringing the emotional dimension of the body and its intentionality to the forefront of phenomenological thinking, Scheler prefigures postmodernists such as Merleau-Ponty and Foucault.

Albeit spiritualized, we cannot ignore the emphasis that Scheler places on love, which he characterizes as the highest emotion. If we then view Heidegger as another pathway leading from phenomenology, we find that he relocates the dimension of emotions within the accompanying dispositions that earmark the manner of our being "thrown" into the world. Emotions are not either mentalistic or subjective, since they point instead to the manner in which human existence discloses itself as already situated within a pregiven set of circumstances. Heidegger takes Scheler's criticism of Husserl's intellectualist bias one step farther by showing how the projective character of understanding must always be conjoined with the thrown dimension of dispositions. And to complete the transposition in which "world openness," a term Scheler coined,[30] replaces consciousness as the hallmark of being human, Heidegger relocates the vortex of emotions within the composition of care: facticity, existence, and falling. If we construe love on a primordial level commensurate with care, then we can see why human beings inevitably fall short in their quest for control over its wide spectrum of feelings. Accordingly, "love" is not simply an affect or emotion we can "master," as, for example, an outstanding golfer such as Jack Nicklaus or Tiger Woods can be said to surmount the influence of anger (over bad shots) within the circumscribed context of that game. As Giorgio Agamben states: "Love suffers all of this (in the etymological sense of the word passion, *pati, paskhein*). Love is the *passion of facticity* in which man bears this nonbelonging and darkness, appropriating (*adsuefacit*) them while guarding them as such. . . . This why . . . according to Jean-Luc Nancy's beautiful phrase, love is that of which we are not masters, that which we never reach but which is always happening to us."[31]

In reconsidering the myth of the "fall" of humanity, and the fact that the acquisition of original sin is in some way a narrative about the human predicament involving sex, we should not conclude that this narrative conveys something "bad" or evil about sexuality. In his 1928 lecture, "Phenomenology and Theology," which he dedicated to Rudolf Bultmann, Heidegger emphasizes that guilt as the hallmark of human finitude, precedes sin.[32] Heidegger's differentiation between guilt and sin would seem to be a rather trivial point, and perhaps one of the most easily overlooked in this lecture. According to him, sin is a moralistic concept that rests on a specific commitment of faith. Guilt, on the other hand, pertains to the general character of Dasein's situatedness, and to the challenges that the individual faces as always presented with the task of becoming an individual. Thus in linking sex to the conditions of thrownness and finitude, Heidegger, ironically, provides a way of decoupling the concern we show toward our sexuality from moral categories of "right" and "wrong." And through its moral neutrality, guilt points to sex as one of the various controversies and enigmas springing from Dasein's search for individuality. Conversely, sexual matters may be among the most painful predicaments in which human beings become "entangled" in their falling, not because sex is bad, immoral, and "sinful," but because the "meaning" it has for one's identity becomes most problematic when the risk of forsaking one's self, of losing oneself (e.g., in compromises, etc.), runs the highest.

Heidegger, then, links sex to Dasein's potential for selfhood, keeping in mind that the self is not a soul but, rather, may include in its openness the range of feelings and emotions that arises with the facticity of one's situatedness and embodiment. Ironically, two schools most opposed in the treatment of sexuality, natural law theory and evolutionary biology, both place a premium on reproduction, despite the fact that the former discounts God's existence and the latter affirms it. Though reproduction may serve the random processes of natural selection, on the one hand, and the mirroring of God's glory in human form on the other hand, either approach places the concern for sex on a generic, rather than an individual, level—of the procreation of species, whether naturally or divinely conceived. The individual level at which Heidegger broaches the issue of sex, however, has another important implication for its unfolding in terms of relationships, as a dimension of solicitude. Specifically, moral discussions, traditionally defined, would not be especially relevant for any phenomenological treatment of sex, for example, blanket prohibitions against premarital and postmarital sex. In this context, solicitude has a twofold importance in suggesting parameters for intimate relations between the sexes, but not simply for legislating right and wrong. Sexual intimacy entails acknowledging the singularity of the other, in such a way as to return to the other the maximum capability proper to his or her being (i.e., seeking his or her unique possibilities). But is this emphasis on allowing the other to exercise choice not just another way of acknowledging the importance of "consenting" relations between adults? Our phenomenological approach would not simply reject this contention, although there is more at stake. For solicitude also entails curtailing the imposition of my own beliefs and values on others, of allowing the other to be as other, in order to cultivate a relationship that accepts the controversy and disagreement inherent in the process of each "coming into its own."

A relationship that gives priority to such ownedness may not necessarily be bound by the mandates of a conventional institution such as marriage, it is safe to say. In stating that a married philosopher is a "comedy," certainly Nietzsche called into question the universal necessity of this institution.[33] Even when we accept marriage as a viable possibility, its limitation lies in the concession, in recounting Rilke's rejoinder quoted previously, that "togetherness" can be maintained only when each partner grants to the other periods of "separateness." But would we then want to conclude that the experiment of multiple relationships, even of promiscuity, would be the preferred path for seeking sexual fulfillment? Frederick Elliston has argued as much in emphasizing that Heidegger's concept of authenticity implies a license of individuality.[34] Yet hedonism and the pursuit of pleasure for its own sake appear to be as far removed from Heidegger's analysis of authenticity, with its stoic tone of the importance of "giving oneself up to death," as anything could be. With the suggestion that embodiment and sexuality actually signify human finitude, we could as easily argue that exclusive or monogamous relations (though not necessarily sanctified by the institution of marriage) are more preferable and rewarding than are promiscuous ones. Insofar as Heidegger defines freedom in terms of finitude, he states in *Being and Time*: "Freedom [lies in] . . . tolerating one's not having chosen [other possibilities] and one's not being able to choose them."[35]

Affirming the limitation's of one's existence defines the innermost meaning of Dasein's potential to be guilty, the hallmark of human finitude. Far from suggesting deficiency, these limitations distinguish Dasein's admission into the abundance of possibilities that existence bestows upon the self as it comes into its own. Dasein comes into its own, however, when it ceases to be defined by the narrow pursuits of the "they," and instead finds in the expanse of openness the wider vistas, the "*worauf*," or "whereto," in which it can continually unfold the uniqueness of its individuality. Once again our discussion of embodiment, in this case, as concretely experienced through sexuality, yields another illustration of the grammar of middle voice: only by facing the limitations of its existence, including the closure of death, can the self abide within the openness of existence. Dasein, however, discloses the "there" through the enactment of its temporality, in projecting itself upon its own possibility of being-toward-death. Thus the self's openness becomes more encompassing as it is reconciled with its finitude and acclimated in its attunement to the transitoriness of its temporal sojourn in the world. This transitoriness conveys to Dasein the urgency of its choices in such a way that as the trajectory of transcendence, the whereto of the temporal dimensions brings the self squarely into the ecstasy of the moment (*Augenblick*).

The self is inherently ecstatic, and bodying forth is one way in which it can experience this mode of "carried awayness" or transcendence. When we recognize that the nearness of Dasein's incarnatedness marks the distance of the "whereto," and finitude determines the trajectory of transcendence, we discover that characterization of the self with a metaphor of "ecstasy" whose meaning may be illustrated most graphically by the orgiastic experience of sex. Yet we do not wish to make the inference, as many poststructuralists have, that sexual idioms determine the character of Heidegger's ontological discourse. This may very well be the case. For those of us who explore the phenomenon of sexuality as a facet of embodiment, the opposite proves compelling: that sexuality indicates certain formal dimensions of care, and, conversely, that temporality as the meaning of care defines the distinctive modalities by which human beings experience (e.g., the pleasures of) sexuality. Thus the pleasurable reward of an orgasm is always overshadowed by the transitoriness of its occurrence, and the fleeting ecstasy of the flesh attests to the finitude of the self's temporality. In "Sex, Time, and Love," M. C. Dillon argues, in a Heideggerian spirit, that sexual passion is shaped by a temporalizing process in which the future holds open the possibility of satisfying the self's desires, and the past reveals the transitoriness of their fulfillment.[36]

Whether one falls in the camp of evolutionary biology or natural theory, there have been frequent attempts to address the relation between sex and love. While evolutionary biologists decouple love and sex, natural law theorists seek the convergence between them, for example, in advocating marriage as the proper context for engaging in sex and hence for reproduction. Heidegger, however, proceeds along a different path, insofar as he challenges the priority of any anthropological, sociological, biological, and even theological concept of love. On the contrary, he prioritizes the ontological character of care. Heidegger does so not to deemphasize the importance of love but instead to allow for the possibility of considering it on par with the ontological constitution of care, that is, in terms of temporality, transcendence, and finitude. In this way, Heidegger diverges sharply from Ludwig Binswanger, who criticized the former for underestimating the importance of a social experience of love as the dynamic of interpersonal relationships. In *Zollikon Seminars*, Heidegger responds to Binswanger's criticism in the following way:

> Because care is merely conceived as a basic constitution of Da-sein, which has been isolated as a subject, and because it is seen as only an anthropological determination of Da-sein, care, with good reason, turn out to be a one-sided, melancholic interpretation of Dasein, which need to be supplemented with "love."
>
> But correctly understood (i.e., in a fundamental-ontological sense), care is never distinguishable from "love" but is the name for the ecstatic-temporal constitution of the fundamental characteristic of Da-sein, that is, the understanding of being.
>
> Love is founded on the understanding of being just as much as is *care* in the anthropological [psychological] sense. One can never expect that the essential determination of love, which looks for a guideline in the fundamental-ontological determination of Da-sein, will be deeper and more comprehensive than the one seeing love as something higher than care.[37]

One implication of the neutrality of Heidegger's phenomenological stance is to avoid a moralist bias in one direction or another, for example, of hedonism versus marriage, the pretext of any ideology. Yet the way in which a concern for individuality may shape one's perspective on sex allows for the *possibility* that love may be interwoven into the fabric of one's sexual experiences. The major difficulty with addressing this possibility, however, is that Heidegger has little more to say about love than sex, with the exception of his 1936 lectures on Schelling that address more of a cosmic rather than a personal form of *liebe*. In contrast, Spinoza linked sex and love, claiming that the latter must be governed by "adequate ideas" in order to avoid the individual's enslavement to erotic desires or "inclinations."[38] In Heidegger's case, perhaps the best indication of the power of love may not lie so much in the permanence of its fulfillment but once again in the transitoriness of its occurrence, in the potential for its loss. Love is of such a character that it welcomes the clash of the other, thereby seeking "harmony" only through the counteradmission of strife, as Heraclitus remarks.[39] As pertaining to care, and thus as governed by thrownness, the character of love is to accept the relinquishment of the desire to control the "beloved," even if and not in spite of the transitoriness of the relationship that the shadow of death inevitably casts.

Regarding love and death, Freud addressed this curious juxtaposition, as did Rilke and Nietzsche. For Nietzsche, love becomes a pervasive concept such that through *amor fati* it rises to the level of the celebration of each and every moment in the eternal recurrence. In citing Nietzsche's discussion of "free death" from *Thus Spoke Zarathustra*, Heidegger suggests that the "joy" of existence is intimately tied up with one's readiness to "give oneself up to death."[40] That is, the authentic projection of being-toward-death demands a relinquishment of the so-called "possessiveness of love," as a mode of the "clinging to existence" that Heidegger maintains typifies Dasein's tendency to "flee from death" and hold onto the level of life it has reached. In simple terms, love is defined as an openness to the other, which thereby becomes most effusive when (1) the self seeks the highest degree of individuality, and (2) it heeds the conditions of finitude, including the transitoriness of death, which allows it to defeat the will of possessiveness and respond to the singularity of the other. As Rilke emphasizes, love cultivates individuality rather than denies it: "love . . . consists in this, that two solitudes protect and border and salute each other."[41]

Love is first and foremost the acceptance of loss. While resonating somewhat with the romantic ideal of love, this statement has ontological meaning primarily as a declaration of human finitude. But this is where Heidegger's notion of embodiment, as ontologically defined as a dimension of being's manifestness, differs significantly from Merleau-Ponty's account of the body as a mode of intentionality, as "motility," as a (physical) presence to the world.[42] Indeed, due to the temporal modality of manifestation, the meaning of incarnatedness does not simply lie in presence, except when counterbalanced by the opposite possibility of absence. Thus everyday locutions such as "absence makes the heart grow fonder,"or "we only truly appreciate someone after they are gone" carry significant weight as indications of the essential finitude of love and human relationships. Indeed, insofar as concealment is necessarily a part of the openness of my discovery of the other, there is always a reservedness and withholding that preclude any perfect knowledge and complete appreciation of the other. A mystery inevitably lingers in the experience of love that is part of the concealment of being itself. This mystery may be the source of much poetic lore and inspiration behind the so-called "romantic" and "unrequited" love that Goethe explored in *The Sorrows of Young Werther*.[43] But the mysterious depth of love is also a fact, insofar as it sustains a devotion to the other, even after the physical presence of the other is gone.

In popular circles, intimacy becomes a catchall phrase to describe the close compatibility of two sexual partners. But what intimacy actually entails is that the closeness implies a desire to engage in a continual rediscovery about the identity of the other. Because of the fact that all discovery is finite, and hence *remains opens as a* possibility, there remains an element of masking and concealment so that in the movement into openness, a mystery always remains. The prevalence of this mystery thereby allows for a special mode of exchange, or in the popular rhetoric, "communication," by which each partner can relate without using words. Thus nonverbal exchange, for example, what Merleau-Ponty describes as the silence of the caress, distinguishes this mode of sexual intimacy.[44] To be sure, Heidegger does not describe this phenomenon as such. But he does emphasize that language originates at a prepredicative level, and thus gestures in the sense that Merleau-Ponty describes, belong to the essence of language.[45] Even in *Being and Time,* where Heidegger neglects the problem of embodiment, he still emphasizes that bodily indices such as "right" and "left"—which refer to the positioning of one's hands—acquire significance against the backdrop of the preorientation, directionality, and deseverance of being-in-the-world.[46] Thus a wink can convey sexual desire, because of a prior opening forth of a world in which that gesture acquires its signifying power. And of course a person's deployment of that gesture points to incarnatedness as issuing forth—bodying forth as such—into the area of language, the signification of embodiment. Echoing Julia Kristeva, Jennifer Gosetti describes this linguistic dimension of incarnatedness as the "rhythm of words" or "bodily speech."[47]

Time, in conjunction with space, ultimately yields the conditions of embodiment. So when embodiment ceases to be essential to individuality, as in death, then the materiality of the world still intercedes in the vacuum left by the other's departure. That is, the other may still become present through his or her absence, whose locus extends from the four quadrants of the world rather than confined to physical coordinates of proximity. Through absence, the other may become present again, not just in photographs and other pictorial representations but in the recollection of those ancestors who harken forth in the "ones to come," as Heidegger suggests in *Beiträge.*[48] This is not to say that the other is "immortal," either in the literal sense of the Christian soul reunited with God or in the figurative sense of which Gabriel Marcel speaks of a commemorative "presence" (although this view is closer to Heidegger's).[49] Even when death as such is not the source of loss, as in "long-distance relationships," "breakups," and divorces, the possibility of absence foretells the story of love and romance.

Perhaps in the arena of love, as nowhere else, we experience the fragility and vulnerability of life. The cliche that few things last forever recalls the fact that temporality is finite; but the *pathos* of this transitoriness is perhaps felt no more profoundly than when the self confronts the fleeting character of love, of intimate relationships. Longevity, as it were, can still be a desirable end within relationships, for example, marriage ensures that both partners embody trustfulness and a willingness to renew their commitment to each other. Heidegger coined the term "self-constancy" to distinguish the interval of "stretching along" by which Dasein discovers that the meaning of existence unfolds across the entire arc of its existence. Indeed, meaning arises as Dasein discovers a direction arising from the reconnection of the past with the future, whose intersection is the self's ecstatic eruption into the moment as the individual takes a specific course of action. The renewal of commitment, as may be exemplified in a "healthy" marriage, hinges upon the enactment of self-constancy by each of the partners. Heidegger, of course, relied heavily on Kierkegaard's notion of repetition to draft his concept of authenticity as Dasein's way of stretching itself along between future and past. Allowing the circle of interpretation to swing in the opposite direction, we can say that Heidegger's vision of self-constancy distinguishes the ontological precondition for the renewal of commitment, which in marriage each partner practices in the name of fidelity. And we would define fidelity, in temporal terms, as a reciprocal commitment of the partners throughout the unfolding of their historical existence.[50] Again, Heidegger would not be endorsing marriage, much less same-sex partnership, as much as identifying the precise exercise of responsibility that each individual must exhibit as the key to securing the bond of any relationship. Thus monogamy is not simply an option that one chooses and then puts aside, such as selecting an insurance company. Instead, the choosing is such that one must be prepared to venture the risk of that decision in which the preference for an exclusive relationship reemerges as hanging in the balance.

Yet Heidegger would imply that if marriage were the best option for developing a specific relationship, then the beginning of its success hinges upon each individual's already coming into his or her own. In other words, one cannot be of benefit to anyone else in entering into a relationship of truth and reciprocity unless one has also developed a measure of self-responsibility and self-understanding. In his 1930 lectures on Kant, Heidegger states: "*Self-responsibility* is the *fundamental kind of being* determining distinctively *human* action, i.e., *ethical praxis*."[51] Two years earlier, in his 1928 lectures on Leibniz, Heidegger remarks: "Freedom makes Dasein in the ground of its essence, responsible [*verbindlich*] to itself, or more exactly, gives itself the possibility of commitment. . . . As a result of this commitment, Dasein commits itself to a capability of being toward-itself as able-to-be-with other in the ability-to-be-among extent things. Selfhood is free responsibility for and toward itself."[52] Selfhood then includes responsibility, and hence in whatever relationship Dasein pursues, there is a tendency to exercise the greatest degree of commitment, that is, fidelity. Trust and truthfulness then become the yardsticks for the responsibility each partner assumes by his or her relationship to each other. To quote Rilke: "Love is at first not anything that means merging, giving over, and uniting with another . . . [i]t is a high inducement for the individual to ripen, to become something in himself, to become world, to become world for himself for another's sake, it is a great exacting claim upon him, something that chooses him and calls him to vast things."[53] But, to consider the observation, what happens when this fidelity breaks down?

The obvious instance of this breakdown would be a so-called transgression such as adultery. But at issue is not so much the morality of adultery, or even of promiscuous sex in general. As Wasserstrom points out, the problem with adultery is not so much the character of the sexual behavior as the suggestion that a promise to another person, or a commitment, has been broken.[54] Indeed, the phenomenologically relevant factor is the deception that the adulterer practices in order to keep his or her partner from discovering the "affair." Conversely, the advantage of an open marriage lies in avoiding from the outset this stage of deception, because the marriage agreement includes a mutual acceptance of each spouse's alternative sexual partners. Thus adultery becomes a problematic decision for the individual, insofar as such an action may seem to weaken his or her commitment to oneself. Ontologically speaking, the falling that would seem to come into play would not simply involve a lostness in one's carnality but instead an ensnarement in a continual propensity to cover, conceal, and disguise the affair in the eyes of others. People commit adultery, and various prominent ones at that: from great philosophers to famous politicians, and it is irrelevant here to seek some position of exalted "self-righteousness." But the fact of the circumstances surrounding such "falling" remains clear: adulterers dissimulate; and perhaps the most objectionable aspect of this behavior, when viewed from a non-Christian perspective a la Nietzsche, is the hypocritical character of such an act: of preaching *monogamy* and doing the opposite.

Does the prevalence of adultery, then, suggest that sexuality is intrinsically tied to falling? Obviously such a statement would be false, particularly when we view the negative way in which sexuality is construed by the Judeo-Christian tradition. The act of adultery, of course, is prohibited by the Ten Commandments. And St. Paul advances such memorable statements as: "It is better to marry than to burn in lust." In attempting to correct the imbalance of importance that the Western philosophical and theological tradition places on the spirit, Nietzsche rebukes St. Paul's exhortation by proclaiming: "Modern marriage has lost its meaning—consequently, one abolishes it."[55]

In a technological age where the search for self-fulfillment, if not gratification, prevails over the interests of the family, the institution of marriage becomes increasingly problematic. Be that as it may, there are aspects of romantic love, of the fickleness of its steadfastness and devotion, that illustrate an important dimension of care, the self's tendency to "fall" into the web of its own preoccupations. As an ontological structure of care, falling is connected with the dispersion that Dasein experiences in its embodiment. And the materiality of this dispersion harbors a tendency toward concealment. Thus it is because Dasein is already prone to dissimulation, insofar as the possibility of untruth or covering up belongs to care, that an individual becomes capable of the kind of *dissimulating* behavior that we attribute to adultery. There is a recent aphorism that "An erect penis knows no conscience." What is at issue in adultery is not simply the urges taking over to the detriment of reason or common sense, but the underlying expression of care that sustains that behavior, namely, covering up or lying. The vernacular description of adulterous behavior as "cheating" implies that at its heart the act includes a propensity to lie, dissimulate, and cover up.

There is perhaps no human experience that dramatizes the joy and pathos of our embodiment more than sexuality. But bodying-forth is a complex phenomenon that includes care and its dynamic of revealing-concealing. And it is the fact that sexuality extends into the social arena that illustrates, through partnerships and their dissolution, loyalty and infidelity, how the fact of our embodiment brings us before the cusp of the tension of truth and untruth. And how we confront this twofold points back to how each of us as Dasein already stands in a posture of self-interrogation. Sex turns out to be not only one of the greatest pleasure of life but also one of the greatest mysteries. And this is true because as a basic instance of our embodiment, sexuality refers each of us back to the mystery of his or her origins and the continual enigma as to the identity of the self, the possibility of coming into one's own. If such were not the case, then sex would not pose the kind of ubiquitous problems that it does.

Thus infidelity is not simply a desire gone awry but instead points to basic tension of human existence whereby one is always challenged by the task of coming into one's own. In sexuality, this challenge is doubled by the fact that the self's proprietorship of coming into one's own always occurs in tandem with its relation to others. As John van Buren emphasizes, in his early lectures on Aristotle, Heidegger stressed that the facticity of the self becomes concrete through the *ethos* of its "speaking-with" and "being-with" others.[56] As the lived-out, relational sense of facticity, the language of relationships reveals idioms of the proper and the improper. These idioms suggest that how we deal with our sexuality plays out on the stage of the larger drama of revealing-concealing, which pertains to Dasein's being and, ultimately, to being itself. As Giorgio Agamben, who attended Heidegger's "Seminar in Le Thor 1966," states: "Lovers go the limit of the improper in a mad and demonic promiscuity; they dwell in carnality and amorous discourse, in forever-new regions of impropriety and facticity, to the point of revealing their essential abyss."[57] Agamben thereby expresses a view of sexuality that mirrors much more the Greek vision of sex as an instance of the tragic transgression of limits than a Christian portrait of violating moral standards. Sex, then, is not simply ontic in its relevance (desire and reproduction) but instead bears out the tension between the two, of the ontological difference as such.

Given this connection to Dasein's being and to the ontological, sex has always posed a perennial problem to human beings, even going back to the mythic days of Adam and Eve. As Rilke suggests, we are still not sufficiently learned in our dealings with sex to have a full appreciation of its importance for human beings.[58] The voice of the poet resounds with a similar message in *Sonnets to Orpheus*: "Neither has love been learned."[59] Perhaps Rilke more than Heidegger, appreciates the importance of sexual difference and its contribution to the mystery of sexuality. And this differentiation becomes more explicit when we began to question, as Julia Kristeva does, whether the importance of the feminine element has been suppressed within a phallic-centered, patriarchal Western culture, civilization, and philosophy. In many respects that becomes an issue for postmodernists and deconstructionists to debate, particularly given the fact, as John van Buren has suggested, that Heidegger occasionally falls back on ethnocentric and chauvinist stereotypes (e.g, the "wife" whose primary lot in life is to "sow at the table").[60] Kristeva provides a unique perspective, however, because she integrates a concern for the Heideggerian motif of temporality into her discussion of the unique way in which a woman experiences her mode of embodiment. Specifically, "woman's time" includes an explicit tie to the materiality of the earth, for example, the duration of pregnancy, and to natural cycles of menstruation in monthly intervals.[61] This female temporalizing helps create the space of difference in which the differentiation of the sexes can play itself out. Luce Irigaray offers an interesting perspective on this differentiation: "It is not only around the earth that we must turn but around ourselves in order to be capable of opening ourselves, including dialectically to another. . . . The unity of the being as human should then be measured with respect to the unity of the relation with the other taking account of difference."[62] While addressing further my relation to the other, Irigarary states: "The attentive approach to the other gives me a real and a meaning still to come and unknown for me. . . . It is only bestowed thanks to the fidelity of each to oneself."[63] Following Irigaray, Patricia Huntington speaks of a "sexual incarnation" in order to identify the distinctive modality of care that women experience in such maternal acts as feeding and "weaning"a baby.[64] To quote Krell: "Men and women, joined as mortals, give one another whatever 'man' can be. If not a minor theme after all, it is still in a minor key. Its dominant tone is not heroic coupled by which desire would be drained utterly and the Other appropriated once and for all."[65] As long as this interplay flourishes, there will be an accompanying mystery of the sexes.

Can the mystery of sexuality, of our embodied condition, provide an indication of the mystery of being? If we take Rilke's statement seriously and approach sexuality less as an instinct than as a phenomenon of the understanding of which is still unfolding, then we can point to the inception of the future as the stage for addressing this mystery. One of Heidegger's foremost students, Herbert Marcuse, points to a future where the "eroticism" of humanity can occur in a way that liberates us from those Victorian inhibitions and constraints, which Freud recognized as an important factor in the development of many sexual pathologies. Although abandoning Heidegger's terminology of radical finitude, Marcuse nevertheless offers an interesting portrait of eroticism as a striving to transgress boundaries:

> What distinguishes pleasure from the blind satisfaction of what is the instinct's refusal to exhaust itself in immediate satisfaction, its ability to build up and use barriers for intensifying fulfillment. Though this instinctual refusal has done the work of domination, it can also serve the opposite function [to] eroticize non-libidinal relations, transform biological tension and relief into free happiness. No longer employed as instruments for retaining mean in alienated performances, the barriers against absolute gratification would become elements of human freedom; they would protect that other alienation in which pleasure originates—man's alienation not from himself but from mere nature: his free self-realization.[66]

In *Contributions*, Heidegger refers to the "ones to come" in order to distinguish the tension in which we stand to the future and to suggest that being itself is that whose clearing (*Lichtung*) first casts the light of understanding (*Verstehen*), is what "gives us to understand," even in the most personal and murky region of human sexuality. In emphasizing the need to reformulate *die Seinsfrage* in the first introduction to *Being and Time*, Heidegger states that being is the most indeterminate concept and also the most obvious. We might draw a curious parallel with the phenomenon of sexuality, namely, that it is both the most inscrutable of all human experiences, the hardest to get a handle on, and yet also the most personal and provocative. As Heidegger states, as "ontically closest," Dasein is also "ontologically farthest."[67] And it is the unfolding of this dimension of inscrutability and mystery that implicates our embodiment as an issue that correlates with the task of reasking the question of being. Indeed, it is because that issue bears upon the specific circumstances of our finitude, including our mortality, that our way of addressing it can become a new springboard to ontological inquiry. When reinscribed in terms of the idiom(s) of embodiment, finite transcendence reemerges as an erotic striving to reset the boundaries of the possible, to transgress the limits between what is acceptable and forbidden. In accordance with the language of Heidegger's ontology, we appeal to imagination to mark the source of this special mode of creativity, the topography of the erotic. Imagination (*Einbildungscraft*) arises as an impetus to transgress the restrictions of convention and to circumscribe new boundaries of meaning, intelligibility, and even permissibility.[68]

EROS, IMAGINATION, AND THE PORNOGRAPHIC

Let us now turn from how the fact of sex expresses itself in our daily lives to the ontological implications of that phenomenon. Initially we saw how an ontology of human existence as thrown illuminates the pivotal role that sex plays in human experience. On the basis of that insight, we must now consider, conversely, how sex can illuminate the dynamic of being, that is, the way in which its (i.e., being's) unfolding in terms of embodiment, *or as* incarnality, distinguishes the diversity of its manifestation. We move, as it were, within the sweep of a circularity in which a hermeneutics of facticity illuminates sexuality and the concretion of the concern about *eros*. Love finds in incarnality a formal indicator of being's power of manifestation and appearance. Such a formal indicator, however, harbors its own impetus for self-articulation, whose basic idioms acquire their meaning against the backdrop of tradition and its transmission through the ongoing conversation in successive generations. To borrow from Hegel, one such idiom would be the "language of tragedy."[69]

In myth and literature, let alone the factual realm of people in politics, tragedy seems to follow on the heels of sex. The myth of Adam and Eve paints this tragedy in terms of exile from paradise, from the Garden of Eden. As Ricoeur emphasizes, however, the Adamic myth hinges upon the breakthrough of a certain kind of knowledge, of good and evil, an awareness of the suffering, as well as the bliss, accompanying our sexuality.[70] The emergence of such understanding, almost a painful revelation of what has formerly been concealed, typifies the myth of Oedipus as well, including such modern renditions as O'Neill's *Desire under the Elms*.[71] The revelation of sexual difference, to employ Derrida's term rather than Ricoeur's, points to the emergence of a predicament that will punctuate the entirety of the human situation and distinguish the precariousness of our predicament. Even in contemporary politics, as the legacy of President William Clinton illustrates, the lure of sex obtrudes to mark the "downfall" of the rich, the successful, and the powerful. In *Being and Time*, Heidegger "formalizes" this mythic condition for the potential of a downfall by identifying "falling" as an essential component in the structure of care. And precisely because there is falling, there can be entanglement in that toward which one falls, that is, in light of our previous discussion, vulnerability to addiction. Though one might question whether there is, medically speaking, such a malady as "sexual addiction," there is nevertheless sufficient evidence that points to a compulsive need that certain individuals have to be in a relationship, a codependency.[72]

In recovering tragedy as a key cultural idiom, Heidegger incorporates a narrative into his ontology that distinguishes the tension of being's revealing-concealing as a kind of conflict, as a "drama" that is historically carried out and in which human beings participate by undertaking decisions. But how does a concern for sex also figure into this narrative, not only as pertaining to the human predicament but also as shaping the idioms for being's self-expression? We gain a hint from Heidegger's 1929–1930 lectures on animals, in which he distinguishes between an ontological desire for openness and an ontic craving for satisfaction vis-à-vis an immersion in and a utilization of beings. An ontological desire can be construed as a variation of *eros* that draws (the self) forth into the expanse of possibilities, what Heidegger first describes in *Being and Time* as the *worauf* and ecstatic outsidedness of the "ahead-of-itself." In his lectures on Plato in the early 1930s, Heidegger explicitly identifies eros as an ecstatic movement into the openness of possibilities, as embodying the trajectory of transcendence as a surpassing outward and beyond.[73] Eros, in this sense, is an ontological desire that welcomes otherness and seeks refuge in the open rather than in a narrow perspective of self-preoccupation and gratification. Eros may also include the physical intimacy of sexual love, insofar as the individual stands out beyond himself or herself in response to the other, and hence forsakes the control over his or her wishes in favor of the discovery that communion with the other may provide (i.e., as a passage into the openness). As Plato realized, and Heidegger reaffirms, the self-questioning of philosophy is as much a form of eros as it is sexual love, to the extent that both originate within the open and accent the play of possibility as such. Moreover, *philosophy is inherently erotic*, if by that we understand the quest to test limits whose enactment spawns a wider expanse of possibilities. As such, the love of wisdom, *philosophia*, is a response to an invitation to participate in this openness.

Ontic craving, on the other hand, defines an attraction toward what is already manifest and how that can be utilized for an advantage (e.g., the satisfaction of hunger, or a mate for reproduction).[74] This ontological-ontic distinction, however, becomes especially relevant in sex: for as finite, we are already caught between *an erotic impetus to emerge into openness and a countertendency to identify with and utilize what becomes opened up*. Sexuality, then, is a special kind of inducement for the self to enter an expanse of openness, while the ontic craving for satisfaction works itself out in the opposite field of control and domination (especially over others), as Jean-Paul Sartre graphically describes.[75]

What we might call the experience of "sexual tension," then, may also be indicative of the basic drama of humanity's experience of being as an emerging into and retreat from openness. The tension is that which, originating from thrownness, transports human being into opposition between truth and untruth, and thereby makes the self vulnerable to a kind of ontological slippage called "falling." From the earliest myths at the dawn of civilization until Freud, humanity's experience of sex has always been colored by tragedy. The fact of this tragic dimension, as inscribed in the facticity of Dasein's historical existence, is more than just the "ontic" way in which human beings become susceptible to lust. Instead there are profounder vicissitudes we experience that accompany such lust. Insofar as these include denial and dissimulation, sins of omission and deception, they stem from a negativity so primeval as to arise from an abyss, an *Abgrund*. But this negativity not only shapes our tendency to be immersed in beings but also harbors the potential for the interruption of this proneness to "fall." Because of the dual tension between the ontic and the ontological, the self's submission to the passions of the flesh can never be simply reduced to a complex of biological urges, for residing in the openness of the erotic impetus to transcend is the countertension of narrowing the scope of slipping back into the narrowness of craving in all of its destructive implications.

As Heidegger states in his 1931–1932 lectures on Plato:

> for this reason the *bodily constitution* of man is fundamentally different to pure nature. It is primordially inserted in the striving for being. It is not the case that man is first an animal and then something else in addition. Man can never be an animal, i.e. can never be nature, but is always precisely over the animal, or, precisely as human, *under* it (whereupon we can say that man becomes 'like an animal'). Since nature does not have the inner elevation of *existence* which belongs to being human as *being out beyond oneself* [*Über sich hinaus-sein*], it is incapable of *falling*.[76]

Correlatively, the allure of an escape into the attraction of beings, which propels us in our myopic pursuit of sex, invites a countermovement of self-awakening, discovery, and understanding. The tragic dimension is such that the destructive consequences of falling must be first played out as a prelude to the "protagonist's" accepting an insight previously withheld, a new form of self-revelation. In *Letters to a Young Poet*, Rilke summarizes this double-edge character of human sexuality. "Sex is difficult; yes. But they are difficult things with which we have been charged. . . . If you only recognize this and marriage, out of yourself, out of your *own* nature and ways, out of your *own* experience and childhood and strength to achieve to sex wholly your own (*not* influenced by convention and custom), then you need no longer be afraid of losing yourself and becoming unworthy of your best possession."[77]

In this context, Zarathustra's words "*Incipit tragoedia*" carry a lot of weight.[78] Indeed, only the self-submissive act of "going under" prepares the way for the eventual transformation of "crossing over." Put simply, sacrifice lies at the heart of tragedy. Ontologically speaking, this sacrificial act is nothing else than the admission that openness is always bounded by an encounter with mortality. That is, an encounter with the possibility of death overshadows the enlightenment of any moment of self-discovery and self-revelation. But what does this have to do with sex? Everything. For sexual relationships are essentially about limits and boundaries, how to set them, how to push and even transgress them, and, finally, how to reinstate them. Insofar as the negotiation of these limits requires that the individual develop greater self-understanding, sexual transgressions are essentially an experiment—however dangerous and destructive—with the finitude of Dasein. And a reconciliation with this finitude allows the expanse of an ontological openness to reign, which rescues the self, as it were, from (the clutches of) a destructive pull of "ontical craving" that fragments the individual in his or her pursuit of various sexual obsessions and compulsions.[79]

Is there any distinctly human potential that epitomizes the ability to transgress and reset boundaries of the possible which, by its affinity for temporality and finitude, constitutes a vessel of disclosedness? More pointedly, the "power" in question would not only serve this ontological role, it would also double in an ontic fashion with what the tradition has historically equated as a producer of "fantasy." And of course the only candidate which, in its economy, can include such polyvalency is imagination. Perhaps the simplest instance of this is the role that fantasy plays in stimulating physical arousal, both for males and females, as a conduit of sexual expression. Acting out different personas, or "role-playing" between couples, suggests how imagination transposes the physical event of lovemaking into a wider arc of expression and meaning. Role-playing then becomes a kind of mimesis of a couple's sexual encounter, which allows imagination to reset the boundaries, as it were, in which the acts of intimacy can be undertaken.

We might ask, as Lawrence Hatab has, why even preserve the concept of imagination, when in many ways it holds a trace of subjectivism that may render it somewhat obsolete?[80] But the issue of embodiment, as it pertains to sexuality, shows why the process of imagemaking becomes important in providing a bridge between the ontological (imagination as shaping the horizon of transcendence) and the ontic (imagination as a flight toward the fantastic, even taboo). Heidegger's famous retrieval of imagination in the Kant book illustrates how this originator of time and, hence, of disclosedness shapes the finite horizon for any understanding of being (transcendence). When developed in its full ontological power, as Heidegger does in the Kant book, imagination provides the occasion whereby being is raised from its restriction to the proposition and transposed into a new relation in which language re-emerges as a partner to unconcealment.[81] By discharging this ontological power, imagination also marks the furthest vistas of the *worauf*, the arc of transcendence, where the contraction and expansion of a horizon of possibilities occur. We can construe this vacillation between the two as it is enacted through imagination, as a kind of "play." Because this play takes it cue from possibility, its emphasis lies more on what is not merely given or "present," or what is "absent" and withdrawn. Following Rousseau, John Sallis describes the play of imagination as "extend[ing] the measure of the possible."[82] Because of this inherent creativity, as it were, imagination can give birth to the "fantastic," to the genesis of the "surreal," a presencing rooted in the counterpull of absence. While imagination catapults us to these fanciful heights, we welcome its creativity precisely because, as factical beings, we are steeped in the conditions of finitude (time-space), that is, *incarnated in the flesh*. As such, imagination is an offspring or a corollary or our "incarnatedness."[83] To be sure, Heidegger does not explicitly make this declaration. Yet in the Kant book he does imply as much.[84] The the basic thrust of his destructive retrieval of transcendental philosophy is to overcome the polarity of thought and sensibility by rediscovering in the synthetic power of imagination the unity of both: a receptive spontaneity and a spontaneous receptivity.[85]

But what is at stake in the arousal of human sexuality? Psychological studies make evident that sexual stimulation, in men as well as in women, depends as much on an active fantasy life as on simple physiological responses. As I have already mentioned, the use of role-play in spicing up a couple's sex life is one such example of the importance of creating fantasies. And there are even more extreme instances, in which the fantasies themselves seek new mediums and ever-more "illicit" scenarios of expression and representation. Indeed, we cannot ignore the significance that erotic images have played in human sexuality since the dawn of civilization. By the same token, we cannot underestimate the proliferation of these images through a highly specialized, even commercial, industry of film and Internet: the erotically graphic, that is, *pornography*. When tailored to the special craft of sexual experimentation, of testing the limits of erotic expression, imagination spawns pornography as almost an inevitable outgrowth of its creativity. Where would civilization be without the graphing of sexual images upon the landscape of the possible, a topographic of the erotic, in short, pornography? Perhaps, ironically, Heidegger's radical retrieval of the imagination leads to the necessity of this question. Through the vehicle of imagination, pornography constitutes the body's way in participating in art, a form of disclosure that invites innovation and creativity. Indeed, the *topos* in question, as developed through the play of innovation, provides a material avenue for entering the openness, a *mimesis*, as it were, in which the body serves as a place of unconcealment. The graphic display of sexuality, the exploitation of the body's differentiation into the sexes, constitutes a celebration of our embodiment that human beings are uniquely positioned to enjoy.

In *Introduction to Metaphysics*, Heidegger cites the tragic characterization of human being as the "uncanniest of the uncanny."[86] No doubt a dimension of this uncanniness, of this strangeness, becomes apparent in the way that human beings cherish sex precisely when divorced from the need or wish to reproduce, and, indeed, they go to great lengths to extend the play of the erotic for its own sake through various pornographic mediums. The imaginative portrayal of sex indicates that sexual activity is not simply an extension, as it were, of the organs themselves. Rather, the fact that the activities themselves try to probe the boundaries of convention and acceptability means that eroticism is like a new frontier in which we experience our disclosedness (and covering up), a landscape in which new possibilities for play can unfold. Human sexuality, unlike the corollary for animals, is an "imitation" of nature, a form of mimesis, that transforms the basic difference between male and female into an imaginative, even innovative, pursuit of ever-novel possibilities for consummating the same "natural" act (of intercourse, etc.). Due to this creativity of imagination, our incarnatedness, precisely at the juncture where we experience it most passionately and poignantly, is ecstasy through and through, an "ecstatic play" and a "dance" between the sexes.

But do not animals, in their elaborate ritual of "courtship," also exhibit a kind of play and dance? Or does such a characterization of "courtship" itself betray an "interpretation" of a behavior that we ascribe to ourselves, and, by analogy, to animals? Without getting into a debate as to the priority of nature versus culture, we point to the human proliferation of pornography as a key demarcation point of how human beings display the uncanniness that they do. Pornography is not just an industry of culture, but is a variation of imaginative creativity that, erotic in its form, is always prefigured by and in service of a deeper-rooted mode of disclosedness. To be sure, we can debate the so-called ethics of pornography, and whether its most "graphic" forms objectify women, as feminists such as Helen Longino have argued.[87] And a concomitant, though often overlooked problem is the development of pornography less as an art and more as an industry. In the latter case, under the "they's" influence and its reinforcement in technology, pornography becomes problematic as a medium of addiction, as its instantaneous and ubiquitous access over the Internet testifies. These criticisms must be taken seriously,[88] if only to the extent that they redirect us to consider the ontological origins of the "graphics" themselves, a mimetic art, which draws upon the basic modality of openness. In celebrating the ecstasy of the flesh, pornography makes explicit how sexuality harbors the tension between eroticism and tragedy, play and commitment. Most of all, pornography gives expression to sexual desire, making explicit its inscription within a language of disclosednesss, the gesturing of the flesh, and the flesh becomes word. In this strange transposing of *the word as flesh and the flesh as word*, we discover that our embodiment stands forth in an ecstatic trajectory.

And since we are already "carried away" in this ecstasy, we can only address it by going along with its movement, that is, by undergoing a kind of "leap."

In *Contributions to Philosophy*, Heidegger first alludes to the "leap" as a creative movement that departs from any traditional reliance on "grounds," seeking instead to recover Dasein's origin within the openness.[89] This movement is also a displacement that transposes the foci of Dasein's existence from the qualities that make it human to those that are determined by its relationship to being, for example, the temporal openness of transcendence, the middle voice of an openness born from confronting the closure of death. Ironically, in *Contributions*, Heidegger makes one of his last allusions to the creative power of imagination when he reconsider the import of the Kant book. In emphasizing that the soul is not the seat of imagination, Heidegger suggests that imagination arises through the temporal enactment of human finitude, coinciding with the "clearing" of time space that we experience as situated, embodied beings.

> Indeed: *As thrown projecting-open grounding, Da-sein is the highest actuality in the domain of imagination*, granted that by this term we understand not only a faculty of the soul and not only something transcendental (cf. Kant book) but rather *enowning* itself, wherein all *transfiguration* reverberates.
>
> "Imagination" as occurrence of the *clearing* itself.[90]

In *Contributions*, the leap now configures the movement of displacement in an analogous way in which imagination does in Heidegger's destructive-retrieval of transcendental philosophy in the Kant book. Where, then, does the undertaking of the "leap,"as Heidegger first describes it in *Contributions to Philosophy*, lead us?

Perhaps an answer cannot be readily given, except by those who are still to come, who are more at home, as it were, in the tension of "radical alterity," which helps propel the "leap." By the ones to come, Heidegger refers to those creative individuals who could prepare for the "other beginning," in which the negativity of being's historical self-concealment reverts into the conservatorship and sheltering of its truth. The "turning" suggests a momentum in which history reassumes its importance through the arrival of the future, and, conversely, enowning allows for the appropriation of the origins of Western thought in new and manifold ways. This double joining of inception and reinception, of first beginning (with the Greeks) and the "other beginning," disrupts the direction of history in such a way as to allow a curvature to occur, the full sweep, as it were, of the turning. In the turning, the questions that have formerly been held in abeyance in the subterfuge of metaphysics—such as that springing from the *ethos* of ethics—can reemerge in a primordial way. Traditional ethics may imply a plan or a theory to construct rules of conduct according to the constraints of metaphysics, including a preconception of human being as defined by rationality or endowed with a soul. But an original ethics, according to Heidegger, begins with a questioning concerning human being's relation to being, and a self-questioning of the question, in such a way as to redirect ethical inquiry to the *"how" of Dasein's dwelling in inhabiting the earth and providing a place for unconcealment to occur.*

What some ethicists have rather mundanely described as "obligation to future generations" may have an interesting twist from Heidegger's perspective, when we consider that the outstretch of the future yields the meaning of the deeds of today and yesteryear. In the next chapter, we will reopen the question of ethics as it pertains to the dilemma that springs from our incarnatedness, including the guardianship of the earth that we bequeath to future generations.

Chapter 3

Ethos, Embodiment, and Future Generations

In the *Foundation for the Metaphysics of Morals*, Kant distinguishes between a "holy will," which is always pure, due to the necessity of its coincidence with the moral law, and a "good will," which is pure when it conforms to the moral law by withdrawing self-interest.[1] Only in the latter case, says Kant, can we properly speak of obligation, of the will's self-imposition of the categorical imperative, because only under the limitation of human nature, where there can be discrepancy with the moral ideal, can the constraint of obligation apply. Likewise, Heidegger emphasizes that it is due to our nature as finite beings that the possibility of ethics becomes a question at all. Kant, however, sought to ground ethics in the atemporal, noumenal realm of freedom (i.e., an uncaused or a spontaneous will). In his destructive retrieval of Kant's ethics, Heidegger, on the other hand, redefined freedom in terms of finitude, whose origin he had already equated, as the former had done in the *Critique of Pure Reason*, with temporality.[2] Thus to raise the question of the possibility of ethics, Heidegger takes as his point of departure a mode of temporality from which issues the form of decision making as such, namely, resoluteness. In this way, he repeats Kant's attempt to seek autonomy or "self-legislation," as the form of freedom as such, albeit with the special twist that it is the adherence to the limitations that temporality imposes (i.e., resolve), which makes possible self-responsibility rather than the denial of time. In his lectures from the summer semester of 1930, Heidegger summarizes the linchpin of this radical retrieval of Kant's ethics: "Practical freedom as autonomy is self-responsibility, it is the personality of the person, the authentic essence, the humanity of man."[3]

The transposing of the axis of human freedom from an atemporal basis to the finite openness of temporality, which follows the "*Umschlag*" or "overturning" that is accomplished through metontology, may require a further stage of development. "I designate the set of questions [arising from this overturning] '*metontology*.' And here also, in the domain of metontological-existentiell questioning, is the domain of the metaphysics of existence (here the question of an ethics may properly be raised for the first time)."[4] For Kant associated the negative influence of self-interest with inclination, which he in turn equated with the bodily impulses of lust and greed that were subject to the physical chain of cause and effect. Insofar as Heidegger relocates the origin of freedom in temporality (rather than the opposite), we might wonder if the concreteness of this focus is truly achieved until embodiment, with its affective dimension, is also restored in a positive sense as exemplifying an aspect of the limitation of decision making, of thrownness into a situation or the constraints imposed by a dilemma. Indeed, if Heidegger seeks to recover the dynamic of moral decision making in terms of temporality, and if embodiment is a facet of this finitude, then it must also be necessary to address the incarnatedness of ethical action. By taking this further step of restoring a positive sense of embodiment as integral to the *ethos*, we would lend additional concreteness to Heidegger's destructive retrieval of the Kantian ethic.

This chapter will be divided into two parts. First, I will reopen the question of ethics as it unfolds upon the stage of the embodied self who grappled with the crisis form of limited choices. Then I will reformulate the question of ethics on a concrete level, where the finite exercise of self-responsibility turns into a historical decision about our obligation to "future generations." To be sure, some ethicists would balk about reference to such obligations; how can you consider the welfare of those who do not "yet" exist? *Yet, because Heidegger develops a concept of temporality that gives weight to the future prospect of the "ones to come" as assuredly as he does to those existing today, he can entertain a question that others might dismiss out of hand.*

The Incarnatedness of Ethical Action

In embarking upon the path of ethical inquiry, the primary trend in continental philosophy today has been to emphasize the process of decision making over the promulgation of any extant values, if only because of an interest in capturing the dynamic inherent in such acting and deciding (verbal sense). Much of our life situation informs us that this dynamic arises from the fact that ethical decisions entail a certain degree of urgency, which in turn involves our being confronted by some dilemma or other. In Heidegger's case especially, the concern for the ethical is not closed off by the promulgation of a pregiven set of norms. On the contrary, a vector of openness shapes that (ethical) consideration by a question directed at the decision maker himself or herself, a self-questioning of the possibility of change to which one is delivered over to in undertaking the risk of acting—the unfolding of the decision as to who one is and *can* become. The paradox of traditional ethics is that it seeks directives in the hope of resolving a dilemma when the state of affairs or life situation suggests just the opposite: the refusal of any ready-made solution that prompts a response cutting to the crux of *finding oneself* in a quandary.

Though Heidegger may not address the paradox of ethics in this way, in *Beiträge zur Philosophie (Vom Ereignis)* he identifies a unique disposition, namely, "distress," which corresponds to the aforementioned response.[5] Can distress provide the key to marking the dislocation, the "paradigm shift," of ethical inquiry in which the placement of ethics on a cognitive plane as a search for norms and standards gives way to accenting the dispositional dimension that evokes moral responses? In the following I will attempt to answer this question affirmatively and show how an apparently negative disposition or attunement (*Stimmung*) can provide a positive catalyst for moral self-awakening. To the extent that this is the case, it will become evident how a specific configuring of an ethical situation, what is commonly called a "dilemma," should be of chief importance in appreciating the dynamic of decision making and, conversely, why a preliminary concern for human finitude should orient ethical inquiry in terms of the limitations or constraints imposed by such a situation. Thus we will discover—*and advance this as our thesis*—that a Heideggerian entree into ethics becomes increasingly possible by radicalizing his early concept of finitude from *Being and Time*. This radicalization involves translating the temporal-spatial enactment of existence into a language nuanced with the distinct way in which we are bound to a body,[6] our "*earth-boundedness*," such that human "dwelling" (and our dispositional involvement in it) can form the predicate of any ethical decision.

This section will be divided into three parts. First, I will consider how Heidegger's analysis of distress constitutes a turning point in the effort to radicalize his concept of finitude. Second, I will show how Heidegger's attempt to address time in conjunction with space allows for a sense of "embodiment" as the "outsideness" of social-terrestrial inhabitation. Third, I will establish how the compass of human dwelling provides a new axis to orient moral decision making in such a way as to mark the paradigm shift in ethical inquiry in the direction of addressing our dispositional responses to specific dilemmas.

A.

Heidegger may not have been the philosopher of the emotions *par excellence*,[7] But as early as the *Basic Problems of Phenomenology* (1927) he did recognize that there was more than an accidental link between the dispositions and ethics.[8] Dispositions become significant not because they serve as a preferred candidate—in contrast to ethics—to provide a "foundation" for ethics. On the contrary, they point to that dimension that turns ethical inquiry into a question about ourselves, which challenges the pretense that such a foundation is even possible, namely, our finitude. As Heidegger emphasizes, the expression of obligation in the form of a moral law *can* be binding, only because one is limited, that is, finite, in such a way as to allow for (the imposition of) such constraints. While Kant may have mistakenly sought a foundation for ethics, he implicitly saw that its centering on a rational principle such as a categorical imperative could hold only by acknowledging a corollary response—expressing our finitude—that communicates such a claim of authority, that is, a *feeling* of respect.[9] "Kant's interpretation of the phenomenon of respect is probably the most brilliant phenomenological analysis of the phenomenon of morality that we have from him."[10] Whether or not we wish to contest the importance of ethics, we cannot deny the relevance that dispositions play in allowing a sense of openness to shape the topography or landscape of ethical inquiry.

For Heidegger, distress pertains to our encounter with finitude rather than to its designation as an a priori structure (Kant), which we experience through our incarnation in culture and history. Incarnation is the proper term to describe not only our (finite) composition as temporal beings but also the unique modality by which that temporality conjoins with space to allow for a place (*Ort*) of unconcealing and openness to which concealment also belongs. Finitude ceases to be an exclusive dimension of temporality, as the focus of his destructive retrieval of Kant demonstrates, but instead reemerges to include the counterbalance of negativity stemming from the reciprocity of time and space, that is, time-space (*Zeit-Raum*). This creative dynamic or tension means that we experience the wage of a struggle with negativity as offering deliverance only in the risk of peril, a "venture" intrinsic to all decisions.[11] Our incarnation is the "stress" we feel due to our temporal-spatial boundedness, the weight of being bound in this way—the concrete repercussion of which we experience as "distress." The distress is the pull of negativity, its penchant to dislocate us (from the "familiar"), which we experience as the "gravity" of our situation. We thereby experience distress as a disjointedness in the flow of ordinary events, in which tranquillity gives way to urgency, and the outlines of a predicament or controversy emerge.

Traditional morality approaches a situation as if overdetermined by options of choice in which guidelines suggest the path to a solution. But according to the disjoint of distress, a different topography of any such situation emerges. Indeed, any enactment of a decision must already be counterbalanced by a proportional accentuation of "undecidedness." For this polarity alone recalls our essential "incarnatedness" in which the "heroism" of choice resides in the admission of its frailty, and the predisposition toward goodness hinges on confronting evil. As Heidegger illustrates, Kant spoke of the "heroism" of moral respect as striking down the baseness of self-conceit and self-love.[12] But that Kantian response is not fully transposed in the area of conflict, in which the certainty of any outcome of a decision hangs in the balance, and distress prompts bracketing ready-made solutions in order to pave the way for an encounter with otherness and an awakening to the "gravity" of its claim upon us.

In a lecture course from 1937–1938 that parallels *Beiträge*, Heidegger reserves the term "distress" to describe the way in which human beings are catapulted into an unsettling situation and confront the "not" of radical finitude.[13] In these lectures he pinpoints the "not" or negativity that lies at the heart of all dispositions.[14] At first sight we might think that distress has little to do with ethics. And indeed, Heidegger does not explicitly make this link. Yet as is the case with any disposition, distress propels the self as "thrown" into the forefront of a situation, in such a way as to call attention to its furthest margins where the contours of the *ethos* first arise. By experiencing distress, human beings enter the breach of a crisis, in which all of the variables that comprise the frailty of human existence—ambiguity, conflict, accident—become most pronounced.

Unlike fear, which has a definite object, the "not" of distress is on a par with anxiety. Like anxiety, the distress that obtrudes upon the self points to the metabolic character of the situation as it sheds its facade of familiarity for what is most unfamiliar. Correlatively, the self undergoes a displacement of its sense of the familiar so that it can be removed from the surface of its immersion in beings and reinserted into an unfathomed depth from which the manifestness of "what is" emerges. But is not that dual way of dislocating and transposing more or less what happens when Dasein confronts the "nothing" of anxiety? The answer is yes. However, the description of distress adds another facet to the attempt to elicit the trajectory of Dasein's thrownness into the world. Specifically, distress speaks more explicitly to the topographic setting, the dimensional configuration of the *topos* as an expanse that not only has breadth but also depth (e.g., the depth of neediness and solitude).

The cultural legacy of human being's descent into these depths is the stuff of tragedy. Yet even tragedy cannot command the import it does without the attunement (*Stimmung*) that predisposes us toward the fragility of our condition as finite beings. As such, distress becomes the dispositional throwback to the Greek experience of the tragic side of human existence, the mixture of providence and fickleness. The Greeks provide the legacy of the hero's struggle with the polarity of redemption and loss, enlightenment and ignorance. Because tragedy chronicles the inherent uncertainty of human action, distress arises where knowledge about the precariousness of one's situation is lacking. Given this tragic scenario, distress marks the juncture where the self occupies the transitional zone of the "between," sustaining its existence within the tension of life's extremes. "This distress, as such a not knowing the way out of or into this self-opening 'between,' is a mode of 'being,' in which man arrives or perhaps is thrown and for the first time experiences—but does not explicitly consider—that which we are calling the 'in the midst' of beings."[15]

Distress points to the demarcation of the expanse of world, to the constellation of the "there" as such, which yields the area of human action. Human action requires the introduction of this intermediary zone or the "between," for the power to act stems from our participation in a larger process of openness and cannot be reduced to a product of the will. The arena of human action, however, precedes the compartmentalizing of the world into disparate spatial regions. On the contrary, space must now be differentially distributed in such a way that whole and part are inextricably connected. Thus each distribution of a spatial area is already a composite expression of the world (i.e., as a locale that human beings inhabit). Conversely, the (human) body is not reducible to *res extensa*, an extension of geometrical space. But, as Heidegger suggests in his 1942–1943 lectures on Parmenides, embodiment in a *phenomenological sense entails an expanse of meaning and possibility*—like the craftsmanship of the hand—rather than a mere physiological structure.[16] Yet what about the importance of time; is that not to be our primary focus? As it turns out, space enters the forefront of inquiry with the need to radicalize the concept of time, to elicit its concreteness in defining the *topos* from which human action unfolds. In lectures from 1937–1938, which qualify as a prelude to the *Beiträge*,[17] Heidegger redefines space explicitly in conjunction with time, as "time-space." "This space (time-space)—if we may so speak of it here—is that 'between' where it has not yet been determined what being is or what non-being is, though where by the same token a total confusion and undifferentiation of beings and non-beings does not sweep everything away either, letting one thing wander into another."[18]

Because of this element of vulnerability in distress, it points less to the consummation of a choice as its inception. Put another way, distress is the temporalizing of the transition as such in which the recognition of the lack of any directive (of "not knowing") can illuminate the mode of guidance. Temporality can no longer be constellated as the medium of presence that permits a perfect conformity between an ethical standard, for example, the moral law in Kant's sense and the agency of action, the will. On the contrary, absence overrides presence to allow for an intermediary stage of development to occur in which to cultivate the dimension of responsiveness, which both precedes and diverges from its mechanical assimilation to any preset standard. The "between" where we undergo distress then becomes this haven of preparation.

As such, the distress of the "between" is a unique configuration of time-space, which points both to the unique constellation of a "place" of action and to the "interval" in both the preparation and execution of the decision. Given that the initiative to act must exhibit the dimension of the "between," moral action can no longer simply involve a linear movement. For such a movement would have for its pattern time as pure presence, the organization of time into a discrete series of instants. In contrast, primordial temporality evolves in a circular way, which allows the counterpoint of absence to shape a new trajectory of action. If the encounter with a dilemma involves a search for new possibilities then their novelty may rest on a period of incubation so that they can reemerge at the point called for by the breach or rupture, the point of crisis, in a situation.

Thus a moral response can never simply result in the most expedient choice that seeks comfort in the quickest resolution of a dilemma. On the contrary, any response must inculcate a dimension of "preparation," which bypasses the impulsive quest for "certainty" in favor of the steadfastness of vigilance. In this way, temporality allows for the creativity which, because it originates from the wider expanse of openness, can highlight those possibilities that most meaningfully speak to the difficulties of the situation. Distress thereby entails the allocation of a time, a temporal allotment, in which the transition from the "comfort" of quick solutions gives way to the deliberateness (e.g., as in prudence), forbearance, and vigilance of a moral response. In distress, temporality temporalizes in a radical manner, in such a way as to shift the landscape of moral freedom and outline a more expansive and yet definitive arena of decision making.

Time and space thereby remain inseparable in contributing to the constellation of that openness through which our inhabitation of *ethos* an first occurs. The analysis of distress leads us to this inseparability as the key to redefining ethical action beyond the scope of the metaphysics of presence. Let us then undertake the second part of our analysis, in which we consider the relevance that time has in shaping moral discourse.

B.

In his *Ethics*, Aristotle suggests that the distinction between "full" and "natural" virtue allows for the articulation of the how and why of moral action.[19] The ability to discuss what we do in a moral context seems to be an important part of ethics, even though the accrued "wisdom" (*Sophia*) remains practical rather than "theoretical." But this fact may not so much indicate the need to interject a further measure of rationality in ethics as provide a clue to the equiprimordiality of speech and deed, of their common root. Indeed, while modern thinkers divorce the two, the ancients emphasize their jointure. And why should this ancient perspective be so compelling? In Heideggerian terms, it is because acting is a way of participating in a larger process of disclosure of which language is a vital component. For example, to act in behalf of others is first and foremost to "solicit" their concerns, which implies heeding certain gestures. And these gestures acquire their relevance in connection with the encompassing structure of significance or the world, the demarcation of the human situation as a whole, rather than from isolated speech acts. That is, Dasein's coinhabitation of a world whose concerns may overlap with its own implies that the ecstasy of the self is cast forth into the outsidedness and exposure of the flesh.

Does such "embodiment" suggest a clue that points to the correlation between saying and doing? Insofar as the world comes to be revealed more at a dispositional level than through reason, a possible candidate may be distress. In suggesting that distress exhibits a "negativity" that is creative rather than "depreciatory," Heidegger gives an example of silence. "Not every negation is negative in a depreciatory sense. Silence, for example, means the absence, the 'away,' and the 'not' of noise and disturbance."[20] But what importance does silence have as an example that can mark the crossover between humanity's inhabitation of an *ethos* and its participation in language? Indeed, is not silence the abeyance of all speech, the diminishment of its power? In Heidegger's case, the opposite appears to be the case. *For silence is a unique form of inhabitation in which I become "at home" in my incarnated condition, striking a balance between answering to myself and welcoming the solicitation of others.* Thus silence defers the desire to speak in favor of the capacity to hear, in such a way that the conveyance of the word hinges on our disposition to heed it. Hearing is not a passive occurrence, but instead is a primary form of empowerment that first disposes an individual to act. The so-called discernment of moral decision making and action implies an attunement that prompts an awareness of a given situation. As Heidegger states in one of the most powerful passages from the *Beiträge*: "Whoever does not know of *this* distress has no inkling at all of the decisions that are ahead of us. The decision is made in stillness."[21]

If there is any historical precedent as to how speech can exhibit the same judiciousness that is integral to decision making, it surely lies in Aristotle's analysis of *phronesis*. To exercise balanced judgment is already to participate in an ethical domain of discourse. In his early lectures, Heidegger offers his most provocative statement of where to look to discover the discursive dimension of action given Aristotle's clue. As Gadamer reports, when a student asked Heidegger what *phronesis* is, he thumped his desk and exclaimed "It's the conscience!"[22] As a silent plea, conscience exhibits one of the three components of Dasein's disclosedness, along with dispositions (e.g., distress) and understanding. But conscience is a peculiar kind of discourse, because it seems to lack a discursivity that reaches beyond the self as such. We cannot be too hasty, however, in forming this conclusion. For the negativity of conscience, like that of distress, also has a positive dimension. According to Heidegger, "conscience speaks by remaining silent."[23] Even while the self remains the focus of conscience's call, as an instance of language, conscience exemplifies the priority of hearing over speaking. In an ironic way, conscience points to the disclosive power of speech, insofar as speaking hinges upon hearing, and hearing forms the cornerstone of Dasein's capacity to engage others in dialogue.

Exactly what moral relevance does the call of conscience have? This is a more difficult question to answer than it appears. For Heidegger dissociates conscience with the prescription of any moral mandates. Indeed, only because Dasein can impose a claim upon itself, and heed a voice that originates apart from its immersion in instrumental concerns, can it as an individual acknowledge the binding character of a moral command. Herein lies the key to Heidegger's phenomenological readaptation of Kant's emphasis on autonomy and his belief that self-respect provides the basis of respect for the moral law.[24] As such, the call of conscience becomes the vanguard of responsibility, understood literally as the self's capacity to issue and heed its own directive, a form of "self-answering" (*Selbstantwortlichkeit*).[25] As Dastur states: "Consequently, it seems to me that Heidegger's position, which consists in depriving all content from the silent call of conscience, remains within the strict line of Kantian thought. . . . It is thus because it does not call for this or that, but uniquely to *be, according to another mode, or to will otherwise,* that the call has a formal character, just like the Kantian imperative."[26]

While arising from the self's silent plea, the disclosive power of discourse harbors an understanding about Dasein's constitution as care that equally extends to others. Hence, in heeding the call of conscience, Dasein's actions double as gestures that harbor its ability to articulate the relevance of what it has done. Put another way, by exercising self-responsibility, Dasein already enters a forum that enables it to discuss the moral concerns raised by its actions. And this forum is not an existential structure in addition to Dasein's openness but instead is simply its discursive, dialogical dimension. Thus conscience yields the forum—as the deferral of speaking in favor of hearing—in which the discussion of ethical concerns first becomes possible. As early as his 1924 lectures on Aristotle, Heidegger emphasized this priority as harboring the key to (1) language and (2) the constellation of a forum of ethical discussion and political debate.[27] As Heidegger points out subsequently in his 1926 lecture course, *Grundbegriffe der antiken Philosophie*, Aristotle recognized that the being who is capable of speaking (*logos*) is also capable of action. "'This very same determination of human being turns up again in Kant: the human being that can speak, that is, act with grounds.'"[28] In commenting on the preceding passage, Franco Volpi suggests that this equation of "speaking" and "acting" provides a "hint for interpreting the existential called 'discourse.'"[29]

When we look at the root meaning of conscience and compare it to *phronesis*, the two concepts may not appear interchangeable. After all, conscience has Germanic roots in Kant's idea of an "inner court," the self's compliance to the moral law.[30] Conscience in this sense implies a measure of "certainty," while for Aristotle *phronesis* entails an encounter with the profound unpredictability of the situation. This contrast becomes important, because in the former case, the phenomenon rests upon a configuration of time as pure presence and of the self as simple reflexivity, while in the latter case temporality unfolds through its affiliation with absence and through a relational modality of the self as akin to otherness. Despite a Kantian ancestry, the key to conscience lies in harboring a dimension of nonpresence, as providing an example of the absenting character of time.

Conscience is not simply a rule of conformity but the receiving of an invitation to make a commitment, to exercise discretion insofar as the self responds to the discrete utterance of the call. The responding is a way of reciprocating for the "power" with which one is endowed, a power that one does not possess directly, for example, the capacity to choose or freedom, but which one participates in only through its conservatorship, transmission, and appropriation. Thus the so-called "certainty" of conviction that conscience exhibits is forged across the gulf of the uncertainty of confronting the manifold variables inherent in any situation. The self-attestation and certification of heeding the call occur in proportion to the self's confronting the profound unsettling (distress) of its entanglement in a dilemma. Resolute self-choosing, which "unlocks" the intricacy of the situation, is the essential fruition of the self's heeding the call of conscience. Through resoluteness, Dasein must always return to recover its relation to itself (e.g., as in renewing a commitment). As John van Buren remarks in distinguishing the link between Heidegger's analysis of conscience and Aristotle's appeal to *phronesis*, "As the conscience that cannot be forgotten and is thus a constant renewal of care, *phronesis* is epitactical, ordering, commanding. . . . In interpretively concretizing moral ends, it discloses the 'practical *aletheia*' of the *kairos* and simultaneously issues in a decision."[31]

The axis of Dasein's identity thereby shifts in the direction of absence as well as presence. And this interplay of presence and absence marks the intermediary zone of the "between" (*Zwischen*) in which the voice of conscience can be heard, the exercise of choice can unfold, and the expression of the ethical relevance of any action can occur. We have now seen how the enactment of ethical choice implies language, and hence how temporality facilitates our participation in the disclosive power of the word. Let us consider how we become capable of exercising responsibility toward others, and thus how a kinship with otherness shifts the "ownership" of time to include its "enownedness" of us, in which membership in a community defines the axis of self-identity as much as individuality does.

C.

Almost every discussion of ethics in contemporary continental philosophy emphasizes the primacy of the other. No doubt much of the reason for this development stems from Levinas's influence and his criticism of Heidegger's subordination of ethics to ontology. But if a concern for the other is so focal to ethics, which has a concrete footing in temporality, then Dasein's temporalization must facilitate its interaction with others. Yet it is at this juncture of questioning the permutations of temporality that Heidegger's thinking seems to slip into ambiguity. We must not only ask how time can sustain the self's uniqueness, as Heidegger does through his analysis of temporality, but we must also consider how temporality can reveal various possibilities that point to the *diversity* of the others among whom the self exists.

For the most part, Heidegger shows how temporality combines various processes of unification, particularly in his analysis of Dasein's transcendence. Thus he considers (1) the unification of the structures of the care and the integrity of the authentic self, (2) the preservation of the self's identity in culture, (3) its historical ancestry as belonging to tradition, and (4) the preontological organization of its understanding of being (*Seinsverständnis*)—time as the root for the manifold senses of being. But what remains worthy of question is how temporality can serve as an "index" of diversification as well. Indeed, time is not simply a monolithic structure that encompasses all facets of care, for temporality also spawns the ellipses in which each of us experiences a span of allocation—the interval "between" birth and death, natality and mortality—in a different way.

In his 1928 lectures on Leibniz, Heidegger addresses this temporal nexus when he alludes to the instantiation of existence vis-à-vis Dasein's thrownness into distinct circumstances.[32] Not only must time permit this dispersion, it must also introduce new possibilities by which to sustain the "to be" of existence, the bearing of the fact ("I am")[33] of care itself. Facticity means that Dasein is already beset by the diversity encompassing it, such that it can be most alone even while in the company of those with whom it shares the same mode of being. In this regard, Dasein's being-a-self is always predicated upon its occupying a world with others. Thus the seeming paradox arises that diversity is always part of the equation by which the self can experience its solidarity with others. The diversity of human existence stems from a temporal enactment of care, the doubling of Dasein's identity as both a descendant and an ancestor. Dasein's plurality is not simply a function of its being numerically distinct—such as a Leibnizian monad, for it is equally the case that as thrown the self always belongs to a tradition of which it is not the author and hence is the beneficiary of an origin that it shares in common with both descendants and ancestors. Too often thinkers construe the plurality of human existence as an extension of a pregiven social world. But if the social world is to be dynamic rather than static, then it can have no other foundation than the variables that allow for its preservation and evolution across the eons of history. The self's identity is then etched in the crucible of this historical conflict, fully "incarnated" in the jointure of time-space. Thus the bedrock of human individuality "towers forth" in the guise of the self's singular way of occupying the crossing between past and future, its occupation of a social world in which the voices of both ancestor and descendant can be heard—the expanse of time-space.[34] While freedom corresponds to the self's resolute decision making, the individual experiences himself or herself as free primarily within the context of interacting with others. As Sherover argues, if the ontological character of freedom must be ontically experienced, then the primary "test" of what it means to be free occurs through the self's exercising responsibility in its being-with-others.[35] As Raffoul remarks: "It is in such a nexus of responsibility, facticity, and otherness that the site of ethics, of an 'originary ethics,' is to be situated in Heidegger's work."[36]

In his discussion of tradition, heritage, and legacy, Heidegger points to Dasein's capacity to appropriate its origins as a key to its inculcation of diversity. Since Dasein's origins are never simply given, our access to them must be deferred through their allocation of a time, a temporal allotment, which permits their retrieval in the future. This mode of temporal deferral, postponement, and incubation (*Incubationszeit*),[37] speaks to Dasein's essential finitude. Given its constellation through the interplay of presence/absence, the self as finite can experience its origins only through a temporal process in which the preservation of these origins hinges on their transmission and appropriation. Because history provides the genesis of new possibilities, and these possibilities bear the contingencies of each age, Dasein can rediscover its origins only by affirming the multiplicity of the scenarios for retrieving them. The abundance of diversity is thereby sheltered in the inevitable withdrawal of Dasein's origins. While diversity is the hallmark of Dasein's finitude, it also bears the downside of that negativity. That is, the importance of diversity as the stimulus to social interaction can be as lost to Dasein as any other mode of its enactment of care. Hence, it is part of Dasein's facticity that its encounter with diversity is a source of conflict, trepidation, and even defiance in the face of its tendency to comply with the uniformity of the status quo, the "they-self." While in a mathematical sense diversity suggests a majority, its actual observance may instead be in the hands of the minority. Although this observance implies dissent, the search for diversity unfolds as both a departure from and a return to that origin in which it is ingrained, namely, tradition. Heidegger reserves the term "*Auseinandersetzung*" to describe the way in which Dasein can be both a critic and an exponent of tradition—as descendant and ancestor—addressing both its shortfalls and merits from opposing directions.

Because its own continuity hangs in the balance, tradition engages the participation of its interlocutors. History provides the forum for this critical exchange or *Auseinandersetzung* by underwriting the genesis of new idioms in which to recast the most perennial issues and questions (e.g., the question of being). Insofar as the deployment of new idioms is crucial, the vehicle for cultivating diversity must always be the word. Or put another way, the word resounds in the voice of the other who confronts me by eliciting another dimension of the world, society, and natural environment that we inhabit together. The other can be a participant in a dialogue (*Zwiesprache*), insofar as language arises by giving precedence to listening and the silence of the becomes punctuated by the utterance of many voices. Because multivocality contributes to the power of *logos*, which is a way of "self-gathering," language becomes the chief way through which the assembling of human beings into a community occurs. If this is the case, then world reappears as the confluence of time, which allows for the self-gathering and dispersion of the various ways in which each of us inhabit it. Once again we return to the issue of temporality as an index of diversity. But does this index yield those very gestures by which we display concern for the ethical welfare of others? To answer this question, we must recall our inquiry into a unique constellation of issues: language, temporality, and responsibility.

Time not only allows me to inhabit a world but is also an issue in how others co-occupy that space of inhabitation. The finitude of time-space summons me to show solicitude toward others, because I can only exist as a member of society. But because I am also allowed the option to be indifferent toward others, my primary preoccupation can be with fulfilling instrumental concerns. To be sure, time aids in this fulfillment, but only derivatively as a function of what I can do with it. In this way, we experience temporality by calculating its duration chronologically, in which the primary challenge lies in countering its "lack," its insufficiency, and its inevitable dissipation. In contrast, the primordial temporality that intercedes as the expanse of my inhabitation (time-space) serves as an emissary of the "between," which first enables me to occupy a world with the other and the other to emerge as a participant in my world openness. For example, when I allocate time in order to help someone in need, the other emerges into my sphere of concern as capable of being helped, as welcoming my solicitous response. The time of the other, then, directs me to my participation in the temporalizing process and hence to the genesis of time as such from which my own existence emerges. Hence, the exercise of solicitude redirects me to my own temporal origin. By acting in behalf of the other, I can then experience my "connectedness" with time or the span of its allocation for me (its "stretching along"),[38] rather than its contraction and dissipation in the pursuit of instrumental ends.

In this regard, a chief gesture of solicitude lies not only in "leaping ahead" of the other to safeguard his or her capacity for choice but, reciprocally, in putting the other's good on a par with or even ahead of my own. And insofar as my acting in behalf of the other returns me to the root of my temporal connectedness, I find myself through my affinity for the other. As Heidegger emphasizes at the close of *On the Essence of Ground*, Dasein can "attain itself as an authentic self" only by "surrendering its I-ness" in behalf of responding to the other.[39] In ethical terms "sacrifice" becomes possible, insofar as the time that grants me the opportunity to act in behalf of the other unfolds in the moment (*Augenblick*), and I dwell in the moment only to the extent that I "give myself up" to it by affirming its inherent transitoriness. Thus the "economy" of time entails that it regenerates itself precisely insofar as I relinquish myself to it, and this "nonwilling" (i.e, "letting be") creates the "space of openness" (*Spiel-Raum*) through which I co-inhabit a world with others. As Aristotle remarks: "The excellent person labors for his friends and his native country, and will die for them if he must; he will sacrifice money, honors, and contested goods in general, in achieving what is fine for himself."[40] Does Heidegger leave room in his thought for an ethical phenomenon such as "sacrifice," apart from his aforementioned appeal to the tragic role of the hero who wrestles with the overwhelming power of unconcealment?[41]

For the most part, we discover that Heidegger's text breaks off at the point where the sacrifice can become the focus of discussion. Though he emphasizes the importance of solicitude, for example, in *On the Essence of Ground*, he states that the constitution of Dasein as care implies nothing specific about whether Dasein is "egotistic" or "altruistic."[42] And what about the importance of distress as marking the crossroads of the "between" where the cusp of decision (*Entscheidung*) unfolds? While indicating a key dimension of our embodied condition, distress only indirectly conveys the double gesture of care as a way of both relinquishing itself and providing for others, *the nullity of "fleshly incarnation"* that harbors the abundance of any selfless or "sacrificial" act. Ironically, *On the Essence of Ground* is one of the few texts where Heidegger, in alluding to the "heart of Dasein" (*Herz des Daseins*), intimates a link between solicitude, sacrifice, and the character of human embodiment.[43] Perhaps this is an indication of why Heidegger's thinking, despite having profound ethical implications, retreats at the juncture where it becomes necessary to accent the singularity of the other. Thus the question of cultural and racial diversity, or of the diversity of origins different from the West, remains problematic for him, along with those who are among the historically "downtrodden."[44]

Still, in considering the phenomenon of distress, as the interface between language and disposition, dilemma and decision, I have sought to push Heidegger's thought to the limits. The illumination of these limits actually serves to show how provocative many of his insights can be when transposed within an ethical context. Indeed, it is by leaving Heidegger's thought that we can return again to it with a deeper appreciation of the clues he provides for reexamining the dynamism of moral responsibility. In this way, Heidegger's thought finds its place within a kind of "sacrifice," which relinquishes its claim of privilege in ethical matters for the sake of a profounder rendering of the *ethos* as a response to the vicissitudes of our fleshly incarnation. Can we characterize this sacrifice as a guardianship that defers our own desire for instant gratification in favor of bequesting the bounty of the earth to future generations?

The Ones to Come

What are our obligations to future generations (if any)? At about any juncture in his thought, where a concern for ethics arises, it does so in the form of a question. As Charles Scott emphasizes, this interrogative posture sets apart Heidegger's approach to ethics from all of his predecessors, for it is the turning in the question of being itself that creates an avenue to address ethics rather than presuming the applicability of norms by privileging reason, the soul, the I, or society.[45] Even where Heidegger intentionally remains silent about ethics, that silence serves as a pause of caution, indeed, a summons to approach the topic interrogatively rather than expositionally. The summons is analogous to the call of conscience, in the sense that, whether as the focus of action or thought, it awakens us to the capacity to be responsible prior to any declaration of right or wrong. We must then translate obligation as responsibility, as a call in the sense of a responsiveness to, or readiness to answer for, the how of our occupation of the *ethos*. The *ethos* defines Dasein's place of inhabitation, which it occupies in proportion to its readiness to "let being be" and submit to the task of cultivating the truth of being.

Insofar as Dasein is historical, and its relation to being is conditioned, it thereby suggests that the meaning of individual existence resides as much in possibilities of the future as in the present and the past. The fact that the self is who it is only by reaffirming its heritage entails that the appreciation of one's deeds may hinge on the arrival of a future from which one is absent, having passed away. Correlatively, one's merit as a human being may then depend on the possibility of becoming an ancestor, so the transmission of heritage from one generation to another yields the vitality of existence and the self's succession by others (through death) plants the seeds for future tribulations. As Nietzsche frequently stated: "Some are born again posthumously." Heidegger's concept of history, as outlined first in *Being and Time* and subsequently in *Contributions to Philosophy*, is inherently *generational* in a twofold sense: (1) Dasein's identity is necessarily transposed into the orbit of history, insofar as its commitment to be an individual renews its ties to its past, to its ancestry, and (2) the preservation of origins lies in their transmission and appropriation, such that "life" stems from the birth of history, and the individual is essentially a product of this historical genesis.

Could the genesis of history point back to the finitude of Dasein's temporality, including the inevitability of its being-toward-death? Ontologically, origins imply limits, and in terms of life, natality implies fatality. As soon as Dasein is born, it is old enough to die, to paraphrase Heidegger's citation of Luther.[46] For Heidegger, birth arises as the interval in which as thrown Dasein is already preoriented toward the possibility of death. Just as death marks the juncture of the withdrawal of all possibilities, so birth distinguishes the counterpoint of their limitation over which we have no control. But while negativity distinguishes both of these poles, the negative is equally positive in the sense that the delimiting of possibilities at (the point of) their inception also gives the measure of their abundance. The double vector of the unfolding of birth and death, in which the closure of the latter yields the openness of the former, means that the "gift" of life is bestowed upon us only by assuming the risk of its transitoriness. But does birth or natality have anything to do with the physical origin of an individual's life, as death does with its end? In his 1939 lectures on Herder's account of the origin of language, Heidegger suggests how, even at the breach of its own birth, the human being includes a preorientation to language.[47] In its natality, the newborn is already developing by virtue of its potential to inhabit language, sustained in its capacity to speak, such that crying heralds the baby's unique manner of emergence into the world.[48] Of course, Heidegger rejects all exclusively "biological" explanations, and, in the context of *Being and Time*, attempts to distance himself from any association that we may have had earlier with Dilthey's "life-philosophy." For him, the double movement of history, in arriving from the future by repeating the past, dictates the emergence of origins rather than a naturalistic concept, as could be found in evolutionary theory. Thus Heidegger seeks in natality the counterpoint for the inception of possibilities, in which "birth" is something Dasein experiences only retrospectively by undergoing the process of "stretching itself" along between beginning and end.

In his discussion of birth, we see that Heidegger seems to avoid the issue of embodiment at the juncture where we might most expect him to open the question. Yet it is equally easy to be misled by the commonsense, everyday bias, which equates embodiment with physicality when phenomenologically the issue hinges as much on our experience of it or how we are affected thereby. If birth is the perennial act of incarnation, then to be born of the flesh is to undergo the dispersion and particularization of having been transplanted into a specific set of circumstances, of which having these parents versus others and this physical profile versus that one will define the *facticity* of the self. Facticity, however, is more than just the personal enumeration of facts about one's "origins," as one might relate on an insurance form of medical biography in a doctor's office. On the contrary, the factical emerges as challenging the self to seek its own identity, and to do so by reclaiming those ancestral ties that allow one to plot a course of future development. In opening forth and spanning the extremities of past and future, the self's temporalization enhances its current activities or gives them a measure of fulfillment or completeness. Thus the corollary of the self's material dispersion, as reclaimed in the repetitive movement of resolute self-choosing, lies in becoming "rooted" in one's situation.

The notions of rootedness and dwelling, while not completely suppressed from *Being and Time*, are not dominant either. The dynamic of the self's temporalization suggests their occurrence, but only indirectly in a way that still presupposes a detailed depiction of space (*Raum*), which remains forthcoming in his lectures of the 1930s. But would not it be strange indeed if one of the keys to incarnatedness would lie in something that is neither merely biological or even exclusively human? As Heidegger states in the Kant book: "*More original than man is the finitude of the Dasein in him.*"[49] In this case, that primordiality consists of that venture of disclosedness, which is uniquely correlated with language and which heralds the birthing process or gives it a voice of celebration: the giving of a name to the newborn. As Heidegger suggests, in an ontological sense, naming is an invitation for allowing something to become manifest, and perhaps much of the so-called miracle of birth lies in the newborn's irreducible novelty in the eyes of the parent whose admiration becomes vocal through the assignment of a name. As Arendt states: "With word and deed, we insert ourselves into the world, and this insertion is like a second birth."[50] As embodied, the experience of natality belongs essentially to Dasein, as Heidegger suggests in his 1928–1929 lectures in *Introduction to Philosophy*, even though he emphasizes the opposite temporal spectrum, or mortality.[51]

The metaphysical tradition associates language with reason, the power of which supposedly separates human beings from animals. Language would then seem to fall on the intellectual side of the metaphysical dualism in opposition to sensation and corporeality. Yet in *Being and Time*, Heidegger is already subverting that dualism even with his most tempered remarks about language: "The primordial goal of philosophy is to restore the force of the most elemental words."[52] The efficacy of language hinges as much on the cultivation of an attunement that allows us to hear what is being spoken, as in the conveyance of ideational content. And herein lies one of the most underestimated links to the problem of embodiment to be found anywhere in Heidegger's thinking: the priority of hearing over seeing. Historically, the philosophical tradition equates seeing either with the sensuous presentation of some object to perception, as in empiricism, or with the intellectual appearance of an idea to reason, as in rationalism. In either respect, seeing still presupposes some aspect of outward manifestation and presence. Hearing, on the other hand, allows for the differentiation between the message and its conveyance and reception. Thus in the emphasis on hearing, there is already the reminder of the possibility of the withdrawal and concealment of what is said. Indeed, the disclosive character of language necessarily includes hearing, for the latter keeps in play the dynamic of withdrawal in contrast to manifestation. By harboring the tension of presence-absence, language—apart from its degeneration into a statement form—can qualify as the proper abode for truth.

In this regard, perhaps Heidegger would have agreed with the spirit of what the former coach of the Alabama Crimson Tide, Dennis Francione, voiced to his players when he remarked: "Hearing is more important than speaking; that's why God gave you two ears and only one mouth." For Heidegger, hearing necessarily precedes speaking, because the word arises as a response to the claim of being, as a tribute to its manifestation. In the call of conscience as well, care issues a summons in which the abeyance of the "they's" idle chatter, the uncanniness of silence, facilitates the disclosedness of Dasein. Hearing attests to the self's attunement to its situation, standing in reserve so that it can receive the invitation of being and attend to the diversity of its manifestation(s). Put in other terms, hearing transposes Dasein into the openness so it can relinquish its tendency to represent beings in a generic fashion and welcome their plurality. Hearing, however, is not just a passive reception of auditory sensations but instead is Dasein's active engagement in allowing self-discovery to occur, its acclimation to novelty. In this sense, hearing is the foremost ecstatic dimension of incarnatedness. Animals have much acuter auditory power than humans but do not necessarily have as their origin the attunement that allows apparently random noises, for example, in a musical score, to resound as melody. Thus Beethoven may have been physically deaf when he wrote the Fifth Symphony, but the disclosedness of his attunement gave an even keener tonality to the melody he "heard" and thereby conveyed in musical notes.

It is because hearing precedes speaking, according to Heidegger, that an exchange between human beings or "conversation" becomes possible. Language is a self-gathering, which in terms of the participation of human beings draws human beings together into a forum that allows for the counterpoint of dissent and disputation as well. To reinforce this point, Heidegger appeals to Hölderlin:

> Here language is not understood as a capacity for communication but as the original manifestness of what is, [and] which is preserved by the human being in different ways. Insofar as the human being is being-with [*Mitsein*], as he remains essentially related to another human being, language as such is conversation [*Gespräch*]. Johann Christian Friedrich Hölderlin says: "Since we are a conversation" (*Friedensfeier*). This must be.said more clearly: Insofar as we are a conversation, being-with belongs to being human.[53]

But what is addressed if not disputed, first and for the most part, is how one stands to one's origins and the possibility of articulating this to others who may also question the roots of their existence. Indeed, language is necessary for community. And the future preservation of community depends upon the transmission of heritage, since only because of the common appropriation of origins do bonds among human beings remain intact. Through this appropriation, the "voice of a people" becomes possible, the concrete instance of the historical character of language and dialogue.

Since the appropriation of origins is essentially historical, and in its renewal takes the form of a conversation, the debate is never the privilege merely of one generation. Indeed, the debate over one's ancestry, which animates the "voice of a people," assumes as its predicate *Überliefern*, or the "handing down" of tradition. Handing is an essential possibility of historical Dasein, which can also be raised to the level of a responsibility insofar as Dasein answers to itself by fulfilling the mandate of perpetuating its ancestry and deepening the loyalty to its existence. How do we understand this loyalty, which can have controversial implications in light of Heidegger's political affiliation with National Socialism in 1933? At the very least, the loyalty involves keeping the question about one's origins alive so that future generations can experience a profounder bond that remains through conversation. Insofar as the origins are preserved through their transmission and appropriation, the loyalty to existence translates into the possibility of enhancing the self's "rootedness" in tradition, which allows the spirit of a people to flourish. From this perspective, the question of so-called responsibility to future generations would seem to be already answered.

The apparent self-evidence of the answer, however, leads us in the opposite direction of having to question the question. We find a clue to its question worthiness in referring to the rootedness of existence and to the change in our understanding of it due to endangerment with the onslaught of modern technology. For Heidegger, technology brings to fruition the possibilities inherent in the forgottenness of being. In order to confront this forgottenness, not only by reasking the question of being but addressing our tendency to ignore it as well, we must interrogate the definitive form of its historical development (i.e., modern technology). Thus the question of being turns into the question of technology. In technology, the unleashing of the global mechanisms of production and consumption, which deprives the weightedness of things in terms of the calculation of their use-value, creates a condition of uprootedness. The annihilation of geological distances through mass transportation and communication means that human beings can live anywhere and at anytime, forsaking all attachment to homeland, community, and ancestry. Technology proves "dangerous," because it jeopardizes our opportunity for rootedness. And when we face the possibility of *loss* this of rootedness, we situate ourselves within the historical setting in which the question of responsibility to future generations acquires special relevance.

But what is going to be our key in unfolding this question? Language keeps alive the historical and allows human beings to prepare for rootedness. And it does so not only in the aforementioned way but also by providing the example that governs all other responses to our heritage, namely, the exercise of stewardship or guardianship. We tend to consider dwelling as a way of cultivating the conditions of our situatedness, including the heritage anchoring it, while forgetting that the most vigilant endeavor thereof lies in the simplicity of taking residence in language itself. Thus learning, to be at home in language, proves to be among the most difficult tasks because of the obviousness and innocuousness of that endeavor. When Heidegger remarks that "Language is the house of being,"[54] he recalls the possibility that we can occupy a domicile that is so primordial that it marks the intersection for all other sites of being's manifestation. Specifically, the safekeeping of language through power, the stewardship of the word, would be the foremost instance. Accordingly, Heidegger appeals to the poet of the poets, Hölderlin, to distinguish the special economy between the word, its guardianship, and dwelling: "'poetically dwells man upon this earth.'"[55] It was Hölderlin, as Hans-Georg Gadamer recounts, who "'first set [Heidegger's] tongue loose'" so that he could articulate this economy.[56]

How does this form of dwelling arise in contrast to the relentless drive for control and manipulation that is embodied in technology? The answer lies in the fact that language is already that province into which we are thrown, and hence it epitomizes the degree of powerlessness that we must accept so that we can receive the bounty of being's unconcealment and be enowned by it. We experience this powerlessness in simple ways. For example, when talking, we fumble to find the right word. The lack of control suggests a profounder negativity in which the withdrawal and the refusal of utterance are intrinsic to its obviousness and innocuousness. The self-effacing character of the word stands in stark contrast to the tendency to utilize words as vehicles of expression, analogous to items of equipment to be deployed at our whim and discretion. In this regard, our vulnerability to the word subverts the pretext that technology places at our disposal representational models to organize information in the most expedient and useful ways. Correlatively, the acceptance of our powerlessness over the word gives way to a profounder form of potency: the self-manifestation of being, whose novelty can never be exhausted by the varieties of technological production. Enowning guides us in safeguarding the word, so that by becoming at-home in its province, we can enter into partnership with being (i.e., in deeds such as poetry and thought) and thereby stand out from the whirlwind pursuits of global technology.

When we speak of what is at stake in future generations, the obvious concern is the quality of the habitat that is left to others, which in Heideggerian terms translates into the character of our earthly sojourn: inhabitation as such. In speaking of future generations, the concern for the welfare of the earth, for inhabitation, has its precedent in late-twentieth-century thought through the ecological movement, specifically deep ecology. But we must be careful not to push Heidegger prematurely in this direction. Instead, the emphasis lies not simply in a paradigm shift to "earth-consciousness" but in the turning in enowning that makes such ecological awareness possible, insofar as enowning allows us to gauge less what we "owe" to the future as the preparation for cultivating what is ownmost, of "coming in its own." Thus it is not so much the preservation of the earth that is at stake but the manner of projecting open that brings our earthly origin into question. Such projecting-open welcomes a form of "making" that celebrates the uniqueness of manifestness, in contrast to the uniformity of mass production that reduces beings to a one-dimensional manner of appearing. Heidegger reserves the word "building" to describe this form of authentic or primordial making. Such building becomes relevant to future generations not simply by what it does but also by implicating the temporalization that makes such futurity possible: not the expediency of instant gratification, but the steadfastness of patience.

Though the steadfastness of building could take many forms, we can identify a common thread that accounts for its generational character: craftsmanship. Whether it is the crafting of *poiesis*, the nuanced articulation of thought, or even the *ethos* of dwelling, we discover manifold ways in which the future can come to pass through the sustained endeavors of human beings. Indeed, almost by definition, craftsmanship suggests that it is the potential of "passing down" that lends vitality to art itself and bestows its meaningfulness upon all those who participate in it. As such, building, dwelling, and thinking are inherently generational in their development. But the question arises as to whether we can construe "generational" in a double sense: first, as the dynamics in the transmission and appropriation of heritage that we broadly, though not exclusively, experience as a cultural phenomenon, and second, as the *energia* spawning the diversity of manifestness that we experience by assuming the role of guardian as well as occupant of the earth. How these ways of participating in the creativity of *poeisis*, in the primitive depths of its *physis*, can translate into specific responses that help enrich our way of inhabiting the earth remains to be seen.

In speaking of "future generations," we acknowledge a succession of inheritance that is predicated upon the heir's submission to his or her finitude, to the inevitability of death. But in the temporalizing of "handing down," the emphasis on generations to come suggests that death also serves as a portal of birth, of incarnality. Life thereby exhibits a special economy, so to be embodied is to walk a tightrope between natality and mortality. This economy suggests a temporal cycle in which the replenishment of life springs from its cessation, a *natural rhythm that reminds us of our earthly ancestry, our genesis from the earth. And our generation's giving thanks for the blessing of having "inherited" the earth, by becoming stewards of it, illustrates an authentic way by which Dasein "speaks from the depths of its heart."* For Heidegger, there is no enigma, as there is for some ethicists, as to how we can have obligations to future generations. For the lack of a future generation's actual existence does not make our concern for its welfare, and hence our obligation to it, void and irrelevant. On the contrary, the prospect of futurity grants meaning, through the historical genesis of temporality, to the endeavors of those who exist today. Hence, *our obligation to future generations springs from the stewardship we already exercise toward the earth and the life it sustains*. In harmony with this stewardship, let us appeal to Heidegger's citation of a line from Stefan George's poetry: "'*Listen to what the somber earth speaks.*'"[57] The "somberness" and self-concealing of the earth point back to the depths of silence from which language, as such, originates.

Given these observations, we must first ask what Heidegger understands by the earth,[58] the initial concern of the next chapter. And since the earth defines a major topic in *Contributions*, we might find that another key motif, that of a spring (i.e., a leap), which is also a wellspring (i.e., an origin),[59] provides a hint to a legacy that expands along a zoological as well as a social front, of companionship with animals as well as comradery with people.

Chapter 4

Of Earth and Animals

Is not a discussion of the earth a topic reserved to the science of geology, or perhaps in its relation to other celestial bodies, a concern for astronomy? And yet, surprisingly or not, a reference to the earth makes its way into philosophy, and, in Heidegger's case, comes to occupy a central place. Far from ignoring other such references preceding the development of Heidegger's thought, we should do well to admit their unsettling overtone. First, given Heidegger's allegiance to Kant, we must acknowledge his famous analogy to the shift in perspective from the geocentric to the heliocentric system that provided the clue to his own Copernican revolution. To be sure, superficially the analogy seems to displace the earth's importance. But on a deeper level, the Copernican revolution points to the position of the earth's movement around the sun in order to suggest that the dynamic conditions of human finitude (i.e., time) define the objectivity of knowledge. Second, and even more dramatically, we must point to Nietzsche's parable of the "madman," the deranged individual who takes his own proclamation, that "God is dead," as a catastrophic event of the magnitude of "unchaining the earth from its sun."[1]

If we take our cue from Kant and Nietzsche, then we should take seriously any allusion to the earth in Heidegger's thinking. Indeed, for Heidegger, like his two predecessors, the introduction of a concern for the earth is as "ground shaking," as "abysmal," as any parallel issue that a philosopher might raise. The fact that Dasein is in some way related to the earth, and can dwell upon it, indicates the centrality of its importance, particularly when the problem of the flesh or embodiment provides the focus of our study. For Heidegger, the earth stands in contrast to (the disclosedness of) world and exemplifies the counter-pole of the abysmal element of withdrawal. But because the earth also points to the locus of human inhabitation, and in turn marks our intersection with nature (*physis*), a nagging ambivalence arises: is the earth purely a formal, ontological concept, or does our experience of it also entail its dimension as a "habitat" with at least some of the implications that ecologists later developed? In answering this question, I will show that, in terms of Heidegger's phenomenology, we can only develop an ecological concept of earth in a very limited sense.

This chapter will be divided into two parts. First, I will reexamine Heidegger's notion of earth and consider its relevance to the development of ecology. Then I will show how his parallel concern for animals, while it has ethical implications for safeguarding their welfare, is also limited in its ecological scope. However, the fact that such ecological issues can be raised at all will indicate the extent to which incarnality defines an important permutation of the manifestation of being, particularly as it unfolds through the diversity of nature.

Of Habitat and Dwelling

Heidegger's discussion of the earth is very complex, and yet there is also a simplicity to its message: wherever we look to identify humanity's origins, in art or history, in religion or science, we must acknowledge the fact of the inevitability of withdrawal of these origins. Insofar as we find ourselves either in proximity to or removed from these origins, we experience our inability to gain complete access to them through a thrownness into a pregiven situation. The way in which we find ourselves as embodied and materially bound to the sustenance that the earth offers in terms of food and water constitutes an important aspect of this thrownness. Thrownness, however, defines the trajectory in which we experience the dynamic of the self-concealing advent of being. If this is the case, and, if as thrown we come to appreciate the fact of having a body as earthbound creatures, then, ontologically speaking, the character of our materiality must not be merely material. Indeed, we cannot forget the *to be* of materiality. To be materially also includes the capacity, as Dasein, to take a stand toward that materiality, for example, by occupying a place on the earth and appropriating that domain as one's own. In terms of its materiality, the earth displays a twofold dimension. On the one hand, the earth defines the emergence of the capability of human dwelling, the possibility of cultivating a habitat, of inhabitation itself. On the other hand, earth distinguishes the darkest recesses of any indeterminacy, of a void that gives life and takes it away.

As much as any other philosopher, Nietzsche recognized the inherent ambivalence of the earth in his parable of the "tightrope walker" who plunges to his death. As if to affirm the transitoriness of life, Zarathustra buries the body of the tightrope walker at a base of a tree, recognizing that from the standpoint of the earth, decomposition is an essential part of the cycle of rebirth and regeneration. These Zarathustrian elements of the earth, while consistent with Heidegger's discussion of the same, are not identical either. Zarathustra exhorts us to "*remain faithful to the earth.*"[2] However, in the next sentence, he cautions us, in contrast, of giving in to "otherworldly" aspirations. Due to this way of opposing "this-world" to the "otherworldy," Heidegger classifies Nietzsche's thought as "reversed Platonism,"[3] relegating him to the position of the "last metaphysician West." Heidegger avoids this metaphysical dualism of the sensuous versus the supersensuous; he thereby construes the earth not according to a grammar of "this" versus "other" but as the counterpoint of withdrawal in the horizon of "meaning" that the world provides. In defining Dasein as "being-in-the-world," Heidegger already displaces the metaphysical distinction between the this-worldly and the other-worldly. Correlatively, in contrasting earth with world, he construes the former as preceding the latter as the preontological organization of involvements. The earth constitutes the limitless limit that is placed on any pretext of complete unconcealment and its factical occurrence, the disclosedness of the world. As Gadamer recalls: "The new and startling thing was that this concept of world (as the horizon preliminary to all projections of Dasein's concerns) now found a counter concept in the *earth*.[4] In retrospect, Max Scheler's claim that there is a dimension of beings that exceeds their integration into a chain of equipment—the counter-pull of *resistance*—constitutes a lingering objection to Heidegger's account of world in *Being and Time*.[5] With his appeal to earth, Heidegger may not completely answer Scheler's criticism, yet his discussion of earth does accent the need for hermeneutic phenomenology to reconsider the problem(s) of embodiment and materiality. As a vessel of materiality, the earth arises on the side of concealment, limiting the transparency of the opposite, or unconcealment.

As an inherent restriction on the world's disclosure, the earth appears as the limit of all limits. As Zimmerman states: "Even the scientific-technological will to mastery is impotent in the face of the self-concealing, enduring earth."[6] But when viewed in terms of the dynamics of its own occurrence, that is, in terms of its *materiality,* the earth appears as an abyss. We must emphasize, however, that the abyss should not be equated with an indeterminate negativity. On the contrary, the abysmal also serves as a creative void, the polarity of opposition, where various forces of nature can intersect to produce novelty and diversity (e.g., of life forms). Seen from the standpoint of what acquires (the gift of) life and consequently occupies its surface, the earth is the reserve of fecundity and growth. As such, the earth is the origin of all "organicity." Herein lies the renewed parallel between Heidegger's and Nietzsche's concept of the earth. To quote Gadamer, "The earth, in truth, is not stuff, but that out of which everything comes forth and into which everything disappears."[7] Yet for Heidegger, the organic dimension does not exhaust the materiality of the earth, since that also includes a counter-valence of meaning and intelligibility, or the negation thereof. But that negation, once again, is not simply "nothing," but instead includes the positivity of "protecting," "holding in reserve," "sheltering," as in preserving and "incubating" a mystery—keeping it alive throughout a period of dormancy.

In *Contributions*, Heidegger describes the dynamic relationship between world and earth as one of "strife." Insofar as world is a disclosure that makes explicit the intelligibility of involvements, its strife with earth brings to light the struggle of bringing forth meaning and the limit of its transparency once developed. The battle of wrenching forth the "meaning" of being through philosophical questioning, and the corresponding "violence" enacted in the process, is no exception. But just as in a literal sense the earth provides the surface (and nutrients) for organic creatures to develop, so in a semantic-figurative sense it defines the *materiality* in the limitation and withdrawal of intelligibility. Where do we look to find the embodiment of the revealing-concealing dynamic inherent in intelligibility? Obviously we need look no further than the activity in which we are already participating, namely, language. On the one hand, language would seem to be on the side of meaning, since it corresponds to the opening forth of world. On the other hand, there is an element of materiality of language, not so much in the vocalization of sounds but, if anything, in the receding of those sounds: silence. Put another way, the acceptance of what is "unsaid," its way of sheltering a mystery, if not the inherently ineffable, points to the prevalence of an abyss from which the challenge of wrenching forth "meaning" begins. And in more innocuous linguistic occurrences as well, in the ambivalence of meanings, in the "slippage" of the word, in verbal ineptitude, we experience thrownness as the full force of the materiality of language.

Is the linguistic capability of Dasein tied to its organicity? Is the power of language granted to "earth-bound" creatures (Arendt's phrase), and if so, how, if at all, are humans different due to this ability, in contrast to animals? Is language inherently earthly and apportioned to those capable of dwelling of taking up residence on the earth as an explicit task? As Heidegger emphasizes in the Kant book, human consciousness requires conceptual distinctions of thought to organize the manifold of sense experience, precisely because the self, as finite, must depend upon the manifestation of being in order to encounter them (i.e., in sensuous intuition).

> Finite intuition, as something in need of determination, is dependent upon the understanding, which not only belongs to the finitude of

> intuition, but is itself still more finite in that it lacks the immediacy of finite intuiting. Its representing requires the indirection [*Umweg*] of a reference to a universal by means of and according to which the particulars become conceptually representable. This circuitousness [*Umwegigkeit*] (discursiveness) which belongs to the essence of understanding is the sharpest index of finitude.[8]

In many respects, the philosophical tradition has it wrong in claiming that language, in its affiliation with reason, distinguishes a higher capability of human beings. On the contrary, it is because human beings have an inferior kind of intellect (perhaps in contrast to a purely cognitive being) that they require speech to facilitate the need for differentiation. Indeed, human beings speak due to their finitude, and that capacity indicates more their common occupation of a habitat with animals (i.e., as earthly) rather than their place in a higher, spiritual pantheon.

Interpreted in one light, Hölderlin may more properly hit the mark when he suggests that human beings' "possession" of language serves primarily as a measure of their distance from the gods. Because of this separation, language, as exemplified particularly in poetry, is both the most "innocent" and the most "dangerous" of all occupations, for not only does language disclose, it also conceals. Nietzsche once claimed that "'the poets lie too much.'"[9] We can assess the merit of that claim when we juxtapose the human exercise of speech with whatever animals do. Empirically, there is more and more evidence that animals "communicate," as sociobiologists have shown in the case of primates. But what distinguishes the human capability of speech is not so much a "merit" we can laud over our animal counterparts but a deficiency we alone have. That deficiency becomes apparent in the manner of "cruelty" (Dostoevsky) that human beings show toward their own kind. Put another way, human beings can obfuscate due to language in a way animals cannot, not only because of a deceptiveness as the flip side of uncovering, but, in concert with this dimension of truth/untruth, the inherent ambivalence of the words themselves.

Put simply, human beings are "earthly" not simply because they are blessed with language, but because they occupy it in such a way that through it they can mark the distance between earth and sky. The endowment of language grants to human beings the openness to measure the expanse between earth and sky, to traverse that *chiasmus*, so that they can be even more firmly entrenched in their finitude and resolved in their "rootedness." To designate fully the terms of this quadrant, we must assign the name "mortals" to us in contrast to the gods. The full complement of these terms, in their dynamic interplay, constitutes the "world." The world discloses, but never with perfect transparency, for it includes as one of its complements a strife with earth, that is, a countervalence of concealment whose ground is groundlessness, the yawning abyss. Insofar as language corresponds to world, whose four quadrants mark the expanse of openness, language is the beginning of all inhabitation, of "dwelling" on the earth.

Why is language so crucial? Most simply, language is the most primordial form of self-gathering that makes possible the allocation of any "place." Insofar as any "manifestation" must always be directed toward a place, and being seeks Dasein's cooperation to ensure the unfolding and guardianship of this site (*Ort*), language distinguishes the most primordial "wherein" of any dwelling. Heidegger emphasizes, then, that mode of guardianship that the protection of such a place exacts, rather than simply the physical assignment of a location that defines dwelling as such. The dwelling, in turn, requires the further administration of this stewardship, the endeavor of "projecting open" the place of unconcealment, in accordance with the interplay of the quadrants of the fourfold. We call the materiality of this projecting open "craftsmanship," of which building is a primary instance. Ironically, it is only as human beings dwell and build that we must first become aware of our mode of inhabitation and can in turn address the quality of any habitat, including that construed in an ecological sense. Thus, a habitat is never ready-made, even given the ubiquity of the earth's surface, but arises with the creation of a place of inhabitation. With animals, for example, a habitat for a bird begins with a "nest," and with a gopher a "burrow." Animals have a habitat whose materiality stems from the earth and yet acquires its significance in conjunction with the "dwelling" of human beings and the stewardship they exemplify in creative efforts at "building."

Can we classify Heidegger as an ecologist, or even as a protoecologist? This query should give us occasion to pause—as Zimmerman has recently emphasized—if only for the fact that most of his thinking predated the environmental movement, as least it was pioneered in the United States.[10] It might be more accurate to say that Heidegger's thinking begins the enactment of Western thought, and Western civilization, coming into its own, the adherence of thought to the guidance of enowning as such. This "turning in enowning" opens the way to articulate a "paradigm shift" whose development corresponds to what we today call the "ecological movement."[11] We can thereby call into question (1) our relation to the earth rather than assume it as the totality of nature at our disposal, and (2) the human capacity for dwelling rather than accept the fact that nature must conform to the ends-means continuum of instrumentality by which we fulfill our needs and desires. But what makes Heidegger's thought stand out is its ability to distinguish the historical changes that allow the ecological movement to emerge *as* a movement, namely, the detection of a *crisis* emerging on a global scale. Through the historical dislocation of the turning in enowning, the question of being reverts into the question of technology. The question of technology considers not just the specific development of machinery but addresses machination as such, and, indeed, the scope of its unfolding, the globalization of a corresponding threat to the environment. In "Seminar in Le Thor 1969," Heidegger aptly describes this dynamic of enframing:

> Now the further that modern technology unfolds, the more does objectivity transform into *standing reservedness* (into a holding-at-one's-disposal). . . . Hence the energy politics and the politics of agriculture, which indeed no longer have anything to do with things, but rather with the systematic order of a space within a general planing, directed towards future exploitations. Everything (beings as a whole) from the outset arranges itself in the horizon of utility, the dominance, or better yet, the *orderability* of what is to be seized.[12]

Globalization, however, is a term that pertains not to the effects of technology but to the mode of revealing and presencing, and the countermovement of concealing and absencing, which pregoverns any of these specific effects. Yet it is precisely when the danger, as Heidegger says, takes on this scope that we can direct attention to the threat of the earth's destruction as a possibility as such. Correlatively, only when this possibility arises *as* a possibility can we consider the opposite prospect of rescuing the earth, of protecting it from the onslaught of destructive forces. Indeed, only when metaphysics reaches its extreme point of the forgottenness of being and beings are abandoned to instrumentality do human beings enter into an epoch in which they can address the viability of their habitat, the manner of inhabitation as such. The absencing of being, the dynamics of its withdrawal, brings us to a zero point or nullity where what we formerly took for granted as the ground on which we stand—literally and materially—all of a sudden becomes problematic.

When we project Heidegger's thinking back upon the ecological movement, we discover a double sense by which to construe the earth: as sustaining a habitat, a place of inhabitation, for the disclosive endeavors of human beings and, literally and materially, the soil on which we stand that sustains all life, including plants and animals. As such, a possibility whose origin points back to the turning-in-enowning, that is, the ecological movement, gives further concretion to the multifaceted responses human beings may have in confronting the danger of technology. We might say that the development of this movement constitutes something like a "formal indicator" of the historical coming to pass of a new conservatorship of care or stewardship toward the multiplicity of being's manifestations, including nature. However, this conservatorship is not a given, and a decision (*Entscheidung*) must be enacted in regard to it. Factically, the exacting of this decision can take the form of making further distinctions as to the course for the development of the ecological movement (e.g., of "deep ecology" versus "shallow ecology"). Deep ecology attends to a stewardship (of nature) that aims to cultivate a sense of "harmony and balance," and hence need not be restricted by the desire to fulfill human ends. Shallow ecology, on the other hand, might be interested in cultivating precisely such strategies (e.g., recycling soda cans), and thereby views the conservation of the earth's resources, including water, as serving the means of our own survival. While there is a tendency to place Heidegger in the deep ecologist camp,[13] the salient point may be that either way history gathers human beings together at a crossroads and thereby poses to them the need to decide about the fate of the earth, or the possibility of their "inheritance" of it. Indeed, shallow ecology, insofar as its interests are primarily human centered, answers to the rule of expediency, and this ecological movement favors short-term goals. Deep ecology, on the other hand, because its interests are not exclusively anthropocentric, embraces the motivation of stewardship, and this ecological movement gravitates toward long-term ends pertaining to what happens with and on the earth subsequent to the span of individual lives or even generations. A shallow ecologist might calculate the dangers of the breakdown in the ozone layer in terms of the immediate risk of skin cancer, but a deep ecologist might weigh a similar danger in terms of a long-range problem of the polar ice caps melting, of averting crises that could undermine the possibility of preserving the earth for centuries to come.

But what sense can we make of "inheriting" the earth? If we take inheritance in a strict Heideggerian sense, as "handing down" (*Überlieferung*), then to inherit the earth is to pass down its bounty to future generations. But are we handing down simply for the purpose of securing its use for future generations and "conserving" it for that reason, or are we doing so for a "deeper" motive, namely, of practicing stewardship? An example of such stewardship would be fostering a "kindness" toward our animal counterparts, which in Tom Regan's vision of *The Thee Generation*, suggests a metaphor for a compassionate attitude that acclimates human beings to their role as tenants rather than exploiters of the earth.[14] In this spirit, would handing down, then, not merely pertain to the earth itself, and what bounty, beauty, or resources we could identify, or would it instead be a "legacy" that hinges as much on cultivating stewardship itself, as if it were a craft? In raising these questions, we face the need to exercise a decision about the so-called "depth" or "shallowness" of the ecology we believe to be most beneficial or promoting the "good." As Heidegger states in *Being and Time*, "if everything good has a heritage. . ."[15] That is, the good of inheritance might lie in the transmission of this craft, in which dwelling on the earth would be an indirect, but nevertheless, a desired benefit. The enowning that would govern this act of inheritance, then, would qualify any so-called "ownership" in terms of its "tentativeness," in a way in keeping with our transitoriness. The reciprocal rejoinder of handing down the legacy of the past suggests a special economy in which futurity emerges as a haven to sustain the endeavor of safeguarding the earth. Because history bestows upon us our role as stewards, we are essentially "tenants" of the earth, in contrast to its owners. As Heidegger states in his analysis of Hölderlin's poetry: "This belonging [to the earth] consists in the fact that man is the inheritor, and the learner of all things."[16] The double legacy of inheritance, to which we alluded at the close of the previous chapter, becomes apparent: the enowning of appropriation relegates to human beings in their role as heirs of the earth, granted their capacity to safeguard it, a power that goes hand and hand with the promotion of future generations by acknowledging its dependence on previous ones. In either case, what stands out is the self's ontological capability to acknowledge its mortality and be appropriated into and by the openness through that concession: to let be.

And here the question of the materiality of the earth reemerges. While time is basically what historicizes for Dasein, there is still, from enowning, the reservedness of this temporal movement, an "incubation period," as it were.[17] We speak of geological time, which precedes and supercedes all life, and we speak of paleontological time—as that of the dinosaurs—which precedes and may supercede human life on this planet. Correlatively, there is the question of "cold hermeneutics," as Caputo discusses it,[18] such that the earth is an orbiting planet that may expire in 4 billion years when the sun ultimately burns out (long after all human life, theoretically, would have existed). And yet all of these possibilities, *as* possibilities, still derive their relevance from Dasein's mode of historicalness, and ultimately, from the history of being itself. To the extent that we can refer to "geological time," a time of the earth, the ability to do so still hinges upon the possibility of an awareness of such terrestrial origins, of the *possibility* of the breakthrough of temporality.

An allotment of a period of billions of years becomes meaningful only *given* the possibility, as a counterpoint to this lengthy duration, of the temporalization of *the moment* (*Augenblick*) through which "*es gibt zeit.*" Correlatively, for geological and paleontological time(s) to have their relevance, there must be a potential for a "cosmic awareness," in some instantiation of life or other, which provides a vessel through which the diversity of beings (throughout the universe) can become manifest. Insofar as "there is time," "there is being." And insofar as the conjunction of time and being occurs in the form of history, "there is (also) Dasein." Regardless of exactly which life-form in which it is instantiated, for example, the "Dasein in man,"[19] the breakthrough of an opening for manifestation becomes essential. In *On the Question of Being*, Heidegger cites this passage from the Kant book, although emphasizing the nonanthropocentric origin of Dasein: "But the being (verbal) of man, 'the Dasein in him' [cf. *Kant and the Problem of Metaphysics*, 1st ed. 1929, section

43] is *nothing human.*"[20] In this regard, the materiality of the earth, as it spins on its axis, is a tribute to this necessity, regardless of the precise manner of the evolution of its life-forms. As such, the earth resides in its character as an abyss, and insofar as we accept the inevitability of the evolution of life according to Darwinian theory, there still remains a mystery of the initial translation of inanimate matter into cell-dividing life over 3 billion years ago.[21]

Despite this mystery, the earth itself, both as the surface for dwelling and as the materiality which sustains life, harbors its own inscrutability, majesty, and wonder. The inherent strife between earth and world means that as long as human beings undertake the task of dwelling, they must inevitably be provoked by the self-concealment of earth and the catalyst of questioning that it provokes. Without that self-questioning, the concern for the origins of life, evolutionary or otherwise, could never arise. Without the self-interrogative posture that human beings assume, they would never address the problem of "handing down" for posterity's sake a good or better possibility (of a habitat) for dwelling. Regarding origins and ends, the latter can never be divorced from the former, since it is the dynamic of temporalization that ensures the interplay between the two, the withdrawal of origins, and the futurity of their retrieval. But just as the self-concealment of the earth always overshadows the world's disclosure, so this temporalization must in some way include nature (*physis*) rather than exclude it. As Heidegger emphasizes in his discussions of Aristotle, nature temporalizes as self-absencing presence, as the double play of withholding and reemergence.[22] Whether we are archaeologists interested in biological beginnings, or ecologists concerned about safeguarding the environment for posterity, these inquiries proceed from the temporalization that the inquiry enacts as a creature of nature, whose "creatureliness" dramatizes the transitoriness of life-forms, the projection of the absenting character of death, of the inevitability of ceasing to be and having no further possibilities.

The question of Heidegger's status as an ecologist, then, turns into a query about how matters stand with Dasein's animal counterparts, these "other" so-called life-forms that reside together with human beings on the earth. The traditional privileging of human beings as "rational" animals, and the attempts to differentiate them due to their supposed possession of a higher capacity, such as reason or even speech, have become increasingly problematic for sociobiologists. Indeed, the lines of demarcation between human beings and other creatures, which centuries before were so obvious, have become increasingly blurred with the advancement of our understanding of the capability of primates and porpoises.

While critics may fault Heidegger for an "essentialism" that holds to a view of the "essence" of human being, he differs sharply in this regard from his contemporary, Max Scheler. There remains one important methodological difference in these thinkers' approaches that bears directly on their consideration of the "essence" of human being. In the early part of the twentieth century, Scheler developed a naturalistic phenomenology that privileges human beings over other animals due to abilities they exhibit, including a capacity for transcendence, which leads in the direction of absolute being, or God.[23] In developing a philosophical anthropology, he begins by distinguishing aspects of human and animal behavior and then seeks to extrapolate the *difference in capability*, which emerges as the "thing itself." Heidegger, on the other hand, proceeds from the observation of a fact that is peculiar to the individual, to the personal enactment of existence (i.e., *facticity*), rather than from a comparison of the superiority of one species over another. Human existence is uniquely "indicative" of its own occurrence, and this "formal indication" of facticity means that the hermeneutic-phenomenological description of the human "essence" (*Wesen*) unfolds along an axis (of being) that diverges from any reliance on a *hierarchal arrangement* of beings, including different species and animals forms. While this methodological shift has often gone unnoticed, Heidegger's *hermeneutic* phenomenology turns out to be species-neutral when understood as the attempt to privilege humanity over other species.

While it may be open to question whether Scheler could entertain the evolutionary thesis that human beings are descended from apes, Heidegger could not. *But the reason for this not being able to do so is different than scholars have identified thus far.* Specifically, it is not due to some kind of "specieism," to invoke Peter Singer's term,[24] that Heidegger rejects the theory of evolution. On the contrary, it is because the basic thrust of his hermeneutic methodology, in its emphasis on the example of the individual, is *species-neutral* that he rejects this theory.

Thus when Heidegger ponders the marvels of the human body, he construes it "ontogenetically" as an extension of the human essence rather than either as a mechanical device operating by its own devices or as an organic process functioning through interaction with the environment:

> The human body is something essentially other than an animal organism. . . . Just as little as the essence of man consists in being an animal organism can this insufficient definition of the essence of man be overcome or offset by outfitting man with an immortal soul, the power of reason, or the character of a person [cf. Scheler]. In each instance essence is passed over, and passed over on the basis of the same metaphysical projection.[25]

Instead, the "body" in Heidegger commands attention insofar as its activity contributes and serves as an "indicator" of what is distinctive of its essence, namely, the power to disclose and participate in being's process of manifestation. Through his hermeneutic methodology, Heidegger can appreciate the unique character of the body, unlike an idealist; but, unlike a materialist, he need not adopt the reductionist tendency that pervades most evolutionary models according to which the body is simply a *composite* of physiological features suited for the purposes of (better) adaptation to the environment. Despite the interval of several years, Heidegger makes a statement in his 1942–1943 lectures on Parmenides, which underscores this methodological shift:

> No animal has a hand, and a hand never originates from a paw or a claw or a talon. Even the hand of one in desperation (if least of all) is never a talon, with which a person clutches wildly. The hand sprang forth only out of the word and together with the word. Man does not "have" hands, but the hand holds the essence of man, because the word as the essential realm of the hand is the ground of the essence of man.[26]

Evolutionists might balk at this statement, as if Heidegger would downplay the ancestral link between homosapiens and lower animals. But Heidegger can be viewed less as an anti-evolutionist, provided that we interpret the preceding quote in terms of the counterpoint supplied by Scheler's phenomenology. For Heidegger, the hand's manual dexterity comes to light when joined with its capacity for linguistic dexterity, namely, through gestures that open up a field of significations, for example, when a baseball catcher relays a set of signs to a pitcher by flicking her or his fingers to signify a variety of pitches and locations (e.g., cut fastball up and in). Insofar as manual dexterity and linguistic dexterity intersect, hands do indeed "hold the essence of man."

As we will discover in the next section, the ability to speak is not species-specific, at least in the anthropocentric sense of privileging "man." Yet on at least one important level, which is correlative with human being's way of belonging to language, Heidegger still maintains an important disjunction between humans and their animal counterparts: the recognition of the *possibility* of death as distinguishing Dasein. As Heidegger emphatically states: "To die is to be capable of death as death. Only human beings die."[27] On the one hand, this statement reinforces the essentially chthonic character of human beings, or the fact that they are essentially of the earth, are "earthbound" creatures. On the other hand, in observing animals, it is clear that they grasp death in some form, or at least the nature of "demise," as when a lioness whines when discovering its recently born offspring have been killed by another predator. Even if we accept Heidegger's claim that human beings have a closer affinity for the "nothing" than do animals, can we clearly distinguish the line of demarcation between them?

If we take the ecological question and develop it in terms of the question of how we can differentiate ourselves from our animal counterparts, then we might ask: is there room in Heidegger's thought for "equal consideration" of animals, or at least a concern for animal welfare? In developing this question, we will go a long way toward unfolding the tentativeness of our sojourn on the earth, our unique role as tenants in honoring the simplicity of Rilke's declaration: "The earth *bestows*" (Die Erde *schenkt*).[28] In this respect, we will take a step farther toward uncovering the material fabric that binds us to the earth. And the more we can rediscover ourselves as "earthbound creatures," the more we can shed the problematic legacy of much of the Western tradition: humanism and anthropocentricism. In criticizing the anthropocentric premise of Western philosophy, Heidegger brought the concern for the *ethos*, for our manner of inhabiting the earth, into the forefront as a new point of departure for ethical inquiry. The more hermeneutics shifts its attention to the *ethos* of earthly dwelling, the more radically ethics undergoes transformation by addressing the issues of deep ecology. But we cannot overlook the reciprocal transformation that occurs at the heart of hermeneutic phenomenology itself: the more a concern for nonhuman creatures enters the forefront of ethical inquiry, the more *the key hermeneutic motifs of finitude, embodiment, and inhabitation must be radicalized* in order to keep pace with and help formulate the questions posed by the current environmental crisis.

WHO SPEAKS FOR THE ANIMALS?

From Singer to Regan to Callicott, philosophers have entertained the case for animal welfare.[29] Its defense depends upon overcoming an "anthropocentric" bias, which governs philosophy from opposing directions of Christianity and modern humanism and licenses humanity to pursue the interest of its species to the detriment of others.[30] Insofar as this critique develops tactics found in such thinkers as Hannah Arendt and Hans-Georg Gadamer, Derrida and Heidegger, ethical inquiries into animal welfare often presuppose a "paradigm shift" or "decentering" of the human subject. Specifically, the paradigm shift reorients a normative discourse about animal welfare by providing a new portrait of humanity's reciprocity with nature. In order to coordinate the prescriptive and descriptive modes of discourses, it is necessary to clarify the larger presuppositions that govern environmental ethics, as well as outline specific guidelines to regulate our treatment of animals. In this respect, do advocates of animal welfare merely exchange one set of assumptions for equally problematic ones, or do they succeed in cultivating a deeper appreciation for the affinity between human beings and nature?

In the following, I will attempt to answer this question by arguing that, contrary to those who propose an "egalitarianism" between animals and humanity,[31] it is really the differences separating them that dictate why we should protect animals from acts of cruelty. To defend this thesis, it will be necessary to clarify two assumptions that underlie the animal liberation movement. Specifically, the fact that humans have subjugated both wild and domestic animals for their purposes does not necessarily entail, in contrast, that animals have a potential for or a claim on freedom. Thus the first assumption we must examine is an ontological one: that our ability to choose as moral agents originates in a wider context than the circumscribed domain of human interests. Freedom must thereby be exercised in harmony with, rather than in opposition to, the ends of nature. To support this claim, it is necessary to show that freedom is not a possession of the will or a "proprietorial" right, as modern humanism contends. Instead, it is a gift that human beings receive only by subordinating their interests to the larger process of unconcealment, that is, by allowing the diversity of nature to manifest itself.

The second assumption is more subtle and more endemic to the strategy of ecological arguments. This premise points to the intersection between dwelling as a way of cultivating our kinship with animals and the power that seems to set us apart from them, namely, our capacity to speak. To support this premise, it is necessary to show that, as in the case of freedom, language is a power that enables us to participate in the process of unconcealment and is not confined to addressing human interests. Hence, the fact that animals cannot speak does not signal their inferiority to us, but, on the contrary, entails that our speech can be deployed as much to voice the interests of those creatures lacking that power as to articulate our grandeur. This thesis challenges scholars, such as Simon Glendinning, who argue that Heidegger fails to break with the humanistic tradition, insofar as he maintains a sharp bifurcation between the being of animals and humans due to the fact that we can speak and they cannot.[32] By upholding the *differences* between ourselves and animals rather than the similarities as the basis for a compassionate response toward the latter, my thesis provides an alternative ground to defend the animal welfare movement than does George Cave's. Cave points to a "reciprocal concern" that animals and humans have in cultivating the distinctive possibilities of their being, to the extent that both exhibit an ontological dimension of care (*Sorge*).[33] In either case, Heideggerians have overlooked the fact that the "power" that presumably elevates us above animals does so only by summoning us to answer to a higher mandate; this mandate directs us to deploy our power to "speak" as benefactors in acting on behalf of those that cannot articulate their interests.[34]

A.

While not the overarching concern of his philosophy, Heidegger nevertheless provides a language to address many of the ecological problems that confront us today. He emphasizes the need to preserve the earth, for human beings to act as stewards over it while cultivating a place of dwelling. Yet in recent years critics have begun to question the feasibility of appropriating Heidegger's thought for the purposes of buttressing the assumptions of deep ecology.[35] The sweeping character of his ontology makes it particularly difficult to apply it in a way that speaks to the welfare of earth's creatures. Moreover, the example of his involvement in a totalitarian regime suggests a huge gap between his thought and practice. Given this gap, it becomes especially difficult to adopt Heidegger's philosophy with the aim of developing a "pluralistic" ethic that can illuminate a wide range of social ills, from discrimination against minorities and women to the exploitation of animals.

Yet despite these shortcomings, we can hardly deny that Heidegger's insights into the dangers of Western anthropocentricism still ring true as we begin a new millennium. How can we occupy an earth whose pool of resources continues to shrink and threaten the life whose bounty it has spawned? As members of the human species, we have benefitted from the wonders of technology during the past 100 years. But the irony is that at times we may become the victims of this great progress. Technological advances, from medical vaccines to genetically enhanced food, have extended human life spans and have sheltered us from many of the vicissitudes of nature. Despite its achievements, technology provides methods that postpone death rather than eliminate it. While many "miracle cures" encourage us to forget our finitude, they do not annul the gulf from which time immemorial has separated mortals from the gods. On the contrary, technology poses profound dangers that impel us to view our finitude in a new light, as inhabitants of an earth whose boundaries of land and water continue to recede. Consider the following paradox: the medical advances which provide the seeds for overpopulation in the present may in the future contribute to an "ecological disaster" whose effects are universally threatening.

The problems we recognize under the heading "ecological crisis," however, can only become meaningful as problems, given our inherent capacity for self-understanding and our ability to question our place on the earth.[36] When seen in this light, our finitude is not simply a lack or deprivation, insofar as it also grants us the power to address the problems posed by technology, including the gradual restriction of the earth's habitats. As such, finitude marks the limits of human potential, the expansion and contraction of possibilities. Human beings confront their limits as much pro-actively as reactively; they can thereby anticipate changes nascent in their situation and take steps toward their realization.

Thus freedom accompanies finitude. As we will see, how we develop this concept of freedom will have ontological implications for specifying our uniqueness as human beings as well as determining our affinity for animals. Indeed, the differences that separate us from animals will swing the balance in the direction of promoting their welfare rather than exploiting them according to the destructive forces of technology. As Heidegger emphasizes, the consequences of technology are necessarily global, in such a way that its destructive character does not discriminate between the kinds of animals that suffer—whether domestic or wild—even though the impact on each may be viewed quite differently. It is just as important to stress this point as it is to affirm the key distinction that many ethicists make between the set of problems unique to either domestic or wild animals. Whether electronic tracking, which permits cornering a cougar for the kill, or the injection of primates with the AIDS virus, the effects of technology are obvious. To be sure, we may sympathize more with the plight of domestic animals due to our proximity to them. From a Heideggerian perspective, however, the transgressions against wild animals most clearly suggest what is at the root of all other forms of cruelty against the earth's creatures, namely, the encroachment upon, if not the destruction of, their territory, of the ecological niches where they thrive. In a phenomenological approach to ecology, the earth is a place of inhabitation where the diversity of habitats hinges upon the allocation of space. As Heidegger suggests in "Building Dwelling Thinking," space (*Raum*) "frees" a being to settle where it belongs, demarcating boundaries in which various locations can arise.[37] The loss of wild habitat, whether of food or territory (land or sea), defines the overarching ecological crisis that enables us to put into perspective the plight of domestic animals as well. Specifically, the benefits which they reap from us as suppliers of their food at the same time will compromise them in the vulnerable area where their livelihood hangs most in the balance: in *depending upon us* for the allocation of their territory (e.g., the suffering of the caged laboratory animal).

With this observation, we arrive at both an important similarity and difference between ourselves and animals. On the one hand, we share a common concern for the extent and quality of habitats. On the other hand, we have the additional capacity to address the problems posed by the shrinking of all areas of inhabitation. And this ability stems from freedom, insofar as our "world openness" uncovers various regions of activity and occupation within the compass of nature. In his hermeneutic phenomenology, Heidegger distinguishes between a volitional sense of freedom and freedom in a more primeval form as a "world openness." For him, choice presupposes the unfolding of possibilities and hence the self's situatedness within the encompassing horizon of world. As a human comportment, freedom defines human being's emergence within an expanse of possibilities, its encounter with the diversity of manifestness. The world implies a topography, a distribution of regions or an allocation of space on which all living creatures depend for their habitats. By opening a world, human beings can cultivate this diversity and appreciate the integrity of nature insofar as its creatures reveal themselves in terms of their unique ends. But while animals may exhibit the ends unique to their species, we can address the degree of harmony or conflict revealed in all of the ends of nature.

Depending on the expanse or restriction of our disclosure of world, we can pursue ends that subordinate the interests of other creatures for our own benefit. When this instrumental pursuit becomes all-encompassing, as occurs in technology, the danger arises that animals can be treated uniformly as mere commodities. When we subordinate animals to our purposes, we infringe upon the claim of territoriality that determines their being. Yet humanity's world openness also enables us to step back from our absorption in instrumental ends in order to ponder our role in cultivating the diversity of nature. Indeed, only through the "freedom of transcendence" can human beings consider their place within the nexus of life. In this way, they can become guardians of nature's welfare rather than agents of its exploitation.

In defending a Heideggerian approach to animal welfare, there is a tendency to seize upon a moral intuition that emphasizes a synergy between human beings and nature. This path seems to be the proper one insofar as it offsets the anthropocentric bias of elevating human beings qua rational animals above other animals. A concern arises, however, about whether the application of Heidegger's critique of anthropocentricism turns out to be question begging, because it identifies the animals' likeness to humans as the moral basis (i.e., moral "intuition") for treating them fairly (e.g., the argument for "equal consideration"). Yet from a Heideggerian perspective, we will discover that the more compelling and provocative argument lies in restoring the differences between humans and animals, albeit with a twist that also renounces anthropocentricism. Specifically, that twist involves redefining human freedom to include humans' capacity to dwell on or inhabit the earth rather than as a possession of the will.[38]

As much as anyone, Michael Zimmerman has shown that the parallels that hold between human animal life originate from profound ontological differences.[39] By drawing upon Heidegger's 1929–1930 lectures,[40] Zimmerman argues that human beings, unlike animals, situate themselves within a world openness that allows them to rise above immediate desires and instrumental concerns. In contrast, Heidegger emphasizes that animals are "world poor," insofar as the scope of their immediate environment circumscribes their sphere of interests and hence disposes them to become absorbed in basic activities (e.g., pursing food), a restricted kind of comportment or awareness for which he reserves the term *"Benommenheit."*[41] Yet by the same token human beings can forsake the primordial openness of the world, and by immersing themselves in a parallel kind of immediate preoccupation and "ontical craving" exemplified by animals, they can fall prey to a more ruthless drive than even "brute" animal survival, namely, self-aggrandizement and the will to domination. Human beings become capable of such bestiality through a dereliction of care in which they misappropriate the "potency" that originates from (the gift of) freedom and foster a "prowess" employed for self-serving ends. As Heidegger emphasizes in echoing Schelling, human beings exhibit an equal capacity to descend to a level "lower" than the animals as much as to ascend to a level above them: "'the highest heaven and the deepest abyss'" (*der tiefste Abgrund und der höcheste Himmel*).[42] Due to their finitude, human beings acquire freedom as openness directly in proportion to how they forsake the interests of their will. Thus they become "free" by situating themselves within the expanse of world openness, within the space allocated for dwelling. The freedom that rescues human beings from their animal-like craving is precisely the "power" that enables them to suspend their will within a technological context and thereby rebuff all of the mechanisms, including enslaving animals for instrumental purposes. Heidegger describes this nonvolitional form of freedom as "letting be."

While the term *power* may be used paradoxically, it really entails the difference between an "endowment" or a "gift" implying stewardship, and a "possession" to be deployed arbitrarily at one's caprice or "will." The freedom that sets humans apart from animals, however, may dispose humans to act in behalf of their welfare as stewards rather than with indifference to their interests as masters. Freedom in the form of letting be allows humans to juxtapose their interests with animals rather than arbitrarily subordinate their ends to humans'. Through this more radical concept of freedom, humans can counter the anthropocentric position, which begins from the premise that human beings are privileged over other creatures due to their rationality. In contrast, those in the animal welfare camp discount this premise by accenting the animal's similarity to us humans (e.g., the capacity to feel pain or to exhibit sentience). But, ironically, the best strategy lies not in upgrading the status of animals by blurring their differences from humans but, as undertaken here, seeking a more primordial origin for the exercise of human capabilities. A "non-anthropocentric perspective" emphasizes that the *abilities that distinguish humans most from other creatures are precisely those with which humans are endowed (rather than possess), and hence their exercise extends beyond the satisfaction of exclusively human interests.* In arriving at this radical concept of freedom, we separate the fact of our endowment of it from any axiological privilege or presumption of moral superiority. Freedom as letting be and truth as unconcealment, of course, are reciprocal. Thus on the "practical" front, the displacement of the will as the privileged locus of freedom complements on the "theoretical" front the removal of the assertion as the privileged locus of truth. And the more explicitly we witness the breakdown of the theory-practice dichotomy, the further we distance ourselves from the influence that Cartesian dualism has on shaping modern ethics: the presumption of privileging consciousness as a disembodied spirit and then denigrating nature as the aggregate of material objects devoid of value. An "original ethics," which attends to the *ethos* of our inhabitation, can then emerge in the space created by subverting the volitional, anthropocentric, "foundationalist"premise of modern ethics.

Given the turn to a nonanthropocentric perspective, what separates humans from animals is the freedom that disposes humans to assume guardianship over animals, that is, by suspending humans' will to self-aggrandizement. Borrowing from Eckhart, Heidegger refers to this freedom as "wanting not to will."[43] Indeed, humans are different from animals, but the freedom that epitomizes this difference demands a stance of humility rather than aggrandizement. Thus the freedom distinguishing humans from animals is the impetus to "let be," which allows humans to develop a conservatorship for animals. Rather than viewing freedom as a "property" right, as suggested by the humanistic tradition of the Enlightenment, humans instead construe freedom as a "gift" whose exercise does not coincide with human interests.

To a large extent, the debate over animal liberation fails to develop this distinction, even to the point of never questioning the origin of freedom. Yet the formulation of this question provides the key to the paradigm shift that governs the animal liberation movement, namely, we are most fully human or "authentic" when engaged in acts of stewardship rather than in exploitative pursuits. In becoming guardians, we display the "care" (*Sorge*) that situates us within nature as a whole and fosters the possibility of a harmonious relation to those domestic animals dependent upon us. We can express this harmony in various ways, but the term that Heidegger employs most frequently is that of "dwelling" on the earth.[44] The expression "dwelling" has both romantic and poetic overtones.[45] We must emphasize that dwelling is a mode of human comportment that presupposes freedom rather than being a mystical sentiment.

Authentic freedom cultivates our place of dwelling on the earth, suspending the drive of our human will rather than allowing it to fuel our domination of nature. Freedom in this radical sense concurs with the quest to rescue animals from technological exploitation, as exhibited in both medical experimentation and agriculture. Yet we must still ask whether this ontological sense of freedom, and the corresponding concept of care, implies any "directives" of its own. While our world openness grants us the capacity to attend to the diversity of life, there seems to be lacking any explicit element of governance that would direct us to exhibit benevolence toward animals. The "solicitude" and compassion that the self can show toward others may not immediately extend to our animal counterparts. Is it possible to make the transition to a normative discourse that can articulate a "principle of benevolence," a precept of compassion, in regard to our interaction with animals? Because Heidegger's ontological concept of freedom disposes us to, but does not explicitly sanction, animal welfare, we must examine a second assumption, which involves singling out animals as being worthy of special consideration. That is, how can we ascribe to animals a measure of consideration in coinhabiting a domain with us, when it is the ability to employ language that forms the predicate of any community?

B.

A terminological clarification will yield the path for the remainder of my discussion. Why do I refrain from alluding to "animal rights" and instead speak of "animal welfare"? Not only does the notion of "rights" have a problematic history, but granting the distinction opens up an entire set of problems. Indeed, opponents have argued that animals cannot have "rights," because that privilege is reserved only to beings who can discharge responsibilities and enter into reciprocal obligations.[46] To defend welfare toward animals on the basis that they have "rights" is to fall into the trap of adopting a preconceived notion of what constitutes a "community" in the first place, namely, a consensus determining inclusion or exclusion of membership. But this view is limited by its tie to the anthropocentric tradition of the Enlightenment and its volitional concept of freedom. Despite the Enlightenment's belief in the self-evidence of humanity's grandeur, there may be an inherent arbitrariness in privileging one species' interests over that of another.[47]

The shift away from "rights" implies a new orientation for ethics. Specifically, ethics must reformulate the "good" to include our way of dwelling on or inhabiting the earth, as well as the dynamics of interpersonal relations. In this regard, ethics rediscovers its roots in the *ethos*, in which descriptive as well as prescriptive considerations shape the landscape of ethical reflection. The *ethos* thereby provides the backdrop for transcribing a sense of the good into explicitly discursive or conceptual terms. And while ethics still retains a concern for the good as its primary emphasis, the development of a corresponding vision of human nature becomes relevant. Rather than equating the self with a detached rationality, we must consider ourselves embodied beings situated among the diversity of life-forms. The overcoming of an anthropocentric standpoint, then, goes hand in hand with the radicalization of ethics. As one of Heidegger's students, Hans Jonas emphasizes this "embodied" dimension more than his mentor did. According to Jonas, "only an ethics which is grounded in the breadth of being, not merely in the singularity and oddness of man, can have significance in the scheme of things."[48] We might add that the same holds true in considering the natural as well as the sociological factors that define the nexus of community (e.g., the aspect of gender). Indeed, it is the search for an alternative notion of community that yields the catalyst for developing an ethics of our earthly inhabitation. For the rediscovery of a primordial form of community, as including the material dimension of our rootedness on the earth, constitutes the first step in radicalizing ethics, in developing an "original ethics." To reiterate a quote from Hannah Arendt (another prominent student of Heidegger's), "Human beings = earthbound creatures, living in a community."[49]

Yet in accenting the importance of language, have we not inadvertently identified the factor that separates human beings from animals and thereby discounted the pretext of any "equality" between them? Indeed, many philosophers have pointed to language as the key to human rationality and the cornerstone of the moral agency that humans possess and animals lack. Ironically, critics argue that Heidegger reinforces this humanistic-anthropocentric bias because he states that only human beings can speak.[50] But he does not maintain, conversely, that the primary aim of speech is to delineate the sphere of human interests, for those interests are only one aspect of the manifestation of beings in their diversity. Thus while maintaining that animals lack speech, Heidegger also emphasizes that human beings do not "possess" language.[51] How do we resolve this aporia? Once again, it is necessary to employ our strategy that allows the *differences* between humans and animals to swing in the direction of promoting the latter's welfare rather than the similarities as in Cave's approach.

We must recall that for Heidegger language is not a "tool" that human beings use in order to communicate, but instead it constitutes the disclosedness of the "there." That is, language enables humans to participate in the process of unconcealment, the opening of a world as a differentiated field of meanings. Just as the world governs all forms of human comportment, so human beings depend upon language as an endowment that spawns all of their discursive abilities. As Heidegger suggests, human beings speak only insofar as they respond to language.[52] But the corollary of this insight is also important. Human beings do not possess language, they acquire it. And they acquire it in harmony with an "attunement" (*Stimmung)* that disposes them to foster the manifestness of things, nature, and the welfare of their animal counterparts.

In Heidegger's case, this radical enactment of language assumes the form of "middle voice"—a balance between activity and passivity. For any activity of freedom in which humans engage there is a corresponding form of expression. The grammar of middle voice provides this form to enable human beings to participate in the larger process of unconcealment. The summons to "let be" does not annul all differences but instead awakens humans to the nuances and subtleties in the manifestness of nature. What sets humans apart as unique due to our capacity for speech simultaneously exacts of them a humility to deploy that power in order to voice the interests of those unable to speak, and thereby serves the larger process of allowing nature to manifest itself. Rather than result in a mystical union with nature, letting be spawns a humility in humans' treatment of all life. Human beings cease to be a "subject" for which nature is an "object," and, by dwelling on the earth, they allow nature to appear as that haven of which they are both recipients and guardians. How does this "paradigm shift," then, translate into a deeper compassion toward animals, according to a normative discourse that articulates a principle of benevolence?

The grammar of middle voice redefines humans' relation to language in order to emphasize inclusivity.[53] It provides the schema for an action which expresses concern for the welfare of creatures different than them that nevertheless occupy a common habitat. The speech with which humans are endowed can no longer be deployed exclusively to articulate their interests. Rather, humans' speech serves the greater process of unconcealment and thereby provides an inclusive forum to express the interests of those unable to do so. Thus we can point to an "*ecologos*," or a grammar of inclusivity, in which humans' compassionate actions toward animals become *idioms* that express the interests of nonhuman species and thereby form the cornerstone of a "transhuman ethic."[54] This grammar of inclusivity accents the "conjunctive" form "both . . . and," so humans can express the importance of their interdependence with other species. Hence the leadership ascribed to human beings as speakers is predicated as much on showing compassion toward the most vulnerable creatures as on exercising dominion over them. The "both . . . and" (versus "either . . . or") means that the differences that separate human beings from animals call humans to act in a way that is contrary to "their animal-like craving" of self-aggrandizement and become "shepherds" for their animal counterparts. By upholding the *humility* that allows humans to speak, they can become the voice for those creatures whose suffering otherwise would go unheard. The voice, however, speaks in favor of showing compassion toward animals. For despite rejecting anthropocentricism, Heidegger just as assiduously rejects the liberationist (e.g., Regan) proposal that animals have intrinsic worth, if only because it harbors a hidden metaphysical assumption.

Animals become vulnerable to exploitation when they relinquish their territorial claim and occupy only the space granted to them by the instrumental ends of human beings. Given that we can simultaneously recognize the limits of earth's habitats as well as our potential for self-aggrandizement, our responsibility toward animals arises from the finite nature of freedom. Because freedom is a gift summoning us to dwell on the earth and not a proprietorial right exclusive to us, we deploy it in a way that allows animals to be the benefactors—hence the possibility of "animal liberation." By the same token, the grammar of middle voice—the gestures of care that dispose us to respond to suffering other than our own—entails that we lend our freedom for the sake of those animals dependent upon us. In this way, we acquire the power to speak by submitting to the wider claim of unconcealment, so that the humility of our existence can become a sounding board to address the welfare of earth's creatures. As Heidegger remarks, it is one thing to "use" the earth's resources for our own benefit; it is quite another "to receive the blessing of the earth and to become at home in the *law* of this reception."[55] Given the mandate of this law, our special heritage as beings endowed with language warrants those who propose policies for animal protection, for example, "anti-vivisectionists," to speak on behalf of those creatures who cannot. In this case, speaking unfolds in reciprocity with acting, namely, through our commitment to allocate space in behalf of our animal counterparts, both domestic and wild. In heeding this responsibility, we become "liberators" of animals whose domain gradually shrinks at the hands of technological progress. Animal liberation does not require an egalitarianism between animal and human but instead aims to restore a diversity of habitat for which each has a common interest.

As we already indicated, it appears paradoxical that those creatures incapable of speech can be included in a community that is predicated on a dialogue among its participants. Indeed, the critics who disclaim animal "rights" do so on the grounds that rights extend only to those who can partake in reciprocal obligations. The fabric of a community would seem to include the ability to discharge such obligations. However, the impending ecological crisis adds another dimension to the constitution of a community than might otherwise be acknowledged under anthropocentric premises. The destructive character of technology also becomes an indirect sign of the fragility of that domain we share in common with our animal counterparts. The vulnerability of animals in our technological age reminds us of the transitoriness of our existence otherwise disguised in the march of progress. Animals portend the conservation of life (including ours), the promise of rebirth and regeneration amidst the threat of global destruction. And animals do so through two distinct manifestations of nature, on both domestic and wild fronts. This tension becomes unavoidable, however, insofar as the proliferation of some kinds of domestic animals can upset the ecological balance (witness the conflict between the Audubon Society concerned with protecting birds and groups that champion the cause of the feral cat—a domestic animal that has reverted to a semi-wild condition). Wild animals point to the extra-human dimension of nature over which we have no mastery, while domestic animals remind us of the expansion of community beyond the borders of human civilization.

Here again the power of language underscores the behavior we show toward domestic animals and, by extension, wild ones, which welcomes them within the folds of community, that is, by "calling" animals by name. Such "naming" reinforces the way that, on a biological level, we already "commune" with animals as occupants of one global habitat; through such communion we extend the borders of community to include the welfare of earth's creatures. The language we use is an indication of the kinship we share with animals, the underpinnings of the normative discourse by which we express our compassion toward them. In this respect, the human community cannot be built according to artificial specifications designed to exclude animals from humans' company. On the contrary, a truly global community reserves a place for animals in order to protect their welfare, thereby reinforcing a *bond* with domestic animals (through the "familiarizing" gesture of the name), which is as old as civilization itself. Such a community would unfold in two directions: first, through humanity's disposition to "let be" and, second, through the common interest humans share with animals to maintain the extent and quality of habitats. As Gandhi once stated in pointing to this unique intersection between ecological interests and ethics: "The greatness of a country can be judged by how it treats its animals."

The current ecological crisis had reversed the roles so that instead of humans competing with animals for survival, animals are now beholden to humans. As outlined previously, the two assumptions pertaining to animal liberation cannot be separated from the historical situation in which this ecological crisis unfolds. This historicalness does not mitigate the importance of the concern for animal welfare; if anything, it makes it more urgent. However, the preceding approach varies from the tack taken either by those who argue that animals merit "equal consideration" due to possessing comparable interests to humans (Singer), or those who point to a complementarity between animals as "moral patients" and human beings as "moral agents" (Regan).

Despite the considerable merit of either perspective, each assumes a common ground that sustains both animals and humans and permits differentiating their interests without subjugating one to the other. Put in the terms expressed earlier, how do we bring humans and animals together under a common canopy of concern? I have tried to answer this question by emphasizing a "shared" interest that both humans and animals have in the face of a common opponent—the reduction of both the expanse and diversity of habitats through technology—and hence by showing how those endowed with speech can become the voice for those who lack it. In undergoing this paradigm shift, spearheaded by the questioning developed in deep ecology, we encounter a new unfolding of the ethos in which our animal counterparts enter into consideration as we ourselves do. For the ethical landscape expands in such a way as to include the materiality of our common ancestry, our ties to the earth, our shared vulnerability of the exposure of the flesh. If we bend Heidegger in a Levinasian direction and raise ethics to a level of importance on par with ontology, then we become witness to a "*carnal topography* in which

[we] read the commandments written on the surfaces of the flesh, a *corporeal topology* in which the body is the place from which the *heteros* speaks the *nomos*."[56]

Though in his pivotal essay "On the Essence of Truth" (1929) Heidegger discounts the fleshly dimension of our being-in-the-world, he does emphasize that an "exposedness to beings" lies at the heart of unconcealment.[57] Conversely, by pointing ahead to a revival of the *ethos*, and the exposure of the flesh as the intersection between the cultural and the zoological, *we suggest how incarnality is an important permutation in the diversity of being's appearances.* The accompanying critique of technology, on which this paradigm shift is predicated, however, requires further clarification as a historical possibility of the West. My discussion in this chapter, then, harbors its own presuppositions about the evolving character of our moral understanding and the possibility of its expression through different, even opposing, voices. Such understanding develops, as Ken Wilber emphasizes, by recovering dimensions of the self that Western culture has traditionally dismissed: emotions, corporeality, and nature.[58] We need to clarify the historical backdrop for this development by addressing the kind of political governance that welcomes the voice of the other (including those who can only indirectly speak on their behalf—our animal counterparts).[59]

Specifically, how can we justify assuming a communitarian form of freedom, a "letting be" that elicits a shared interest we have with animals in safeguarding the earth? How does the governance implied in the exercise of such freedom, or a political body, originate? Insofar as our bond with animals reveals our dual origin as terrestrially as well as socially rooted, a "body politic" must assume both a literal and a metaphorical meaning. When we juxtapose the question of freedom with the concern for embodiment, however, a troubling problem arises. Traditionally, freedom has been defined as one facet of a dualism, spirit and intellect, whose opposite, or "determinism," has been defined according to another facet, namely, corporeality and sensation. Given our discussion of the materiality of the body, can we rescue Heidegger's concept of freedom on the other side of this dualism? We will now turn to these perplexing concerns.

Chapter 5

The Body Politic
Terrestrial or Social?

Human beings alone are free. This seems to be a self-evident statement provided, of course, that we assume that freedom belongs to human nature. But what if freedom were broader and more primordial than the set of faculties exercised by "man," and, if exercised in the guise of what Heidegger describes as "letting be," induces a concern that includes the welfare of animals as well as human beings? Indeed, no less a luminary than Friedrich Hölderlin, when seeking a metaphor to describe the poetic search for releasement and liberation, stated: "'Poets be free, as swallows.'"[1] Do we then conclude that animals are "free" too? Rather, we must take Hölderlin's remark as referring to the region in which the swallow has unfettered flight. And that region is opened up by the interplay between earth and sky, which are joined, in Sallis's words, by a "rainbow" whose arc sets each apart.[2] For Heidegger, earth and sky define two quadrants whose interplay, in conjunction with mortals and gods, outlines the openness of world. Seeking guidance from a line from Hölderlin's poetry, "'Everything is intimately interrelated [*innig*],'" Heidegger clarifies the nature of this interplay. "This means: One is intimately appropriated [*vereignet*] to the other, but in such a way that thereby [each] remains in its own proper domain: Gods and men, earth and [sky]."[3] And thus it is to this dynamic of world openness where we must look to discover the meaning of freedom. In making this claim, however, a troubling ambiguity arises, insofar as we consider the full development of Heidegger's thought. Freedom may pertain to (1) the openness of play, but may also correspond to (2) the act of projecting forth the world as the horizon of possibilities, or to the finite transcendence, as he illustrates in *On the Essence of Ground*. Indeed, we discover an inherent polyvalency in the concept of freedom, which gives us occasion to pause.

In this chapter, we will try to unfold this polyvalence by examining the various stages in Heidegger's thought where he addresses the possibility of freedom. First, we will examine the key thesis that Heidegger advances in his 1929 lecture on the essence of truth: that freedom is not a possession of man, but, on the contrary, man is "possessed by" freedom.[4] Then we will determine to what extent freedom becomes possible in conjunction with the embodiment of our thrown condition, in a way that circumvents the traditional dichotomy of free will versus determinism. The more clearly we can redefine freedom in terms of a response to our way of being situated among beings, that is, as a form of "letting be," the better we can succeed in "deconstructing" the last vestige of modern voluntarism.

Deconstruction also has implications for our attempt to recover freedom within the social arena beyond its confinement to the individual will. Just as freedom need not be disembodied through its supposed opposition to nature, so the decision making of the individual need not be divorced from his or her membership in society. On the contrary, freedom will appear according to a special economy in which the preservation of its power increases through its transmission to and exercise by an ever-larger constituency—what we might call the "body politic." As freedom reemerges as the presupposition of the body politic, the character of its materiality will become increasingly clear. Specifically, as the power with which human beings are endowed, our capacity for freedom summons us to safeguard the welfare of animals and the earth, rather than simply to exploit nature. We thereby arrive at the conclusion which, to those modern philosophers who subscribe to the mind-body dualism, would appear paradoxical: specifically, we acquire a radical concept of freedom by showing how its exercise occurs in conjunction with, rather than in opposition to, nature.

The Polyvalency of Freedom

Freedom versus determinism—such is an example of a metaphysical dualism that Heidegger not only circumvents but almost totally ignores. Mind/body and spirit/nature would be examples of Cartesian dualisms that Heidegger, while he does not take them seriously, at least acknowledges. He seeks to retrieve a primordial sense of nature as *physis* (outside of and prior to this bifurcation) in such a way that privileging spirit, at the expense of truncating nature into the totality of physical objects, becomes symptomatic of the forgottenness of being. In regard to the modern problem of freedom/determinism, we might take guidance from Heidegger's response to Kant's chagrin at the "scandal of philosophy['s]" not being able to provide a suitable proof for the existence of the external world. Rather than take seriously Kant's "refutation of idealism," Heidegger states: "The 'scandal of philosophy' is not that this proof has yet to be given, but that *such proofs are expected and attempted again and again.*"[5]

Speaking of Kant, Heidegger *does* address the dilemma posed by the third antinomy, the conflict between freedom of will and the natural chain of causality, in his summer lectures from 1930. Yet once again the motivation is not so much to resolve this dilemma as to rescue the concept of freedom from its segregation in the atemporal, noumenal realm and rediscover its origin on the concrete level of the self's facticity, the set of pregiven circumstances. Rather than relegate freedom to an otherworldly realm, Heidegger re-opens the question of freedom in conjunction with the problem of world. "The problem of freedom arises in the context of the problem of world."[6] Indeed, Kant suggested that the concept of world, the cosmological idea, marks the boundary where two kinds of causality, free will and nature, could be related and yet differentiated from each other. For Heidegger, however, world reemerges as the horizon of the self's possibilities, so its development of them, or the factical exercise of freedom occurs as an affirmation of temporality and freedom, rather than a denial. When we redirect the question of freedom from the concrete soil of being-in-the-world, we discover that Heidegger's ontological inquiry has already subverted an even more fundamental dichotomy than that of freedom and determinism, which the latter bifurcation presupposes, namely, theory versus praxis.

For Heidegger, everydayness defines a unity that precedes the division between theory and praxis, for Dasein's engagement in various activities receives guidance from a preunderstanding of existence and being. Conversely, the development of any thematic understanding of being, in order to remain concrete, must be rooted in the facticity of the inquirer as being-in-the-world. Care distinguishes the "pre-unity" of Dasein's being. And, if it is also the case that the concept of the will is subsequent to care, and thus is already determined by the theory-praxis split, whereby will constitutes the root of praxis, then willing arises as an expression—albeit a derivative one—of care. Correlatively, if modern philosophy takes willing to be the seat of freedom, then Heidegger's position must be that the unity preceding willing, or care, for example, the projection of "that for the sake of," harbors the concrete origin of freedom.

> Willing and wishing are rooted with ontological necessity in Dasein as care. . . .
>
> Care is ontologically "earlier" to the phenomenon we mentioned. . . . In willing, a being that is understood, that is, projected upon its possibility, is grasped as something to be taken care of or to be brought to its being through concern. For this reason, something

> willed always belongs to willing, something which has already been determined in terms of a "for the sake of which."[7]

While the activity of willing may have an affinity for freedom, it is the will's relegation to a faculty of the human subject that makes it problematic. As Heidegger states in *Being and Time*, "The underlying totality of care shows through in the phenomenon of willing."[8] Specifically, "that for the sake of which" (*umwillen*) defines the formal structure of freedom. In upholding this formality, along with willing (verbal) as a formal indicator, Heidegger takes a subtle but crucial step forward toward defining the nature of freedom. Indeed, the formal structure "that for the sake of" does not necessarily have a scope that pertains to my interests in exclusion to another's, the egocentric connotation that some senses of willing might have. On the contrary, in this formal sense it would seem equally plausible that the umbrella of concern could encompass the welfare of others, as in "solicitude." That is, Heidegger suggests that "that for the sake of which" as a form of existence pertains fundamentally to being-a-self, albeit not to the exclusion of the others. For being-a-self already implies being-with-others, or the structure of "*mit-sein.*"

There is, however, perhaps an even more important consideration that distinguishes the formal character of "that for the sake of." Implicit in the sense of willing as freedom is the disposition of a power, or potency, which in terms of care first comes to light as Dasein's "can be," or the potential to be (*Seinkönnen*). Concealed in this sense of potency is the positing of a deed, or what we might commonly call an "initiative." Heidegger does not deny these senses, but at the same time, it is in recognizing their incompleteness that we begin to observe the turning point in his inquiry into freedom. For it is not only in willing that freedom may become evident, but, paradoxically, in the possibility of the abeyance thereof, that is, in the "exercise" of reservedness and restraint. This "nonvolitional" element of the will, if we can call it that, becomes apparent when Heidegger distinguishes between authentic solicitude as a "leaping in ahead," which *restrains* from any imposition (of direction) upon the other, and inauthentic solicitude as "leaping in for,"[9] which imposes control upon the other and deprives the other of the singularity of his or her potential to be. The dimension of reservedness turns out to be intrinsic to the "can be" of human existence, and serves as a formal indicator to a deeper root of freedom beyond simple volition.

A.

One of the most overlooked factors in discussing Heidegger's concept of freedom is its development in terms of the grammar of "middle voice." The grammar of middle voice defines the balance between activity and passivity, spontaneity and receptivity. When the tradition defines freedom in terms of volition, spontaneity becomes the key factor in distinguishing its mode of enactment. But the grammar of middle voice rebalances the relationship between spontaneity and receptivity in order to displace subjectivity as the locus of freedom qua exercise of the will. Thus freedom involves accepting as well as affirming, giving (myself) up as well as asserting who I am. For in question is whether or not freedom has an extra-human origin, and, as such, entails a power that we acquire rather than simply (willfully) exercise. And that power will in some way be related to being and in its own way solicit our help in the dispensation of its openness. However, we first experience that dimension of enowning in terms of the coming into its own of the self, in which Dasein seeks its individuation by projecting forth the inevitability of death.

Dasein's authentic being-toward death provides an important example of how the grammar of middle voice shapes the self's experience of freedom. As we have seen, in "giving itself up" to death, the self receives in return an understanding of its unique possibilities, so it becomes "free" for its existence in proportion to accepting the limited scope of its possibilities. As the first act of freedom, Dasein becomes "free" for death, and because the anticipation of death brings forth the whole of its being, it is thereby "freed" for the unique possibilities of its existence. Thus freed, Dasein comes into its own through its encounter with otherness, with the "radical alterity" of death, in such a way that the contraction of a limit redirects the self into the wider expanse of its *own* possibilities. Three key presuppositions of Heidegger's subsequent inquiry into the essence of freedom arise from this analysis of "free death": (1) that Dasein's experience of freedom is essentially connected to its finitude and (2) as finite, freedom requires a "site" for its enactment, the facticity of human existence through which new possibilities emerge, and (3) that freedom, by unfolding within and through an expanse of possibilities, is interchangeable with openness.

The importance of the first presupposition becomes immediately apparent in the chapter of *Being and Time* following the existential analysis of death, the discussion of the "call of conscience." For Heidegger, Dasein's attesting to its readiness to face death takes the form of wanting to have a conscience or choosing to choose, that is, resoluteness. As such, authentic resolve constitutes the factical embodiment of freedom as the unlocking and holding open of the possibilities of a situation, including a basic self-awakening and responsiveness that translates into "taking action" in salient way(s). Because of its facticity, resolve is a form of decision making that also divides and separates, waiving some possibilities in favor of others, an openness that occurs always in tandem with a counter-prospect of foreclosing other alternatives. Though this element of foreclosure may appear to be only negative, the negativity as such has a positive element: for an openness of limitation, which selects and discriminates, gives direction and even rootedess to choices rather than an unfettered kind of choosing that cannot prioritize, differentiate, and settle among the various options—the plight of Kierkegaard's aesthetic individual. As Heidegger states in his 1936 lectures on freedom, which echo a statement quoted in chapter 2 of the second division of *Being and Time*: "To choose means to relate oneself to possibility, to prefer one to the other. Thus, to be able to choose means to have to be finite."[10] Resoluteness makes possible will(ing), and not the reverse. The so-called efficacy of willing, as a form of acting that is engaged with the possibilities of a situation, depends upon an accompanying openness. That is, the openness yields not only the expanse of possibilities but also provides the measure of their importance, so as to give direction to any decision. In simple terms, we could say that a "good" decision is more informed by openness than a "bad" decision is. We need not construe good and bad in moral terms. Rather, a "good" career decision is one whose enactment enhances Dasein's uniqueness, the potential for coming into its own, by allowing the openness to draw forth the "richness" of its possibilities. And the demand of openness is always balancing self-determination with responsiveness to the concerns of the situation. In this respect, the grammar of middle voice prevails, the combining of passivity and activity, receptivity and spontaneity. Yet the authentic self who comes into its own by virtue of this openness does not have a monopoly on freedom. If the openness did not include other ways in which freedom could be enacted, for example, the solicitude that safeguards the other's freedom, then the self could not be free. Indeed, the economy of freedom is such that its preservation hinges on its transmission and appropriation in diverse ways.

In resolute decision making, Dasein experiences freedom through the facticity of its taking action (i.e., as a form of praxis). As Heidegger states in his 1930 lectures on Kant: "The factuality corresponding to the idea of freedom is that of praxis."[11] In its facticity, freedom pertains directly to the authentic self. But what about the possibility of Dasein's understanding of being? Is there not corresponding to this development a specific instance of freedom? But how is it possible to understand being except through its differentiation from beings? As Heidegger states in his 1928 lectures on logic, "We thus term this distinction that first enables something like an understanding-of-being the *ontological difference*."[12] In *On the Essence of Ground*, Heidegger suggests that Dasein first experiences the ontological difference by projecting the world as the horizon of possibilities. He reserves the term *transcendence* to describe this act of "world-making."[13] Through transcendence, the ontological difference becomes factical. The enactment of transcendence, the projecting of "that for the sake of which," he calls "freedom."

In this context, freedom implies Dasein's ability to distinguish between being and beings and to abide within that difference. The differentiation between being and beings defines the dynamic character of that openness by making explicit, in a way only presupposed in the phenomenon of resoluteness, the difference between the openness as such and what emerges (to become manifest and be encountered) within the space of opening forth. In the Kant book, where Heidegger discusses at length Dasein's transcendence, he calls this area of openness a "free-space" or "play-space" (*Spiel-Raum*).[14] Not only must various beings emerge in this free-space so Dasein can encounter them, but, because it is *a* being, the self must also depend on this openness in order to benefit from its own capability of "awareness." Thus self-reflexivity is not a given, but, as Raffoul illustrates, it must depend upon a prior openness.[15] Accordingly, Heidegger emphasizes that the self, because it must be surpassed along with beings-as-a-whole, comes to be constituted in the act of transcendence itself. On the one hand, the self projects "that for the sake" over beings-as-a-whole, and hence a primordial sense of willing remains intact. On the other hand, the freedom of the initiating act (of will) only becomes determinate and factical through the accomplishment of transcendence, in which the self benefits from the abundance of possibilities emerging at the periphery of the world toward which the self transcends.

Freedom thereby acquires a double sense as (1) the encompassing power from which being-in-the-world originates and (2) the factical concretion of that power through the self's engagement with the possibilities of the situation (e.g., choosing to choose). The double sense, however, is not accidental, because it parallels the ontic-ontological distinction that Dasein embodies. We might say that freedom occurs at the intersection of the ontological difference. And it is because freedom arises at this crossroads that it can, as it were, speak to the distinctness of Dasein's relation to being and, indeed, be indicative of it. Due to this relationship, we can say that freedom has an extra-human origin, as arising through a partnership with what is experienced as "other" to man (i.e., being). The absencing of being provides the counter-focus through which beings can become present, and from the standpoint of the self in which the experience of freedom is actively embodied, to be free is to welcome the diversity of manifestness. The self, then, is not free as an atomic unit, since it is only as an occupant of the world (which it helps "make" through its transcendence) that it acquires this power. As being-in-the-world, Dasein is free only by also acknowledging its potentiality embodied in the other, so authentic solicitude becomes an instance of experiencing freedom through otherness. Because the need to welcome diversity, including the otherness of the other, stands at the heart of freedom, the self always exercises freedom as it occupies a specific site; such a place of inhabitation includes a historical specific situation and an accompanying domain of social exchange (i.e., culture and politics).[16]

Freedom arises beyond the self and yet has its facticity through it. If this is the case, then we learn something about the self: that it is social as well as individual. Thus Dasein is always a participant in freedom rather than the solitary possessor of it. At the time, freedom is no more a function of society than it is of the individual, for apart from the coming into its own of authentic selfhood, society can quickly degenerate into collectivism, into the uniformity of the "wishes" of the "they" that extinguishes the voice of individuality, of dissent from authority. Does conformity to the expectations of the "they," then, lead to the kind of facile wishing that diminishes freedom? In extreme cases of compulsion, which occur in various scenarios of addiction, this would seem to be true. But does not inauthentic Dasein then make choices? The answer is yes, but in a derivative way that still presupposes the source of capability, the dynamic in the expansion of possibilities from which the impetus to choose, the deciding to decide, first arises. Conversely, should we then equate freedom with the authentic self? Perhaps the most appropriate answer would be this: in terms of the self's experience of it, freedom begins with authenticity, but in terms of its origin and scope, it does not end there.

For Heidegger, freedom cannot be reduced to the individual's exercise of choice any more than it can the deliberations of many individuals who comprise society. Indeed, a macrocosm of the individual, or society, still does not equal freedom. As we will discover in the next section, freedom makes possible society. That is, something like a *polis* becomes possible because of the way in which it facilitates (1) maximum participation among its members and (2) safeguards the individual's access to freedom. The extra-human origin of freedom becomes increasingly evident, for we are its beneficiaries only to the extent through a reciprocal admission of our dependence upon it (e.g., as a willingness for which to be answerable). It is surely a cliche that responsibility always accompanies freedom. What Heidegger adds to this elemental insight, however, is that reciprocation, a dimension of responsiveness, attests to the extra-human origin of freedom: we are participants in freedom through the dispensation of its power rather than the monopolizers of it.

In his pivotal essay from 1929 "Concerning the Essence of Truth," Heidegger refers to the "freedom to be free."[17] In this context he develops his notion of freedom as letting be (*Seinlassen*) in order to distinguish its coincidence with truth as unconcealment. In his 1930 lectures on Kant, Heidegger reaffirms this discussion, albeit by underscoring the facticity of freedom: "The letting-be-encountered of beings, comportment to beings in each and every mode of manifestness, is only possible where freedom *exists. Freedom is the condition of the possibility of the manifestness of the being of beings, of the understanding of being.*"[18] Once again, a double sense of freedom arises, the dual vector of its unfolding: as given and administered, as granted and exercised. Thus freedom always has its factical embodiment in decisions and deeds but cannot be exhausted by them. The power of freedom is always administered through a modality of ownership, but that enowning is enacted with a countervalence of the difference between being and beings. The economy of freedom is such that the more freedom belongs to the self's ownedness, the more explicitly Dasein is devoted to eliciting the plurality of manifestness: letting be. In its factical embodiment via social relationships, the more explicitly freedom is "my own," the more others must be able to benefit from its "power," share in its potency, or participate in its unfolding. In this special economy of freedom, we see what is at stake in the presupposition governing its bestowal upon human beings: the condition of finitude as such.

The finite character of freedom becomes explicit in the way that power always implies some conditions for its allocation, and this is doubly so given that human beings are the guardians of freedom rather than its simple possessors. As Heidegger states in his 1930 lectures on Kant:

> Man is only an *administrator* of freedom, i.e., he can only let-be the freedom which is accorded to him, in such a way that, through man, the whole contingency of freedom becomes visible.
>
> Human freedom no longer means freedom as a property of man, but man as a *possibility of freedom*. Human freedom is the freedom that breaks through in man and takes him up unto itself, thus making man possible.[19]

Conversely, finitude is not simply a restriction that diminishes, but, because it corresponds to the manner of the appropriation of freedom, to be finite is also to be "empowered" by the potency of the "can be" and by the dynamic of being delivered over to possibilities. Human finitude is not only determined by the limits imposed upon us by death but also by that whose corresponding withdrawal includes the (counter) momentum of granting (openness) (i.e., being itself). Giving and taking away and granting and refusing define the inflection of middle voice that enlists an attunement, a way of co-responding, hence, the ownedness is always more than "my sphere of influence and interest" and involves an allocation whose scope includes increasing possibilities of distribution and diversity. Thus the finitude of freedom lies in its economy, in the manner of its allocation. Insofar as freedom becomes factical, we are free to the extent that we participate in the allocation of its power, in essence, by "letting be."

It is not only the case that Dasein can only experience its freedom in conjunction with limits, as in becoming free to accept its mortality, or in the resolve of cultivating one possibility to the exclusion of others. Freedom is also ontologically limiting as that which must first and foremost be presupposed so ontological inquiry can get underway. The fact that fundamental ontology already presupposes truth, which coincides with freedom, already indicates the latter's character as a presupposition. As an enactment of disclosedness, of projecting open, philosophy issues from freedom, as the groundless ground of its origination. The presuppositional character of freedom then becomes evident in a key quote from *The Basic Problems of Phenomenology*: "Let us rather in the whole of the present course try to establish philosophy on its own basis, insofar as it is a work of human freedom."[20] Precisely because freedom is what allows philosophy to begin, as its presupposition, it is precisely what must be thematized last, in returning to that beginning and radicalizing it, as it were, in following the curvature of the hermeneutical circle. Heidegger points to Kant's admission of a problem of circularity in *Foundation for the Metaphysics of Morals* in which freedom emerges as the supreme presupposition of morality,[21] although moral praxis alone can confer actuality upon freedom, as analogous to the hermeneutical situation of fundamental ontology. In his 1930 lectures on Kant, Heidegger argues that the attempt to arrive at freedom as the presupposition of philosophy transposes its focus, in such a way that its chief topic, designated by the "and" conjoining being with time, is reincorporated back into the essence of freedom as such. "*The problem of freedom is not built into the leading and fundamental problems of philosophy, but, on the contrary, the leading question of metaphysics is grounded in the question concerning the essence of human freedom.*"[22] Unlike in Kant's case, can this "presupposition" also provide a clue to the embodiment of freedom?

By upholding the presuppositional character of freedom, Heidegger stands apart from the existentialist tradition that succeeded him. Indeed, Heidegger is not Sartre, for the latter assumes that human beings have absolute access to freedom, maintaining the bias of its inherently human, even "subjective," origin in the exercise of "choice." Ironically, however, Sartre seemed to accentuate the role of the body much more explicitly than Heidegger does. In its presuppositional character, freedom is constantly problematic: a threefold dynamic of appropriation, transmission, and preservation. But where do we discover the clue to this threefold dynamic if not in that active dimension of disclosednesss, where finitude joins with that of being: the absenting presence of temporality? We might put the matter another way: if freedom is inherently presuppositional, and if time provides the nomenclature for being, the declension of the words by which we can articulate its "meaning,"[23] then we must look to what, ontologically speaking, is equally presuppositional, namely, temporality.

But has not the philosophical tradition tended to cast time more in the role of the enemy of freedom rather than the ally? This is true, insofar as we construe time derivatively as a linear sequence of "nows," in which case it would serve as a deterministic model so that what has happened in the past dictates in advance what will occur in the "future." As is apparent in Kant's discussion of the third antinomy, determinism presupposes a linear model of time as a nexus of cause-and-effect relations. According to this linear model, it is not time as such that dampens the possibility of freedom, as a specific temporal dimension, that is, the irretrievability of the past and hence the inability to impart change with the succession of moments. Conversely, if the past could in some way be retrieved, if not literally, then we might find a clue to how temporality and freedom are compatible. Moreover, that clue would yield further hints as to how exactly freedom comes to be "embodied," or more precisely, comes to be exercised within the thrown situatedness of historical being-in-the-world. In question is what at first appears from the standpoint of modern philosophy to be the antithesis of freedom, or necessity. In necessity we discover the link to the past and, in fact, to time-boundedness. At the conclusion of modern philosophy, at the end of metaphysics, Nietzsche appears as the figure who grappled with the problem of retrieving the past, and, in the guise of his doctrine of the eternal recurrence, sought in the "moment" a window of decision for choice that could arise alongside necessity.

Heidegger discusses the doctrine of eternal recurrence at length in his lectures from 1938, and in *What Is Called Thinking*? (1954).[24] Vis-à-vis the passing of time, Nietzsche characterizes revenge as "time's revulsion against the past and its 'it was.'"[25] The key to overcoming revenge, which Nietzsche describes as the "rainbow after long storms," is to turn "every 'it was' into "thus I willed it.'"[26] The past cannot be literally reversed, of course, but its retrieval is possible as including a meaning whose origin arises from the future. The past reemerges as having a significance that extends from the future and is validated by the will's self-affirmation of the "moment" in which each moment complements every other moment. Thus whatever meaning the self experiences in the moment stems from its future directedness, which rediscovers the significance of what has happened by acknowledging its impact on shaping the present. The present, in conjunction with the imminence of the future, would lack the depth of meaning with the omission of any other (past) moment, including the suffering that may have been produced by it. Each moment, then, has a relative degree of necessity, not in a predestined or deterministic sense but insofar as willing or choosing redeems the past by making its meaning hinge on its rediscovery in the future. Such is the case with Nietzsche's vision of the eternal recurrence of the same, of the cyclical movement of time.

According to Heidegger, Nietzsche unraveled an important enigma in which freedom, in the guise of the eternal recurrence, could occur alongside necessity. The potential for choice is always granted in the moment, insofar as the enactment of choosing conjoins the dimensions of future and past. The choosing in the moment reshapes the (meaning of) the past through its return from the future, and necessity is thereby conferred on "each and every moment" in agreement with the exercise of choice itself. Thus freedom arises in conjunction with necessity. What we gauge as necessity, however, emerges only in retrospect—not beforehand as in some doctrine of predestination when viewed from the perspective of eternity—as we recover the significance of the past along the curvature of time as a whole. Nietzsche characterizes the acceptance of this necessity in terms of "*amor fati.*" In *Ecce Homo,* he states: "My formula for greatness in a human being is *amor fati.* That one wants nothing to be different, not forward, not backward, not in all eternity. Not only bear what is necessary . . . but love it."[27] While various modern philosophers view fate and freedom as incompatible, Nietzsche construes the two as complementary. But their complementarity, as Heidegger makes explicit in *Being and Time,* depends upon a concept of *primordial time,* whereby history originates through the repetition (*Wiederholung*) of the past.

In chapter 5 of the second division of *Being and Time,* Heidegger states: "Once one has grasped the finitude of one's existence, it snatches one back from the endless multiplicity of possibilities which offer themselves as closest to one—those of comfortableness, shirking, and taking things lightly—and brings Dasein into the simplicity of its fate [*Schicksals*]."[28] In alluding to "fate," Heidegger recalls the sense of fatedness that is to be found in the Greek experience of the tragedy, of the hero who, having confronted adversity, discovers the true meaning of his existence. The experience of fate in this sense has connotations of revelation, disclosure, and self-discovery. Heidegger's recollection of Greek tragedy places his view of fate on a radically different ground than that of modern philosophy. We might characterize the difference in this manner: in modern philosophy, fate describes the way in which the past (pre)determines the future, as if closing off in advance the possibilities that can emerge. In the ancient sense of fate, on the other hand, the past is carried forward in the future, to be transformed (by its appropriation) in new possibilities. Thinking's way of continually responding to its beginnings, to the historical granting of its origins, constitutes a supreme act of freedom. This freedom is the empowerment that thought acquires by heeding the reciprocal claim (*Anspruch*) of enowning, of coming into what is most its own.

In the ancient sense of fate, the future conveys an "openness," while in the modern sense it signifies a "closure." Thus Heidegger emphasizes a kind of fate in which the past serves the development of the possibilities of the future rather than denies it. Temporality is essentially a movement and implies a directedness, albeit not necessarily a linear one. The "*worauf*" of the ecstasies of temporality overlaps, interplays, and mutually implicates each other in order to allow a directedness that may imply "purpose," but a purposiveness that unfolds by reclaiming the origins as transmitted and transcribed in futural possibilities. For example, a student whom I taught eighteen years ago at another academic institution—perhaps out of gratitude for past benefits—reemerges from the future to donate funds in support of the 2004 North American Heidegger Conference. "This [form of repetition] is how we designate Dasein's primordial historizing, which lies in authentic resoluteness and in which

Dasein *hands* itself *down* to itself, free for death, in a possibility which it has inherited and yet has chosen."[29] In one of his most graphic statements which underscores a personal experience of fate, Heidegger states the following in *On the Way to Language*:

> The term "hermeneutics" was familiar to me from my theological studies. At that time, I was particularly agitated over the question of the relation between the word of Holy Scripture and theological-speculative thinking. . . .
>
> Without this theological background I would never have come upon the path of thinking. But origin always comes to meet us from the future.[30]

Indeed, the reclaiming of one's thrownness in relation to such an origin projects open the future as a new frontier of discovery. This thrown project, as it were, yields the dynamic whereby temporality moves along a circuitous path so that possibilities held in reserve in the past can reemerge in the future. What we call "novelty" is the breakthrough into the moment of what the future shows to have been prefigured in the past.

Heidegger's appropriation of his *own* past becomes an instance, a concrete testimony to the complementarity of freedom and fate, which he described earlier in *Being and Time*, indeed, the ownedness of how thinking bears directly on his own philosophical development, in such a way as to be completely *self-referential*. And the fact that it can become self-referential in this way, as pertaining to the specifics of his situatedness, suggests that at least indirectly the path for addressing freedom crisscrosses with the concern for embodiment. Insofar as Heidegger himself is an example of how thought is *historical*, of "being-historical thinking,"[31] the philosophical enterprise is always "incarnated" through the thinker's facticity, through his or her thrownness into the circumstances that first prompted a question. The way in which self-questioning is always at the heart of the dynamic of the question of being itself, as Heidegger emphasizes in "What Is Metaphysics?" (1929), attests further to the incarnatedness of the philosophical task. As Heidegger states in his 1930 lectures on Kant: "*The content of the question* of philosophy . . . demands a questioning whose ever more radical broadening implies an ever more certain focus on the individual as individual, placing that *individual in question*."[32] Questioning and questioning the question epitomize freedom itself, insofar as the inquirer takes up the activity of investigation within a concrete historical situation. As such, philosophizing would seemingly constitute a supreme act of freedom.

And thinking, as the specific description that Heidegger reserves for a historical pursuit that receives the claim of being and responds by safeguarding the word, defines an activity that epitomizes freedom most of all. Indeed, only insofar as freedom occurs can we properly maintain that thinking becomes possible as well. But freedom is not merely directionless or without governance, for in originating as a response to being, thinking heeds that solicitation and thereby flourishes in the activity of letting be, of allowing unconcealment to take place. Thinking thereby becomes free at this juncture where freedom converges with truth. At this juncture, as it were, thinking finds its unique mode of lawfulness or logic in which the safeguarding of the originality of the word, of its potential to engender new idioms of expression, defines the essence of freedom. To quote Heidegger:

> The meaningfulness of language by no means consists in an accumulation of meanings cropping up haphazardly. It is based on a play which, the more richly it unfolds, the more strictly it is bound by a hidden rule. Through this, meaningfulness plays a part in what has been selected and weighed in the scale whose oscillations we seldom experience. That is why what is said is bound by a supreme law. That is the freedom [*Freiheit*] which gives freedom to the all-playing structure [*das allspielende Gefuge*] of transformation.[33]

Since the heeding of these new inflections of wording implies an attunement, the freedom of thinking is always bounded by the dictates of cultivating an abode within language, an indwelling within the word. To quote Sallis's unique characterization of how we always assume the challenge of freedom whenever we do philosophy: "The question is whether the beginning of philosophy—every beginning of philosophy, every enactment of philosophical beginning—is not, precisely in this sense, a matter of free thinking."[34] Because appropriation is always at work in this way of inhabiting language, the punctuation of many different voices becomes a further testimony of this freedom (of thinking). For dialogue and disputation lie at the heart of this freedom, insofar as the philosophical endeavor is incarnated within the historical place of human dwelling. Insofar as philosophy is a "work of human freedom," and an admission of the necessity of its (i.e., thinking's) historical situatedness governs this free endeavor, we discover that even at its highest level, freedom, that is, in the guise of thinking, is essentially an embodied activity. At the conclusion to "Letter on 'Humanism'," Heidegger provides an intimation of this when he draws an analogy between the endeavor of thinking and the activity of farming. "With its saying, thinking lays inconspicuous furrows in language. They are still more inconspicuous than the furrows that the former, slow of step, draws through the field."[35] Not only do both of these tasks require an inordinate amount of patience, and hence humility, but both relocate the participants on the topography of the earth and reaffirm the transitoriness of their sojourn there.

But what exactly does embodiment mean in this sense, and can it include a dimension of "materiality"? Does not Heidegger's description of the "solitude" of thinking sound faintly similar to a kind of ivory tower rhetoric? At least Hegel referred to the "labor" of thinking as it takes upon itself the "burden" of the world's history. Is not there a stubborn vestige of "idealism" remaining in Heidegger's thought? Before we answer yes to these questions, we must consider whether Heidegger allows for a dimension of materiality, where the experience of thrownness is felt most acutely, namely, in such dispositions as "distress," as he discusses in his 1937–1938 lectures, and "life-anxiety," as he outlines in his 1936 lectures on Schelling. To be engaged in being-historical thinking is to occupy a specific crossroads where simultaneously a decision needs to be made about what is at stake in the futural arrival of origins, about the possibilities in which the beginnings can be appropriated, preserved, and transmitted anew. Such unsettlement in the face of this decision, the decisiveness of decision, provokes a profound "life-anxiety" in whomever stands at these crossroads. As Heidegger states in his 1936 lectures on Schelling: "Life-anxiety is the presupposition of human greatness. Since the latter is not absolute, it needs presuppositions. What would a hero be who was not capable of letting precisely the most profound life-anxiety arise in himself? Either only a pure comedian or a blind strong man and a brute?"[36] Because of the presuppositional character of freedom its highest accolade requires the presupposition of life-anxiety as well. And in the depth of this anxiety, that the "ones to come" must allow to well up in themselves, lies the materiality of the thinker's facticity or his or her unique form of embodiment. Implicitly, Schelling says as much when he states: "in the contrast between necessity and freedom . . . the innermost center of philosophy comes to life."[37]

In this light, we should not construe heroism in a militant sense of self-aggrandizement, but rather we should view it as an assumption of risk that comes from pressing the frontiers of finitude as such. If philosophy is essentially an enterprise of testing limits, then, through its embodiment, thinking harbors as its material presupposition an affinity for the erotic. As the impetus to challenge limits, eroticism can have an emancipatory role, and, as the unsettling springboard to philosophy, it defines one factical way by which the thinker experiences freedom as the presupposition of thought. We cannot ignore this factical component of philosophy any more than we can deny, as Socrates concedes, that the alluring character of beauty first attracts the philosopher to undertake the arduous rise to the divided line. Indeed, as a permutation of the erotic, the dialogical unfolding of truth "captures" its participants by simultaneously emancipating them. Freedom involves necessity, in which the self is bound by enrapturement and committed to the ecstatic play of truth as revealing-concealing.

Where does thinking occur? Does it occur in the interiority of the mind, as Descartes believed? Obviously not, if we emphasize the centrality of being-in-the-world, as Heidegger does. Thus we would be tempted to say that the world constitutes the proper domain of thought, or, conversely, that thinking occurs "in" the world. But once again, the "in" of world needs to be questioned, indeed, to be thought. As such, being-historical thinking is inherently situated. Yet the "in" of the thinking, like that of freedom, must always be counterposed with the "outwardness" of the ecstasies of disclosedness. For thought, like the letting be of freedom, hinges on a kind of responsiveness that takes it clue from being, and not just beings. Because being is not simply "anywhere," or, for that manner, "anytime," the compass of thought must specify a unique set of coordinates that circumvents the Cartesian dualism of "inner" versus "outer," namely, the "between" (*Zwischen*). That is, thought occupies the spacing of the difference between being and beings; by abiding in that area, thinking responds to the twofold itself, from which originates the key distinctions to generate the primeval idioms for being's unconcealment in language. Insofar as thought endures the tension of this differentiation, the thinker can heed the tonality of the word, the grounding attunement of life anxiety, and thereby experience the thrownness of being-historical thinking, that is, the "leap" into the open expanse of unconcealment.

Leaping—herein lies the enactment of the thinker who is free, the expansive flight that may best approximate the exalted movement of the swallow. The leap, however, does not simply defy gravity, since it is already bounded by that which in advance prepares for its initiation and gives the leaping activity its target, namely, being itself. In other words, the taking flight of the leap is only possible for those terrestrially bound creatures who can distinguish between earth and sky and emerge within the area of openness. Thinking—and that includes the freedom to be such—takes its orientation from the differentiation of earth and sky and, equally, of mortals and gods. As free, the proper domain of philosophy, in which it accepts its mandate, like that of poetry, as steward of the word, is the *chiasmus* of the differentiation of the four quadrants of world. Through this differentiation, the word (of being) can be spoken, and thinking can occur as the supreme act of "letting be," of freedom as such. As Sallis states: "Freedom is letting oneself into engagement with the open, in the open, in such a way that beings can stand forth in their open manifestness, that is, be the beings they themselves are."[38] Because freedom is essentially an involvement or engagement with the singularity of manifestation, it cannot testify to anything else but the finitude of those creatures whose destination it is to dwell on the earth and take up residence there.

In considering freedom in this respect, we cannot forget a distinct manner of its *modus operandi*. If philosophy is first and foremost a "work" of human freedom, then it must also be an occasion for "play." Heidegger speaks of the "work" of art, a *technē* or way of making, which in conjunction with the creativity of *physis* finds limits for the undifferentiated materiality of the unlimited. And through this demarcation, the artwork becomes a vessel for disclosedness, a disclosing that extends as far as the four quadrants of the world and extends back to the singularity of the thing. Through the work of art, the singularity of the manifestness of the thing comes to light as an occasion for the unconcealment of world. And that oscillation *between* the two, within that space of differentiation, constitutes a play that the work of art embodies. The more animated the tension of disclosedness, the more "playful" the art. And its correlation with world means that art stands apart from the ends-means continuum of intraworldly beings, or instrumentality. Conversely, the way in which art cultivates the singularity of the thing, along with its materiality, also contributes to maintaining the tension of the twofold. Without the weightedness of things, this tension would be significantly slackened, and instrumentality would reign. Hence, play is a way of restoring the weightedness of things by circumventing their reduction to use-value or instrumentality.

For Heidegger, art is a unique kind of building, a craftsmanship that relishes in the fancifulness of play. Historically, in which Kant's aesthetics is an example, this fancifulness takes the form of a special kind of craftsmanship, a building through images, or imagination. Indeed, in the *Critique of Judgment*, Kant characterizes the experience of beauty in the work of art as one that incites the "free play" of imagination.[39] The power of imagination thereby stands for a distinct economy in which art, play, and freedom all converge into a single experience. But what bears all of the aspects of this economy, so that imagination epitomizes the wings by which freedom takes flight, for example, in the play of the poetic word? The answer lies in what comes to fruition through the work of art, as its origin and its distinct dynamic of development: disclosedness or unconcealment. Would not imagination, then, characterize a primordial mode of disclosedness? In the Kant book, Heidegger draws a parallel between imagination in shaping the horizon of transcendence, its schematizing *power*, and disclosedness, or the way of allowing sensible objects to manifest themselves to a finite knower. In *Contributions to Philosophy*, as we discussed in chapter 2, he goes a step farther to distinguish a more originary unity between unconcealment and the power of imagination, or, more precisely, to characterize the latter as an instance of the former: "'Imagination' as occurrence of the *clearing* itself."[40] When construed radically in this way, imagination ceases to be merely a mental faculty, or even an inscrutable capacity of the soul, as Kant believed it was. Instead, imagination reemerges, analogously to (being-historical) thinking, as a dynamic originating from the twofold, of being and beings, of world and thing, and hence as a tribute to freedom, to play, to free play as such.

Could the building of images, the play of imagination, be another place we can look to gain an appreciation of our finite embodied condition? Put simply, only a creature bound by the earth, and always recognizing that its death is near, requires such a power as imagination to propel it to look beyond to the farthest vistas, to the most distant horizon. But if the free play of imagination in art points us to these farthest vistas, can we also locate freedom, and hence appreciate the condition of our embodiment, in an all-too-mundane, even obtrusive, activity such as the governance of human beings within society? Is freedom to be found in the makeup, indeed, the creation, of the so-called "body politic"?

The Political Body

Who or what is governed in the body politic? We would assume human beings. Likewise, who is doing the governing? Once again, we would assume human beings. Such would be the conclusion if we were to assume the basic precepts of liberalism, of liberal democracy, whose beginnings reach back into the Enlightenment, including such stalwarts as Rousseau and Kant. As Michael Zimmerman has aptly illustrated, Heidegger rejected liberalism in its various forms; he thereby inadvertently dismissed any ideology designed to safeguard the "rights" of the individual, a move that predisposed him toward a National Socialist program which, unfortunately, harbored a germ of totalitarianism.[41] But before we address the complexities of Heidegger's involvement in politics, let us consider a simple example that brings into question the exclusively human character of political governance. In more and more systems of government around the world, laws have been enacted to grant animals protection under the law. Most noteworthy, in New Zealand, primates have been afforded "equal consideration" with human beings under the law to prohibit any kind of experimentation upon these creatures (e.g., in AIDS research). The fact that the danger of technology is global, and that any community-wide response must be of equal scope, suggests that political governance cannot end with the concern for human prosperity (and perhaps should not begin there either). Instead, the welfare of animals and the environment, of the habitat where we "dwell," must also be given weight in any political deliberation concerning present and future generations of human beings.

The basic criticism waged against Heidegger—to which we will return—is that his thinking occurs on such an esoteric level (e.g., of addressing the truth of being) as to be indifferent to the plight of the individual or even his or her victimization through revolution, war, and genocide. To lend fuel to the fire, Heidegger suggests that from the standpoint of technology, there is little difference between the extermination of human beings in concentration camps and the wholesale slaughter of animals in modern agriculture. As notorious as this statement is, fifty years later there appears to be an element of truth if we consider how technology has facilitated the mechanization of agriculture on a global scale, with horrific implications for the pain inflicted upon livestock. What may be perceived as callous on Heidegger's part turns out to be strangely prophetic in the sense that technology is indifferent to the "life" it victimizes and exploits. But where the political element becomes problematic is not only in preventing this victimization, but, to paraphrase Nietzsche, in diagnosing the rationalization—the form of ideology and self-perpetuating illusion that is itself technologically generated—that "justifies" the perpetration of atrocities.

The allusion to Nietzsche is not without merit. For the politics of "what is today," that is, as underwritten by organizational schemes of technology, works in behalf of the accumulation, if not the concentration, of power, a will to power that is self-empowering. Politics inevitably bows to the "mass man," because organization on a global scale is possible only through rewarding "conformity." Heidegger pinpoints this mode of conformity as the preponderance of the "they-self," the "who" of everydayness that disguises the face, indeed, the voice of individuality. This is not to say that there are not pockets of elitism within this conformity, but that those "elites" rule only as the other side of the coin of conformity, as the beneficiaries of social organization that reduce "care" to one-dimensional interests such as "prosperity." Marx referred to the mechanisms of disguise as serving the interest of the ruling class, as "ideology." But whatever historical factors may instigate conformity to these ideas—regardless of which specific economic illusion may be served—ontologically speaking, the impetus to conform lies in the hands of "they." The passivity of conformance becomes explicit, for example, in the ubiquity of the American dream, a house in suburbia and two cars in the garage, in which people, whether rich or poor, are uniform in their desire to "keep up with the Jones." And while this behavior can be criticized as the insidious product of capitalism in the Marxist sense, the uniformity as such takes a technological form of multinational corporations dictating who the "individual" should be (e.g., be "like Mike" by wearing designer sneakers).

What does this ubiquitous concern for conformity have to do with politics? Through modern technology, politics becomes an extension of the will to power, of control, dominance, and the imposition of power. In the one-dimensional rule of technology, the "they" flourishes. That is, the they-self redefines the persona of society, in such a manner that the desire to achieve power becomes the "norm," and the "standard of deviation" lies in the manifold ways of "competing" to achieve that self-same end. As Heidegger states in "Overcoming Metaphysics": "It is the struggle between those who are in power and those who want to come to power. Everywhere the struggle for power."[42] Because the "they" has the effect of removing differences, a single, quantitative measure of "power" is required, namely, money. The measure is necessarily quantitative, because the mechanization of technology finds in a calculous the surest vehicle of control and domination. *Sex, money, and power* define the triad of interests with which mass society preoccupies itself the most. *Sex is reducible to the other two, because it forms part of the calculous of "materialism" in which people define others as a means to an end and reduce relationships to their use-value within a scheme of machination.*

Politics seems synonymous with power, but does the use of power necessarily involve its accumulation and concentration as an expression of the will? When understood in a more primordial sense, can power be grasped through its ancient analogue of potency, of making possible? Indeed, Aristotle originally defined politics as a concern for what is possible, as administering over the realm of the possible as it involves the human community. Aristotle characterizes human being as the "social animal." As Heidegger states in his 1924 lectures on Aristotle, "In being in the *polis* Aristotle sees the authentic life of humanity."[43] What is possible in a political sense unfolds through a tension between what is beneficial for the individual and what determines his or her membership in the community at large. The goal of the *polis*, or more precisely, its leaders, is to mediate this tension in order to preserve the roots of the community, on the one hand, and yet allocate a space for the individual's pursuit of what is ownmost, in the Greek sense, the fulfillment of the human potentiality, the generic virtues (e.g., honesty, integrity) and the composite good signifying this fulfillment (e.g., happiness), on the other hand.

Governance in the Greek *polis* is closely tied to the facilitation of exchange among members of the community, providing the opportunity to speak out (*Aussagen*) and invite others to participate in the activities of governance.[44] The political body, however, is not simply an aggregate of individuals, since there would be no distinguishing trademark of its practice versus other forms of rule. At the same time, the materiality of the body is more than a metaphor of the mode of organization that draws people together into a community, for having a body means the potential of undergoing the conditions that inhibit its development (e.g., malnourishment) as well as the suffering of the misfortunate who have no ability to correct such adversity. Because such debilitating conditions occur within society it is the body's self-declaration of the hardships that an individual faces, either because or in spite of the political process (e.g, an elite exploiting others under its rule). But whether or not hegemony reigns, the victimization to which the individual is vulnerable—whether directly or indirectly by political institutions—occurs in conjunction with the fact of having a body. In the words of Thomas Hobbes: "Life is nasty, brutish, and short." What is particularly telling about this statement, as it pertains to the fact of embodiment, political rule, and the body politic as the *social embodiment* of discourse,[45] is how it harbors a faint admission of what in the end equalizes all people and gathers them toward a root of commonality: mortality or death. In death, all human beings are equal, and it is to this potentiality, the supreme vulnerability that we all have, that we must look for a clue to distinguish the dynamics of the individual's membership within the body politic.

Death is the most chronic of all human conditions, as it were, which signifies the lot of sorrow and suffering to which we are all vulnerable. But death also forms the backdrop against which we experience the joy and grandeur of life. Hence, the conveyance of the inevitability of death, along with the individual's predilection to heed it, defines the formal relation out of which exchange between individuals becomes possible. That is, the precedence granted to hearing the call of conscience, the pervasive silence requisite for transmitting its message (e.g., the voice of death) formally indicates the self's capacity to solicit a response from the other.[46] Indeed, the possibility of differentiating Dasein into hearer and speaker, which the call of conscience exemplifies, distinguishes the root of all dialogue(i.e., as an exchange between people each as equally capable of listening as well as speaking). The silence inherent in listening and the orality intrinsic to speech comprise the embodied capacity that vaults human beings into the openness so that the tension of their exchange can facilitate keeping open that openness. In other words, dialogue, or the exchange between human beings, is a process in which self and other equally participate in that openness and by forsaking specific claims of "rightness" serve the greater master of truth or unconcealment. The prioritizing of hearing over speaking sets the precedent for the politician's "rhetoric," so his or her success as an orator depends upon responding to the diversity of his or her constituents.[47] If speech has this distinctly participatory element, then can it also exemplify the dynamic of political involvement, the enactment of one's membership in the *polis*?

From the standpoint of everydayness, we might believe that to the extent that politics hinges on discussion, the aim of that discourse, under the popular slogan "majority rules," is consensus. And this view is not incorrect. Yet even then, the principle of consensus must still be predicated on the joining of a diversity of perspectives, the "*sensus communis*," or "universal communicability," which Kant emphasizes in the third *Critique*, and which Arendt subsequently appropriates as a key component of the *polis*.[48] But upon closer scrutiny, we discover that the dynamic of political discussion lies in opposition rather than in simple agreement. That is, it is the tolerance for debate, and for entertaining opposition, that facilitates the political process. Materially, this is the case, because otherwise those who reside on the cusp of political rule would be prohibited from having a "voice." Accordingly, the so-called "minority" would be refused a voice and hence be excluded from participation in the *polis*. Formally, the element of opposition is also primary, because only by inviting contrast and differentiation can unconcealment, as enacted within the factical realm of human exchange, counterbalance the tendency toward concealment. In this way, the dimension of truth can be included within the dynamic of political dialogue. Political discussions, then, depend upon soliciting the voice of the other, the voice of dissent. Only by welcoming this stance of opposition, or otherness, can those who engage in political debate enact the basic form of freedom, namely, letting be. Politically speaking, the letting be of freedom confronts the diversity of voices, wrestling with this diversity in order to elicit a harmony and balance for the sake of the governance of all.

Heidegger's own involvement in the politics of National Socialism notwithstanding, is there any example of his thought that illustrates the kind of disputation through which the alterity of conflicting voices can emerge? Perhaps the most obvious example is his participation in a dialogue with previous thinkers, most noteworthy, Kant. Heidegger characterizes such a dialogue as a confrontation, a placing into opposition, a critical exchange, an *Auseinandersetzung*. As Heidegger states in his 1930 lectures on Kant: "*Philosophical controversy [Auseinandersetzung] is interpretation as destruction*."[49] Due to its historicalness, philosophy advances when a thinker engages his or her predecessors in dialogue. As such a dialogue, philosophical debate throws forth the ecstasies of future, past, and present so that through their tension the "contemporary" thinker who retrieves the past is animated by the possibilities (for thought) arriving from the future. The appropriation of tradition essentially involves a confrontation with it, which rescues latent or dormant possibilities that have never been developed, and seeks their reemergence in the future. Hence, as Heidegger in the Kant book first gave his apt description to this process of retrieval, philosophical dialogue is an inherently "violent" occurrence,[50] for the rescuing of these dormant possibilities necessarily cuts against the grain of tradition, like scissors, in order to loosen up and wrench forth an alternative mode of unconcealment. Moreover, because such unconcealment is still the promise of the future, of its arrival in a new possibility, the violence cuts across the arc of temporalization so that the "present" thinker who is doing the "destructuring" must be equally vulnerable to such upheaval on the waves of the imminent future.

Heidegger's characterization of philosophy as a "violent" enterprise is one of the most profound and yet ominous intimations in all of his writings. That ominous ring becomes most acute when in the 1930s he appeals to Greek tragedy to illustrate the conflict and struggle by which the thinker, and perhaps even the statesman, endures the tension between concealment and unconcealment so that the latter can prevail over the former.[51] At times, Heidegger suggests that the *polis* is a disclosive activity which, for example, seeks to root human beings in a common heritage and thereby foster a kind of dwelling conducive to the manifestness of being. We recall, of course, that being requires a place (*Ort*) for unconcealment, and that the *polis* is itself a site of assembly that draws human beings together. And essential to that assembly is the promotion of conflict, differentiation, the *chiasmus* in which opposition and even dissent (of argumentation) can occur. And hence, at least at the level of disputation, the acceptance of some kind of struggle and even violence would seem to go hand in hand with the creation and administration of the *polis*. Is Heidegger then saying that the *polis* becomes a place of violence, of upheaval, at least to the point of advocating fissures through which being can become manifest and "tower forth" in its manner of presencing?

Levinas advances one of the strongest criticisms in questioning Heidegger's apparent acceptance of violence. According to Levinas, the words that Heidegger selects to dramatize the nature of philosophical discord (e.g., "setting into opposition" [*Auseinandersetzung*]) suggest a rhetoric that places the dynamic of being's manifestation ahead of the welfare of the individual.[52] History plays out the altercation of the conflict between revealing and concealing in such a way as to privilege the narrative of being's disclosure in historical epochs over the heartfelt suffering of individuals who are slaughtered in wars and revolutions. Levinas thereby reasserts his overall criticism that Heidegger privileges ontology over ethics, the generic concern for being over a regard for the singularity of the individual. According to Levinas, the beginnings of totalitarianism, and their politics of oppression and exploitation, arise with the prioritizing of the generic over the singular, the universal over the individual. As a result, the history of politics in the West is a chronicle of excluding minorities from participation in the *polis*, of marginalizing the outsiders, the bereft, and the disenfranchised groups. At the very least, the rhetoric of violence contributes to an amoral climate that accepts the trade-off, whereby economic prosperity often occurs at the expense of others who are less fortunate.

And the lament that as long as there is politics there will always be victims makes the question of where Heidegger stands on the issue of embodiment even more urgent. Following on Levinas's heels, John Caputo has taken Heidegger's apparent indifference to this question as more evidence that he neglects the plight of the sick, the hungry, and the impoverished. Heidegger emphasizes the importance of Dasein's building an abode in language to allow for being's unconcealment but appears indifferent to the plight of the homeless as they suffer unspeakable misery in both rural and urban areas. What else accentuates the fact of having a body but the constant pang of hunger in the pit of one's stomach, one who goes to bed without sufficient food night after night? According to Caputo, Heidegger dismisses the God of love and hence ignores the message of the Christian apostles who express this compassionate spirit by seeking to alleviate the suffering of the disenfranchised factions of society. As Caputo emphasizes, Heidegger upholds Hellenistic virtues of pride and self-mastery rather than Christian virtues of humility and compassion.[53] In a way that Foucault can be given greater credit than Heidegger, the appropriation of Nietzsche's critique of Christianity suggests the cultural genesis of certain genealogies (e.g., the imposition of power elites in the name of control and punishment).[54] Yet there is a "spiritual" backlash to this denial of the body, the mandate of obedience whose violation, as Nietzsche emphasizes, leads to damnation, the subjugation of the self versus its exaltation.[55]

Given the detrimental effects of institutionalized Christianity, the spiritual vision of love, as Kierkegaard recognizes, must be purged of its "ascetic" qualities if it is to provide the springboard for the "leap" of faith, the self's personal relation to God.[56] To be sure, Christianity can also be faulted for emphasizing physical suffering only to seek its transfiguration through the redemptive figure on the cross, as Nietzsche chastises those who "despise the body." Just as Nietzsche proclaimed that there was only "one true Christian and he died on the Cross,"[57] so an appeal to love, while distinctly Christian, cannot be monopolized by that faith, and may historically reemerge in a more relevant way in versions of "heterodoxy" rather than "orthodoxy."

The case in point is Schelling's philosophy of identity and Heidegger's reinterpretation thereof. For Schelling, love exhibits a peculiar polyvalency: the bearing of physical suffering through Christ's incarnation, the *logos* as intermediary, both in the figure of Christ and the word through which the expression of the Divine (order in nature) becomes possible. As such, love brings to expression the tension between the factions of the light of existence and the darkness of ground that become separable in human beings but have their reconciliation in God. Love allows for the defiance and opposition of the particularity of the will in order that it (i.e., love) can become apparent or shine forth through the overcoming of that self-craving. According to Schelling, love is the "letting be of the oppositional element" within the ground, and thereby it occurs in tandem with evil. In turn, evil arises as counterpoint for the appearance of the ruling spirit of love.[58] As Heidegger remarks, "Love is the ruling essence of spirit."[59] But what kind of rule is this, certainly not of imposition and tyranny? The "allowing" dimension of love, which accepts opposition, suggests that there must be an element of decision, or freedom, corresponding to love. The playing out of the alternatives, of the terms of the opposition, distinguishes the dynamic of love, which impacts upon one's life insofar as the choice demands selecting one alternative over another and illustrates the essential finitude of the decision.

Only because freedom accompanies love can there be a kind of order, "rule," or governance distinctive of it. Because factically love always occurs in conjunction with its opposite, the governance of love is one of reconciliation, of communion among those who can equally be opposed. As Schelling states in *Of Human Freedom*, "For every nature can be revealed only in its opposite—love in hatred, unity in strife."[60] The hallmark of human experience, of its finitude, is its vacillation between opposites. Hence, suffering is inherent to the human condition, since only in relation to it can there be any "meaning" to the triumph of its opposite, of joy, transfiguration, and exaltation. In fact, love is a testimony to suffering, and suffering is a testimony to the greatest hardships that human beings can endure. For only by accepting these challenges can human beings resist the tendency of bitterness (in the face of their travails) and cultivate a response of genuine compassion. The exercise of compassion defines a kind of rule in which the frailty of my own situation (without the "grace" of God there go I) serves as a signpost to heed the welfare of others. And in Heidegger's case, the beginnings of solicitude refer back to the expression of the embodied condition we share with others (e.g., the voice of the call). Is there a specific text to which we can refer to find evidence of such an impassioned cry? Perhaps the best example occurs at the close of *On the Essence of Ground*, where Heidegger states: "And only being able to listen into the distance awakens Dasein as a self to the response of the other Dasein in whose company [*Mitsein*] it can surrender its I-ness so as to attain itself as an authentic self."[61]

Surrender and sacrifice—are not they elements of what we commonly describe as "love"? Just as it is a mistake to relegate Heidegger to the camp of the uncaring, callous philosopher, so it is equally problematic to uphold a concept of love that is thinking supposedly should satisfy if it is to have any ethical and political import. Instead, we look more fairly upon Heidegger's thought when we see it as spawning an ambiguity about the material dimension of human facticity, a key component in Dasein's worrying and caring about itself. What is ambiguous is whether solicitude targets primarily the (development of the) potentiality of the other or a restriction if not an abeyance thereof in the form of "need." For Heidegger, need is not simply reducible to one's physical constitution (e.g., hunger), but instead it stems from the negativity by which we are bound by our circumstances. Indeed, whatever one's need(s) may be, one can confront it and make of it an issue of being "to be," only through a corresponding measure of potentiality and possibility. In terms of the self, need is that overshadowing reminder of the extent of one's thrownness, of all that is beyond one's control in one's circumstances, and yet for that "reason" provokes questions about the extent of one's freedom. Need points to the fact that whatever success Dasein attains, in its transcendence, of providing reasons and grounds, it prevails only insofar as the self admits a profounder "groundlessness" to its existence as such.

Needs are to the self, then, like the earth is to the world: the self-concealing abyss, the vestige of materiality that is animallike and *never* "to be outstripped": the irrepressibility of those factors of life (e.g., reproduction, hunger) whose abeyance occurs only with the extinction of all possibilities, or death as the possibility of the impossibility of Dasein. (On a superficial level, even the profoundest periods of thinking may be interrupted by hunger pangs, and the most stimulating lectures may lose the audience's interest after a longer duration of sitting on hard chairs.) As a being thrown toward death, Dasein is only vulnerable to need, and hence to the corollary experience of the self's powerlessness of it (e.g., misery). As Heidegger states in his seminal essay, "On the Essence of Truth," in its "insistent" preoccupation with beings it turns its back on the "mystery" and thereby it is a turning into misery, a "turning into need." For Heidegger, the neediness of Dasein is such that it comes up short before the promise of its potentiality, and, under the sway of this negativity and errancy, it becomes lost in seeking shallow formulas for its fulfillment. In other words, it is as if the more the self gets lost in the tunnel vision of seeking the satisfaction of its interests, or "insistence," the more, paradoxically, it becomes determined by need and the suffering that results from it. Far from denying "need," or human suffering, for that matter, Heidegger acknowledges it and the prevalence of the "misery"—emotional as well as physical—to which human beings are all too prone.

What does Heidegger propose to do about this misery? The presuppositions of his thinking do not point in that direction. Feed a human being and you have fed him or her for a day; teach him or her how to fish and you have fed him or her for life." Such is the cliche that has some bearing on his approach to these issues. Helping is first and foremost an appeal to one's potentiality, to the "can be." Herein lies the central message of "emancipatory solicitude." From Aristotle to John Rawls, "distributive justice" characterizes the attempt to allocate the goods and benefits of society to its members.[62] For Heidegger, however, a narrative about historical conflicts of a people precedes any plan to reconcile differences among members in society. The *polis* is as much a gathering place for enunciating (the voices of) history as it is for resolving the day-to-day problems of society's members. The crisis points of history demand that special leaders emerge who can enact the decision to change society in still unforseen ways. These turning points require heroes, and the leadership of the few, or elitism, seems to be more crucial to the *polis* than the democratic deliberation of the many. Yet as Heidegger emphasizes in his discussion of historicalness in *Being and Time*, the challenge remains for each individual Dasein to "choose its hero,"[63] suggesting that leadership must always be compatible with the self's freedom as it selects the possibilities most in keeping with its heritage. The hero does not advocate conformity but instead returns to the individual his or her own power to choose. In his 1936 lectures on Schelling, Heidegger reaffirms this point: "The highest forms of decision are enthusiasm, heroism, and faith. These forms are manifold and cannot be explained here. But always in every form of authentic decision is the essential knowledge which underlies it and which shines through it."[64]

For Heidegger, then, there appear to be two foci for the *polis*, the self's freedom and its mirroring through the elitism of the leader who stands at the crossroads of history. Given this vertical tension, how society "holds together" across the diversity of its members is not immediately clear. And indeed this question never seemed to trouble Heidegger very much. As a result, he never considered how, in the name of distributive justice, the state must develop its own system of checks and balances to protect the welfare of all of its members. For Heidegger, the *polis* is a historical development that grants to human beings new possibilities to appropriate their origins and to engage in dialogue about them. The repetition of tradition, the appropriation of tradition, becomes, as James Risser states, "the multifarious mixture of past and future which opens up a whole new field of possibilities."[65] Because the origins admit different avenues for their appropriation, the conversations must be equally diverse, that is, must introduce many voices. If there is any democratic element to the Heideggerian *polis*, then it lies in the admission of "multivocality," in the playing out of the exchange of many voices, which at best only implies sanctifying maximum participation among all of the members of society. But obviously Heidegger never advances this "democratic" principle nor articulates it as the cornerstone for founding the *polis*. Subsequent proponents of his vision of temporality, however, most notably Charles Sherover, have attempted to compensate for this omission.

> If each citizen is always engaged in forming the future, while bringing the past into the creation of that future, each free citizen is continually engaged in a temporal time-binding process. It is a continuing process that, at its best, is a common commitment to enhance the socially grounded freedom of its individuated members by using the strength of the whole to nurture themselves and then replenish by creating that future which it will proudly hand over as its legacy to those who come after.[66]

If we look at such formal indicators as "otherness" and "diversity" that help set the parameters for discussing the body politic, then perhaps one cultural dimension to which they point, in conjunction with the appeal to embodiment, is that of "race." From the standpoint of liberal democracy, the concern for race, for racial diversity, is an inevitable fallout of deconstructing the tyrannical implications of National Socialism with its advocation of Aryan superiority. Yet for all of Heidegger's apparent political shortcomings, he did resist the "biologism" of his time, which saw racial distinctions (e.g., cranial size) as an important determination of "man." Where race might become worthy of question, then, lies not so much in isolating an arbitrary set of characteristics that opposes one group of human beings to another. On the contrary, race can become an issue to the extent that our coinhabiting a world with others carries with it, as a fact of our thrownness, diversified ways of being embodied as constitutive of that otherness. Just as an individual may not choose his or her sexual orientation, so too the diversity that comes from possessing different skin colors pertains to the ineluctable aspect of embodiment over which the individual, due to the thrownness of natality, relinquishes express control. From the perspective of facticity, *membership in a race points to a way in which being-with is constitutive of our experience of others insofar as they are exposed or revealed in their otherness.*

Put simply, an important aspect of Dasein's factical dispersion is that each of us, as embodied, displays different skin pigmentation. Indeed, human organicity may be distinctive insofar as each of us is clothed with skin rather than feathers or fur. The tongue-in-cheek Greek designation of man as the "featherless biped" rings with an element of truth, insofar as we accent the importance of our embodiment. Yet we have to be careful to distinguish between radical distinctions and the awareness thereof, the facticity of those differences and how they are assessed as a variable interwoven into the dynamics of social interaction (implying some kind of value or preference). The tendency to assign values or enlist preferences, which Heidegger saw as an extension of the metaphysics of subjectivity,[67] provides the cultural backdrop against which racial distinctions become problematic. The introduction of arbitrary preferences transforms the distinguishing of race into an occasion for selectivity and bias, in short, for all of the negative evaluations that we classify today under the rubric of discrimination. Heidegger thereby criticizes two of the presuppositions on which racial (or even sexual) discrimination rests: (1) biologism and (2) the imposition of values, fostered either subjectively (e.g., Nietzsche's will to power) or objectively (e.g., Scheler's *Wertphilosophie*).[68]

Historically, however, the claim of racial superiority has provided an excuse for genocide. Heidegger thereby runs into difficulty due to identifying with a historical movement, National Socialism, which in its later development under Hitler condoned the extermination of specific nationalities, such as Jews, and even those of a certain sexual orientation, such as homosexuals. To be sure, Heidegger dissociates himself from National Socialism prior to the perpetration of these atrocities. But his reluctance to criticize the Nazi authorities may indicate less a personal shortcoming as a fault line traversing the body politic he occupied: the lack of having an institutional basis for assuming the counterpoint of dissent from the tyrannical reign of National Socialism. Foremost among these institutional checks is the belief in the dignity of each individual, which Kant upheld as the heart of his ethics and which liberal democracy appropriated as the precondition for its form of governance. Race becomes a political issue precisely at the point of the violation of this egalitarian principle, since racial distinctions stand forth most explicitly as the default difference that pits people of various geographical locations against each other. Put simply, differences in skin color become the convenient distinguishing mark on which to attach one group's animosity toward another. Conversely, once this prejudicial tendency is revealed as a root of hatred, the possibility arises to observe racial distinctions as a signpost to recognizing the otherness of the other. Following in the footsteps of Levinas, Robert Bernasconi has shown better than anyone how race can be factored in positively as an "indicator" that distinguishes the other as other.[69]

The fact that Heidegger had little interest in the problem of race, and, indeed, probably could not have, serves to reinforce the flippancy with which he dismissed the institutionalized practice of liberal democracy. Yet perhaps Heidegger might still have some interest in what lies at the heart of democracy, as long as we acknowledge that the premise on which it is predicated need not begin or end with politics, namely, the exercise of "free speech." For him, free speech becomes possible, because speaking is already differentiated in terms of the corollary power of listening. Ironically, it is not the guarantee to say what I want to say that defines freedom of speech, as many of its democratic exponents suggest. On the contrary, it is the necessity of deferring what I say in favor of listening to what else needs to be said, including soliciting the voice of the other, which in essence defines free speech. The primeval differentiation of listening and saying, with an emphasis on the former, is the intrinsic possibility of freedom of speech. In question is not only what we mean by speech but equally the topic of inquiry in this chapter, freedom. The liberal tradition assumes the jointure of freedom and speech, defining the former as the individual's exercise of discretion whose ability of self-expression depends upon the laws of the state. A circularity arises, however, insofar as the articulation of the laws guaranteeing freedom of speech hinges upon a prior constitutional guarantee whose presumed formulation and articulation assume the very practice in question.

Heidegger's thought, however, permits an entryway into this circle, insofar as freedom and language belong together in a deeper unity exemplified by the power of unconcealment rather than viewed as separate abilities. Accordingly, he explains how the word in and of itself merits protection, as an emissary of (being's) unconcealment, and hence can be conjoined with the distinctive capability of freedom, "letting be." Free speech, then, is a way of letting the other be, and as a mode of practice it has an ontological structure corresponding to it, solicitude as a way of inviting the voice of the other and responding to that alterity. The possibility of dissent, even of political dissent, is inscribed in Heidegger's understanding of emancipatory solicitude and of dialogue as a way of encouraging disputation and opposition among participants. Thus we cannot completely discount Heidegger's concern for a political process of checks and balances, if it is a testimony to the exercise of free exchange. We must recall that despite his fascist tendencies, anti-modernism, and even early Nazi allegiance, Heidegger himself recognized that all thinking is situated, and, since it cannot be enacted in a vacuum, it requires its participants to belong to a *polis*. The irony of Heidegger's involvement in National Socialism is that its ultimate preservation, as a form of a totalitarian government under Hitler, requires imposing the rule of censorship; yet the open-ended questioning in which Heidegger engages embodies the opposite of such rule, namely, the spirit of critical confrontation (*Auseinandersetzung*) and dissent. Insofar as philosophy is intrinsically a historical enterprise, and because history is instantiated through the workings of the *polis*, the thinker must exist among the company of others through a forum of free exchange (i.e., the body politic).

This vestige of the thinker's tie to the body politic points back to the materiality of his or her existence. Without a forum for free expression, as it were, there would be no room for philosophizing or thinking either. Heidegger's claim that thought requires speech thereby takes a curious material twist, insofar as our exposure to others, through a forum of critical exchange or *Auseinandersetzung*, anchors the philosophical enterprise as such. Thus the body politic, which encourages maximum participation among its members, is the material precondition for engaging in philosophy. The inhabitation of language, as the self-gathering of diverse voices, traces the outline of the political body. As Arendt emphasizes, the creation of a "public domain" lies at the heart of politics, a form of dialogue and exchange,[70] in which citizens can address an issue from "many sides."[71] Within this public domicile, individuals are exposed to each other, and their cohabitation of language constitutes this exposure—in an analogous way that the possession of a body makes evident the self's thrownness into the world—the body politic as such. Thus language itself, and its manner of constellating the social-political world, constitutes the "pulse" of embodiment, its living, breathing element. Rather than conceding a dualism that distinguishes the soul as that which gives life from the otherwise lifeless body, we can say, as Heidegger does in alluding to Aristotle, "The entelechy of the human being is the *logos* [language]."[72]

In the *Critique of Pure Reason*, Kant gave one of the profoundest accounts of the link between free speech and politics: "Reason depends upon *freedom* for its very existence . . . its verdict is always simply the agreement of *free* citizens, of which each one must be permitted to expression . . . his objections or even his veto."[73] Despite his extended dialogue with Kant, Heidegger diverges from the cosmopolitan spirit that is embodied in the former's remark from the first

Critique. In a famous disputation with Cassirer in Davos, Switzerland, in 1929, Heidegger turns away from this Enlightenment tradition into the uncharted waters of a new breed of the politics of National Socialism, whose principles of guidance remain ill formed. As Paul Tillich summarizes this famous debate in a lecture delivered in New York in 1954: "Two years prior to Hitler's coming to power there was a very interesting discussion in Switzerland between Cassirer and Heidegger. This discussion probably reveals as much about the situation as can be shown, namely, the conflict between one who, like Cassirer, came from Kantian moral philosophy with rational criteria for thinking and acting, and one who, like Heidegger, defended himself on the notion that there are no such criteria."[74] Could this debate with Cassirer have been a key turning point in the future direction of Heidegger's own political uncertainty, insofar as the former defended a neo-Kantian version of the Enlightenment, which the former could not endorse, given the precepts of his own ontology? Indeed, while in his 1930 lectures on Kant Heidegger proposes the *Weltwesen Mensch* who is heroic in his enactment of freedom,[75] freedom begins to take on a form associated more with the scission of historical decision than with the self-legislation of the law of practical reason. In entering these uncharted waters, Heidegger develops a polyvalent concept of freedom whose scope extends in many directions, in contrast to the more simplistic model of liberalism as an outgrowth of Enlightenment political philosophy. But the cost of that development appears rather high: Heidegger's dubious tenure as rector of the University of Freiburg and his entree into the murky waters of a politics bereft of any compass of universal principles of human rights and the dignity of the person.

Perhaps Heidegger's questionable political leanings can be traced to his refusal to embrace a religious source of transcendence, according to the ontotheological tradition of which Tillich's "ground of being" is a late-day illustration. In contrast, Heidegger's appeal to the "last god" in *Contributions*,[76] as the dynamic of revealing-concealing from which the historical epiphany of various divinities arises, seems to historize the divine itself or at least diminish the alterity of its transcendence. Be that as it may, it is not clear, as it has been argued,[77] that belief in a transcendent divinity has provided any better shield against the politics of self-aggrandizement than a philosophy that challenges the presuppositions of faith. Just as the archaeology of historians continues to turn up factual tidbits pointing pro and con to Heidegger's Nazi leanings, so historians' efforts also unearth evidence that the Christian constituency in 1930s Germany did very little to oppose Hitler's uprising.[78]

The body politic remains an intriguing issue when we look at the subterranean elements of Heidegger's thinking and apply further the precepts of his own strategy of destructive-retrieval. No matter how we evaluate the character of his own political involvement, much less the vestige of the politics that his thought suggests, his polyvalent concept of freedom seems as fruitful a point of departure today as it ever has been. If the concept of the self seems to presuppose freedom, and if freedom comes to be enacted within the context of the body politic, then must not embodiment be essential in some way to understand the possibility of selfhood? If we answer this question affirmatively, then we must also acknowledge the possibility that the body politic is not restricted exclusively to the human community, or conversely, *that the threads of the body politic may be interwoven with a concern for the welfare of animals.* For example, the solicitation of care toward nonhuman creatures, as suggested in chapter 4, may become the subject of legislation in order to safeguard those who cannot speak on behalf of their interests—our animal counterparts—from exploitation and other acts of cruelty. The body politic, as the nomenclature implies, must be terrestrially as well as socially rooted. With its dualism of mind-body, modern philosophy might view the following as paradoxical: *We retrieve a radical concept of freedom precisely by showing how its exercise can occur in conjunction with, rather than in opposition to, nature.*

The concern for the genesis of the self, as it includes the ecstatic vortex of embodiment, of bodying forth, points us ahead to the next chapter. In terms of the discourse that will define our discussion, this pointing takes the form of a double gesture: the materiality of "ek-sistence" and the ecstasy of embodiment. How else can we mark the dynamic of this double gesture except through an immanent transformation within thinking? For it is such a transformation that shapes the unfolding of Heidegger's language, namely, the turning of thought, which alone can appropriate physicality as a permutation of being's manifestness and reclaim the body as an idiom for expressing that disclosedness.

Chapter 6

The Return to the Earth and the Idiom of the Body

Beginning with Plato, the body has held a dubious position in the history of philosophy. The inversion of Plato's metaphysics through Nietzsche's this-worldly reaffirmation of sensuality,[1] however, does not successfully bring into question the ontological importance of embodiment. As the last metaphysician of the West, Nietzsche's philosophy allows the body to serve as a clue to a deeper forgottenness of being. Hence, the countermovement of forgetting, the turning around of the question itself or its recollection, implies a dynamic of temporalization that inserts Dasein into the heart of *physis* as the diversity of being's manifestness. In the turning, time emerges as the "name" for being, in such a way as to stand for both the unity and diversity of the possibilities of its manifestness.[2] The question of embodiment reemerges in the turning as a distinct way by which human beings experience the tension of mediating this unity and diversity, insofar as we are included within the whole of beings and yet distinguish the place (*Ort*) for being's appearance. If the turning around of the question underscores the importance of embodiment, then the issue of incarnateness becomes a way to think the turning itself. And the "incarnality of being" would be a way of addressing the openness of being in terms of the dynamic conjunction of space and time (*Zeit-Raum*). As the preceding chapters illustrated, we experience this interface through the primeval gestures of our earthly sojourn, our compassion toward animals, and our stewardship of nature's diverse habitats.

In thinking the turning, what seems to go the way of the metaphysics of subjectivity, the concern for selfhood, reemerges in terms of the enigma of its possibility. Who we are becomes enigmatic, insofar as the self must be rediscovered in terms of its relation to being, a dynamic that arises through the enactment of temporality. If this is the case, then we cannot develop a radical concept of the self without addressing the manner of its embodiment, and, conversely, exploring Dasein's incarnatedness should suggest the way in which we can experience our exposure (as a form of uncovering) of the diversity of being's manifestness, and also of speaking that unconcealment, in which case the body itself becomes an idiom of expression. Language ceases to be a product of some interiorized act of reflection and instead reemerges as accompanying the exposure of the flesh. By the same token, the compass of the self's identity can no longer be confined to the mental acts of an isolated subject; rather, its radius must extend to the web of social and terrestrial relations by which we inhabit the earth and help forge a global community. The overcoming of metaphysics in the turning signals our *return to the earth as a place of inhabitation*.

I will begin by retracing the various ways by which we can experience the manifold permutations of the turning. Then I will consider the illusion of self-mastery, which the metaphysics of subjectivity perpetuates. Finally, I will address incarnatedness as a way of exemplifying the vortex of the self's identity as rediscovered through its reciprocity with being and its inhabitation of the earth. The language of the turning, which is crucial for overcoming the metaphysics of subjectivity, harbors a double gesture: the embodiment of "eksistence" and the ecstasy of the body.

Revisiting the Turning

A.

For decades, Heidegger scholars have debated the meaning of the "turning," batting the issue back and forth like a ping-pong ball. Historical perspective, however, tells us that our understanding of the turning has itself changed throughout the passage of decades, since in 1962 Heidegger first wrote a letter of response to Father William Richardson's query. The fact that this change has occurred is itself an indication that the turning is not an issue available for transparent and immediate scrutiny; instead, the turning constitutes a dynamic in its own right which, rather than simply yielding to our understanding, shapes our capacity to understand as such. Thus we are beholden to the turning in the sense that it instructs and governs our thinking, and hence, conversely, we can "think" it only by following its direction and experiencing the dynamic of its movement. Indeed, we can think the turning given that we concede the historicality of that task itself, that is, the equation of the activity in which we engage with being-historical thinking.[3] The continually recurring obstacle to this endeavor, however, lies in the catalyst that prompts the turning in our way of relating to the origin of philosophy, the transposition in which the forgottenness of being yields to its opposite. Insofar as the impetus toward a "counter-turning" can arise, we must experience this catalyst as a kind of interruption in the tangible effects that embody the forgetting of being, that is, humanity's absorption in the technological manipulation of beings.

The turning includes Heidegger's self-interpretation of his task, of its development, but it cannot be reduced to any single such statement or explanation. This is the case because thinking is being-historical, and as such Heidegger's enterprise must be an instance thereof rather than an exception. Indeed, the turning must first and foremost demarcate the coordinate that locates the inauguration of his project, the task of re-asking the question of being, in its proper historical origin. In this way, phenomenology reemerges as a possibility that is historically prepared for, and hence must be prefigured by a movement of coming into its own rather than as an endeavor with an exclusive authorship. Thus, for example, Martin Heidegger may be the author of *Being and Time*, but this "work" acquires its significance only when projected against the background of the entire philosophical tradition in regard to which he undertakes a destructive retrieval. Thus authorship is really the interplay and articulation of many sources rather than exclusively one, the identity of which coincides with the diversity of thinkers with whom Heidegger stands in the openness of continual dialogue, or *Auseinandersetzung*. Herein lies the first clue to the turning: whatever statements Heidegger makes, it (*die Kehre*) pertains to ways rather than works, and the determination of his task hinges upon what is in question with the "connective" being/time and not merely the title of a book.

Even before Heidegger makes any explicit allusion to the "turning," the possibility of its occurrence already begins to shape the execution of his task as he outlines it in the second introduction to *Being and Time*. Heidegger originally reserved the description "Time and Being" for the projected third division of Part I of *Being and Time*, which, of course, was never formally published. Heidegger's alleged difficulty in completing his *magnum opus* prompted a controversy that perhaps his plan for the execution of *Being and Time* was in some way "flawed," and that, as a result, a radical shift in orientation was necessary in order for him to proceed along the path of radicalizing *die Seinsfrage*. The turning became a description for reversing course in the face of an obstacle that appeared in the attempt to uncover temporality as the transcendental horizon for any understanding of being. Whatever interruption occurs in Heidegger's quest, we might more properly say that the "turning" prefigures and prepares the way for transposing the fulcrum of inquiry. For no matter how we view this breach, as a hiatus in which a change can occur or simply as an unavoidable detour, a turning is already *under way* when the connective "and" joins "time" with "being" in a more intimate way than the original designation "being and time" might suggest.

"Under way" in the turning suggests that its momentum *already* directs the inquiry into being, in such a way that the *grammar* of the "connective" itself becomes primary, the reciprocal relation of time to being. Thus the radicality of Heidegger's task lies in investigating the necessary interdependence between the two, for example, the necessity of preunderstanding being in terms of a temporal horizon rather than addressing each as if they were separate terms worthy of inquiry in their own right. Because of the obviousness with which time has perennially shaped the preunderstanding of being, the philosophical tradition has allowed time to recede into the background of inquiry and has become almost an "afterthought" of thinking as such. Without clarifying the temporal presupposition of ontological understanding beforehand, being appears primarily in terms of one dimension of time, the present, as well as its continuity, permanence, or permanent presence. When the "forehaving" of ontological understanding becomes fixed in this way, the interpretation of being as permanent presence then provides the backdrop for addressing time. Due to an emphasis on the static character of being, time can be constituted only through a bifurcation that privileges one aspect of the present, its permanency, over the aspect, its transience. Being as the Platonic forms, as the Aristotelian unmoved mover, suggests that eternity is the fulfillment of (the constancy) the present, only to be contrasted with a linear model of time as the measure of motion, of before and after.

With this naive juxtaposition of being and time, two levels of forgottenness occur: (1) a neglecting of the preliminary projection of being upon time, and (2) the deriving of a view of time that presupposes an unquestioned view of being. Now wonder, given this double dissimulation, that the philosophical tradition becomes entangled in ever-greater perplexity about what constitutes time. We need to look no further than St. Augustine's famous remark, "that I know what time is until you ask me," to discover how profoundly this is the case. For Heidegger, this double dissimulation takes the form of "forgetting that we have forgotten," which characterizes the entire history of metaphysics from Plato through Nietzsche. If we identify the unquestioned relation between being and time as the premise of metaphysics, then by questioning the grammar of the connective "and," or "time and being," we would transpose the fulcrum of ontological inquiry itself. The result of such a development would be to overcome the negativity of the double neglect, in which forgottenness gives way to "remembrance" or "recollection." Thus time would reemerge as the horizon against which the meaning of being could be projected, and thereby address not in isolation but through its interdependence with being the interplay of all three temporal ecstases from which arises the dynamism of presencing itself (i.e., in a verbal rather than in a substantive sense). Herein lies the first sense of *die Kehre* as a "turning around of the question itself," from "being and time" to "time and being."[4] The designation "time and being" refers to the task set by the unpublished third division of Part I of *Being and Time*.

The turning around of the question itself, however, is a possibility that is prepared historically, and it is not a maneuver that can be artificially orchestrated. The more directly ontological inquiry establishes that being is disclosed through time, the more the inquirer's way of participating temporally, the unfolding of his or her place (*Ort*) historically, becomes explicit as shaping the question of being itself. In making this statement, however, we discover that the momentum of the turning is such that the *retrieval of temporality goes hand in hand with rethinking it in conjunction with spatiality*. The ecstatic unfolding of history always involves the corollary allocation of a place that human beings occupy and whose development is crucial for being's manifestation. This spatial dimension becomes explicit in the way that history originates from coordinates at the outermost extremes (*Worauf*) of our experience of finitude, of thrownness and projection, and thereby it distributes itself in the wedding of the "moment" (*Augenblick*) to the locality of a specific situation. Given this recognition of historical thrownness, ontological inquiry no longer simply addresses being as some thematic object, but instead the attempt at projecting that "meaning" itself becomes an instance of allowing the process of unconcealment to occur, the fundamental experience of "*es gibt.*" Correlatively, history provides the new stage in which the inquiry that Heidegger himself undertook under the rubric "being and time" can unfold. Because the question of being is inherently historical and can be formulated only by undertaking a deconstruction of the history of ontology, the turning around of the question of being itself recursively catapults the thinker into this historical space. To quote Heidegger: "This space (time-space)—if we may so speak of it here—is that 'between' where it has not yet been determined what being is or what nonbeing is. . . . This distress, as such a not knowing the way out of or into this self-opening 'between,' is a mode of 'being,' in which man arrives or perhaps is thrown and for the first time experiences—but does not explicitly consider—that which we are calling the 'in the midst' of beings."[5] In discovering that the tension of the "between" determines the letting be seen of what shows itself, phenomenology ceases to be a philosophical school. Phenomenology then reemerges as a historical possibility, an avenue cleared by the "there is" of being's historical unconcealment, the differentiation of its epochs, and the distinct modalities of their interplay.[6]

Toward the end of the second introduction to *Being and Time*, Heidegger states: "Our comments on the preliminary conception of phenomenology have shown that what is essential in it does not lie in its *actuality* as a philosophical 'movement'. Higher than actuality stands *possibility*. We can understand phenomenology only by seizing upon it as a possibility."[7] Almost half a century later, Heidegger reiterates this point at the conclusion of his essay, "My Way to Phenomenology."[8] Given the momentum of history, and the fact that being must always be disclosed historically, the turning is a kind of rotation, a going around, which redirects philosophy to its origin, to the tension between its abeyance and reinception. The turning is an orbit that brings everything back to its beginning, and more importantly, it correlates the end of metaphysics with the withdrawal of its beginning. As such, beginning and end are not simply separated along a line of chronology but instead are co-present in the arc of the turning, which gathers together and disperses the various historical epochs and subordinates them to an enowning or the gifting of the "it gives" itself. In this way, the first beginning of the Greeks yields to the "other beginning," whereby the entire history of philosophy, to which Heidegger's hermeneutic phenomenology belongs, is encompassed (in advance) by the gifting of being itself.

The turning is a displacing and relocating of origin(s), in which being is delivered over to its historicalness and thereby reemerges as a tension of concealing/revealing where enowning defines this historical development. How can this turning occur except when the negativity intrinsic to the concealing reverts into something positive? In *Contributions*, Heidegger emphasizes that the self-concealing of being also supplies a shelter which, in conjunction with being's historicalness, allows for a preservation, a holding in reserve, and an incubation of the possibility of being's appearances. Thus the period of incubation is also a harboring of a mystery—concealing as self-sheltering—in which being's withdrawal occurs in conjunction with admitting the counter-possibility of its reappearance, and, through this play of contraries, as it were, the negativity of the unthought history of metaphysics becomes a signpost to the positivity of a configuration in which being is joined with thought, and the former unfolds through the claim (*Anspruch*) made upon the latter. We might call this enactment of the turning the "turning in enowning," in which the partnership that being enters with thinking poses the demand of "coming into its own," in which thought is summoned to a special service. This service, in which we are participants in this enowning, might properly be called "stewardship."

Being is that toward which we stand in a relation of reciprocation. Being commissions us to cultivate a place for its manifestation so we can abide within this unconcealment and herald the diversity. But what first and foremost yields this place that, as a corollary to the openness of world, is that which we inhabit before all else? For Heidegger, language constitutes this place, the gathering together that offers a site, the indwelling of all abiding into which we are already thrown and in relation to which all human activities are presituated. Thus the first form of reciprocation, of authentic stewardship, lies in caring for the word. This form of caring occurs in cooperation with enowning, in such a way that to care is to be solicitous toward the origin, the wellspring from which new idioms of expression spring in order to facilitate the singularity of being's manifestation. Only through the inherent creativity granted to the word, in service of enowning, can words acquire the depth of meaning that they do. As stewards of being, we thereby care for language, learning to abide within its play of words while nurturing the diverse nuances of its expression. In lieu of this guardianship of the word, we can distinguish another aspect of the turning, the turning within language itself.

We experience this turning as a transformation in the way of doing philosophy as such. Philosophizing in the traditional sense gives way to thinking, as a measured response to being that heeds its claim by fostering the idiom of the word. Thinking then becomes an adventure with language, on a plane equal to the dwelling on the earth that Heidegger describes as the genuine sojourn of our being-in-the-world. The degree of solicitousness that we show toward the word in turn corresponds to the measure of rootedness we achieve in our dwelling. In the "Letter on 'Humanism,'" Heidegger refers to the obstacle provided by the "language of metaphysics," which made it difficult to arrive at an "adequate saying" in order to accomplish the "turning" from "being and time" to "time and being."[9] His remark not only illuminates the turning but also indicates that the turning around of philosophy itself, including that which is already at work in hermeneutic phenomenology, carves a path that necessarily intersects with language. As such, the change in our relation to language, in which we relinquish our claim of mastery over it in favor of the role of guardian, constitutes one of the most subtle yet profound experiences of the "turning."

The "turning" defines the movement whereby the giving of being can determine thought in a more primordial way than has occurred throughout the history of philosophy. Conversely, the singularity of the "it gives" exacts from thinking a more radical form of being's appearance in language, which in a certain way must suspend the convenience of traditional "concepts" for the "risk" of allowing language itself to speak through new idioms of expression. As Heidegger first emphasizes in *Contributions*, the invitation to accept this risk involves undertaking a "leap." The "leap" is not simply a jump ahead or forward but is as much a dislocation and displacement that seeks to arrive at the origin (*Ursprung*) where we already are.[10] Indeed, as Richard Polt suggests, the "leap" has as much a trajectory of bending back and winding around in the sense of a river weaving back to its source.[11] When viewed from the standpoint of language, the leap has the character of transposing the grammar of the usage of the key words, such as "being," which now must be rewritten in a way that (1) puts in question the obviousness of their conventional meanings, and (2) elicits a new tonality of a ground attunement that allows alternative connotations of these basic words to be "heard" in a new way. This tonality of the grounding attunement becomes the vehicle for being's embodiment in speech, which in *Contributions* it occurs when Heidegger returns to the Old German writing of being as "*Seyn*."

As Heidegger states in quoting Hölderlin, poetry can be the most "innocent" of all occupations, precisely because of the parallel danger associated with human being's entrustment of the power of the word.[12] Because the word has the capacity for "naming," its power lies in opening up a world.[13] But the word also is historical, and hence its capability for world openness hinges upon the restoration of the primeval force of language itself. In *On the Question of Being*, Heidegger undertakes an experiment with language, which sets the stage for Derrida's later exercise of deconstruction, by crossing out the word "*Sein*."[14] The crossing out is a way of illustrating, as it were, language's own way of speaking via a "double gesture," which points back to the manner in which words speak in the first beginning in contrast to how they can speak from the other beginning. The crossed lines then designate the *chiasmus* that separates the two beginnings, the chasm whose abyss must venture to cross, as reappropriating one (beginning) through the "other" (beginning). In this crossing we may gain the truest sense of the "turning" in a double gesture that distinguishes the "salvation" that grows from the impending "danger."

Heidegger frequently quotes these words from Hölderlin's poetry: "*But where danger is, grows the saving power also*."[15] Perhaps the most noteworthy essay in which Heidegger cites these lines is in "The Question Concerning Technology." Why technology? Not only does it point to the harboring of a danger, but an inquiry concerning its "essence" implies a reformulation of the question of being itself. Thus technology marks the intertwining of the various paths that originate from the turning, and hence defines the transformation that is already occurring at the heart of thinking. The intertwining includes: (1) the turning around of the question itself and hence its reformulation through the question of technology, (2) the abeyance of representational thinking in favor of thought's guardianship of the word or the turning in language itself, and (3) the transposing of the danger of technology into its "saving power," or the turning in enowning. If technology allows us to distinguish among these three distinct permutations of the turning, precisely as variations of the same, then the occasion to "think" the turning should coincide with the unfolding of the essence of technology itself.

B.

In 1951, Heidegger first delivered his lecture "The Question Concerning Technology" to the Brenan Club. At that same gathering he also spoke on "The Turning" ("*Die Kehre*").[16] Ironically, scholars have downplayed the importance of this second lecture, despite its translation into English over twenty-five years ago and its inclusion in the same volume with "The Question Concerning Technology." Even more ironic is that in most discussions of the turning, scholars rarely cite the essay that Heidegger wrote bearing the title of this topic. Why this disparity occurs is not immediately certain, other than the obvious fact of the premium granted to the precursory essay "The Question Concerning Technology" and perhaps also the obvious difficulty of thinking the dynamics of the turning itself. Two issues immediately come to mind: (1) What exactly is the danger of technology, and how do we, at the beginning of the twenty-first century, experience it today *as* the danger?: (2) Can we anticipate a catalyst whereby the danger reverts into its opposite or, put another way, how can we think the dynamics of the turning through a double gesture in which the overcoming of the danger *begins* with its appearance as such?

Because of its root in the self-concealing, unconcealing advent of being, technology conceals its own essence, and hence the danger that it embodies. The sum of the various forms of instrumental threats, including weapons of mass destruction, does not equal the danger, precisely because they are variations of technology. Yet we need to distinguish between the danger as it originates ontologically and how it can be experienced factically. This is not to maintain, as some commentators have suggested, that the factual threats are not relevant. On the contrary, these threats are relevant to the extent that they suggest the appearance of the danger, and hence serve as "indicators" of the limits whereby technology "shows itself" incapable of controlling the complex of mechanisms that it deploys. Part of the danger, ironically, is just the opposite, the complacency of believing that technology keeps everything "in line," and that it offers a "ready-to-hand," "within-reach" solution whenever a problem arises (e.g., the invention of an antibiotic to counteract a new virus that has become resistant to the treatment of current antibiotics). Scientists and physicians alike acknowledge the possibility of a "pandemic" of the flu virus, which mutates beyond the ability of all serums designed to counteract it. Indeed, humanity may teeter on the brink of a plague, unlike that seen since the Middle Ages, whose contemporary example Camus describes in his famous novel.[17] The destruction of the rain forests, and the corresponding result of damaging the ozone layer, suggests *our ineptness in controlling major geophysical changes, and hence the possibility of some unforeseen "ecological disaster."*[18] Thus the ontological dimension of the danger pertains to the dimension of concealing intrinsic to technology, which in the *drive to achieve material security creates the illusion of false security, and hence harbors the inevitability of a subsequent encounter with a still-greater potential for destructiveness.*

But what constitutes this destructiveness? Heidegger suggests that the human essence itself is in jeopardy, because in its self-concealment, being abandons beings, placing them in service of technology's calculative manipulation of them. Humanity itself becomes reduced to its role in carrying out these calculative ends, but equally as threatening it reemerges indiscriminately as another instrument to be used and a recourse to be exploited (e.g., as a commodity for work). Thus the danger, in part, appears, we might say, to announce itself, insofar as humanity becomes the "laboring animal." Put simply, humanity is separated from its partnership with being in such a way that Dasein forsakes its capacity in cultivating a place for being's manifestation. Not only does the self cease to experience the singularity of the manifestness of beings, but because it itself is a being, Dasein can no longer partake of that "play space" by which its uniqueness and that of others can appear. And how does the self experience this kind of radical disownedness other than as a sense of "*never dwelling anywhere,*" or of being uprooted from the earth?[19] The danger is this uprootedness, albeit we experience it as the license for wholesale destructiveness that has no limit other than the scope of the entire earth itself. Hence, the danger of technology lies in the globalization of the threat itself. Due to this globalization, Heidegger states that humanity must first be brought to the verge of the "desolation" of the earth.[20] Only then could the initial steps be taken to break the stranglehold of the will to will as such, which seeks ever increasingly complex forms of the accumulation of power and control.

Such a breach, however, is not something predictable. On the contrary, it is its unpredictability that places it beyond the reach of calculative thinking. We can point to such possible scenarios as an "ecological disaster," brought on by the destruction of the ozone layer.[21] Indeed, the possibility exists that calculative prescriptions fall short, and, indeed, humanity itself hovers over an abyss, as it were, suspended among beings themselves in which the "nothing" flashes forth as both the emptiness of destruction and the radical alterity that heralds the arrival of being. And it is in the vacillation between the extremes of this nothingness that the torsion of a displacement (i.e., a "turning") can occur. The breach, the breakdown, which gives full rein to this nothingness, would be analogous to "hitting the bottom," in which ahead of time there is no way of plumbing its depths, the *Abgrund* as such. As Heidegger states in "The Turning":

> Yet probably *this* turning—the turning of the oblivion of being into the safekeeping belonging to the coming to presence of being—will finally come to pass only when the danger, which is in its concealed essence ever susceptible of turning, first comes expressly to light as the danger that it is. Perhaps we stand already in the shadow cast ahead by the advent of *this* turning. When and how it will come to pass after the manner of a destining no one knows.[22]

We can characterize the turning as a kind of prelude to enowning, the event of appropriation, or the eventing of the event. Heidegger emphasizes that this eventing must occur independently of any will to know, since the latter pertains to the calculative aims of technology when it is precisely this manner of willing that must be offset and displaced. "Only when human being, as the shepherd of being, attends upon the truth of being can he expect an arrival of a destining of being and not sink to the level of a mere wanting to know."[23] Though knowing may neither be desirable or possible, it still remains question-worthy as the catalyst for the turning, the curvature in the turnabout from forgottenness to recollection, from refusal to arrival. Perhaps Heidegger gives the best hint in addressing the tension by which enowning draws human "ek-sistence" into a partnership with being. That partnership is such that not only does Dasein belong to being but, in assuming its own role as steward, responds by accommodating that in which being is most in need: bearing out the historical vicissitudes so unconcealment can come to pass. Due to its historicalness, being occurs or happens in and through a relationship (*Seinsverhältnis*), which it itself swings open and sustains. As Heidegger states in *Contributions*: "Be-ing needs man to hold sway; and man belongs to being."[24]

In historical terms, being stands at the furthest point of its withdrawal, as it were, with unleashing the forces of technology. There must be a dual admitting/withstanding of this extreme point, a counterpoint or vector, the orbit of a turning that can be formed, a counter-turning (*Wider-kehre*).[25] But this counter-turning requires a concrete vehicle that is incarnated in such a way that it can both experience the cataclysmic effects of technology and the impotence of its mechanistic replies. An experience of this impotence is necessary in order to transpose the locus of technology's empowerment, away from humanity's search for control, much less the myriad of technological inventions, to the impetus toward unconcealment intrinsic to being and its provision of enowning. In its partnership with human "ek-sistence," being itself must be "incarnated," precisely in the transference and conference to that entity who, placed in the middle, endures all of the ravages of this encounter with impotence, so the will to domination and exploitation can show itself as the empowering of being. At this nullity of time-space, then, the turning takes on a countermovement, whereby humanity experiences the reversion of technological empowerment into the empowering of being, as an abyss that rises to engulf the ground on which it already stands.

Could the self, in a way that directly pertains to its embodiment, become party to an analogous "hitting of rock bottom"? And the "rock bottom" is actually a "downward plunge" into bottomlessness, as if there were no bottom but, on the contrary, the *rising up of an abyss*. And could the self's encounter with the dual vector of nothingness serve not only as a formal indicator but have a material element as well, insofar as the instance in question could be modified, as it were, by the specific historical-cultural conflict of the self occupying the realm of modern technology? And would not the experience of the conflicted self have to be so encompassing, so all-pervasive, that even if the behavior associated with it were not enacted literally by each and every individual, the extent of disapproval of it would still implicate its ubiquity? In the relentless search for security, the attempt to fixate it comes in a concatenation of both hi-tech and low-tech productions, from Internet gambling and sex to various alcohol and drug substances. Thus it happens, around the neighborhood and around the globe, that an individual becomes addicted in one way or another and buys into an illusion that security can be had in a computerized or bottled form, so that the misery of being a mere cog in an impersonal society can be briefly arrested. In a perverse way, technology dishes out the misery and equally serves up the illusion of alleviating it in a variety of artificial forms. As a result of being drawn into this illusion, as personally bearing the brunt of the self-concealing dimension of truth, the individual becomes part of a larger drama in which the danger of technology translates into the downfall of addiction.

Indeed, addiction has such a ubiquitous character that it becomes a metaphor of the body's victimization through technology. The technological creation of ever-increasingly novel forms of addiction meets with the body's unique psycho-physiology of metabolizing "highs" and "lows," of "rushes" and "withdrawals." Now the body becomes enslaved to its own organic processes, in such a way that it seeks more of what it craves in an endless cycle of obsessive-compulsive behavior. The will to will of this cycle, however, seems very difficult to break, and hence the prescription for the patient's overcoming addiction is not good. While new treatments arise, their effectiveness becomes no substitute for the individual's being dashed against the hard rock of fate in the so-called phenomenon of "hitting rock bottom." Only when the individual is brought to the brink of destruction, as it were, and is void of everything, does the potential for a turnaround occur. The void reaches so deeply as to engulf Dasein's preoccupation with things, with beings as such, thereby shaking it free to experience the gift of being's rising forth into unconcealment. At this zero point of bereftness, a turnaround first become possible. The more globalized the effects of technology are and the more pervasive the phenomenon of addiction is, the more humanity bows before the frailty of this bereftness and the more imminent the appearance of the *Abgrund* on which civilization teeters. The experience of the danger as danger is such that the rendering impotent of humanity provides the counterpoint for the appearance of the incalculable, the immeasurable potency of the gifting of being itself, for only when the drive for security is broken and the illusion of its technological satisfaction shattered can the willessness of letting be revert to a new sense of self-responding, or self-responsibility.

But do not "substances" seek to counteract this frailty? Precisely, and in so doing, they contribute to the mask of the illusion of the body's supremacy, thereby yielding further to the dimension of self-concealment. Put simply, addiction becomes the primary way by which a human being, from the proximity of its own existence, experiences what is idiomatic in the dynamics of the absenting, withdrawing, concealing occurrence of technology, namely, that addiction not only rests on a concealment of its own root and origin but more specifically on concealing the concealment itself. Addiction flourishes by concealing its dependence on something derivative for its own existence (e.g., some kind of substance or other), and then it hides its incapacity to control the compulsiveness of this reliance. Just as technology is a concealing that conceals and thereby provides the illusion of mastery, addiction is a way in which the self has direct access to that experience, *participating in the illusion of that mastery, precisely through the medium of the body*. In the form of addiction, the body then becomes the site for the dynamic of self-concealment inherent in the illusion of mastery.

Ironically, the more humanity pursues "quick fixes" that aim to strengthen it, the more human beings become exposed to their own vulnerability and, ultimately, to that before which technology places them. Through its addictions, the body becomes an extension of the "within-reach" rather than the instrumentality of the ready-to-hand becoming an extension of the human being's hands. Technological ways of representing beings, in the timeframe of the specious present (e.g., television) then become occasions for addiction, the compulsive search for the "newest" diversions. As Will McNeill asks: "What makes a television program 'compulsory viewing,' as we say? What compulsion compels the 'compulsive viewer,' the television 'addict,' if not the desire for the new?"[26] Indeed, the body becomes an appendage for the implementation of technology, an occasion for the expansion of cyberspace on a global scale, the hands and eyes stationed before the computer keyboard and screen. But the possibility of hooking into cyberspace is also the possibility of getting "hooked" or fixating on the compulsive activities of Internet pornography and gambling. As the addict's openness becomes increasingly restricted, the expanse of his or her "world" is constrained to the attainment of the "within-reach." Here we employ the term "*Welt*" in a double sense to convey just the opposite of world openness, that is, the occurrence whereby the world withdraws and does not "world." What transpires on the micro level of the addict also occurs on the macro level of technology, the enframing in which world reverts into an "unworld."

Insofar as these addictive pursuits that are performed within the extant distance of cyberspace, the body becomes disengaged from its own ecstatic potential, as exemplified, for instance, in conveying friendship through the "closeness" of the handshake. As addiction becomes more the norm than the exception, bodying forth becomes inverted, transforming our physical existence into a receptacle of the clash between physical stimuli of pleasure and pain. Not only does this conflict arise on a personal level, but it carries over into a kind of philosophical confusion about the origin of either of these emotions. As Heidegger asks rhetorically in the *Zollikon Seminars*: "Take the phenomenon of pain and sadness. For instance, bodily pain and grief for the death of a relative both involve 'pain.' What about these 'pains'? Are they both somatic or are they both psychical? Or is only one of them somatic and the other psychical, or is it neither one nor the other?"[27] In contemporary circles, the reason this question is so difficult to answer is that through our reliance on technological solutions, we tend to treat pain symptomatically and then seek to annul or numb it through medications. As the wisdom of the vernacular states: "Medicate rather than meditate." But today do we not ordinarily view grief, for example, as distinctive of the body's exposure and incarnatedness, to which emotions contribute as bearing on the disclosure of being-in-the-world? Because of technology, human beings live their lives as a trade-off between pleasure and pain, as prisoners of both. Their existence becomes reduced to a one-dimensionally physical level, not in the sense of the corporeal as opposed to the mental but insofar as the satisfaction of sense stimuli becomes the primary reason to live. In turn, pleasure and pain become two masters with different faces and are not experienced as bonds that link us to animals, nature, and the earth, that is, as indicators pointing toward the openness.

Human being's simple identification with pleasure and pain becomes a trademark of technology and a key indicator of an inauthenticity that we experience as a disowning of the body as such. As Heidegger states in the penultimate paragraph to "Overcoming Metaphysics": "It almost seems as if the being of pain were cut off from man under the dominance of the will, similarly the being of joy. Can the extreme measure of suffering still bring a transformation here?"[28] In *Brave New World*, Aldous Huxley provides the most graphic description of this predicament within technology, where soma becomes the drug of choice to eliminate all painful sensations, including the fear of death.[29] Heidegger suggests that pain yields the possibility of transformation only when it is accompanied by a corresponding will to endure, the patience of letting be, rather than a technological willfulness to numb painful sensations through a quick fix or simple remedy.

In his essay "Language," Heidegger appeals to a line from Trakl's poetry to describe such patience: "'Pain has turned the threshold to stone.'"[30] The more dramatically this disowning of the body occurs, the more futile the prescription of physical remedies becomes to break the cycle of addiction and the suffering accompanying it. The futility of the body's addiction, then, becomes the leap-off point for unconcealing the dynamic inherent in the concealing of the illusion of mastery. And hence, through the idiom of the way, the "turning" becomes possible, as it were, when the failure of the cybernetic, calculative model, in showing forth as a lack, an omission, and a deficiency, in contrast allows the danger of technology to appear and be experienced *as such*. "The self-denying of the truth of being, which entraps itself with oblivion, harbors, the favor as yet ungranted, that this self-entrapping will turn about; this, in such turning, oblivion will turn and become the safekeeping belonging to the coming to presence of being, instead of allowing that coming to presence to fall into disguise."[31] In addressing the preceding question, Heidegger concludes "Overcoming Metaphysics" with this response: "No transformation comes without an anticipatory escort. But how does an escort draw near unless enowning [*Ereignis*] opens out which, calling, needing, envisions human being, that is, sees and in this seeing brings mortals to the path of thinking, poetizing building."[32]

Returning to his discussion of Trakl's poetry, perhaps we can gain a hint as to what might provide such an escort. Heidegger points to what moves us, almost paradoxically, to be still in our endurance to pain, the steadfastness and calmness of withstanding the tension of the "dif-ference." In this case, the "dif-ference" is that whose demarcation yields the locus or site for human being to inhabit the earth, the spacing of world and thing. The allowing of this spacing to occur, its manner of letting be, constitutes our exposure to pain or "intimacy." "Then would the intimacy of the dif-ference for world and thing be pain? Certainly. But we should not imagine pain anthropologically as a sensation that makes us feel afflicted. We should not think of the intimacy psychologically as the sort in which sentimentality makes a nest for itself."[33] In typical fashion, Heidegger addresses the essence of pain, which radically defies the presumptuous definitions of it found in the psychological, anthropological, and pragmatic models of technology. Pain is the undergoing of something, yet with a resoluteness of not imposing a time line as to the imminence of the transformation. Thus pain reemerges as the period of dormancy or incubation in which resides a protective sheath for fostering the emergence of a new possibility for change and development. Because the experience of pain is an essential prelude to any immanent transformation, being invites incarnality, in the guise of human existence, to be a key permutation of its manifestation(s). Through its incarnality, being allows the endurance of pain to mark the temporal-spatial crossing where words can arise to say what otherwise remains shrouded in silence, the unspoken mystery. The idiom of the body then becomes the sounding board for speaking what otherwise remains unspoken. The exposure of the flesh through the cycle of natality and mortality, and the absencing that occurs in the experience of pain and the elusiveness of its expression constitute a historical permutation of being's manifestness.

In light of the emphasis on the incarnality of being, let us consider the failure of the calculative model as it pertains to the illusion of "mastering" the body.

Technology and the Illusion of Controlling the Earth and the Body

As a contemporary of Heidegger's, Sigmund Freud identified the plight of twentieth-century humanity with the descriptive title of his book, *Civilization and Its Discontents*. The emphasis should be placed on the last word of the title, insofar as humanity faces the peculiar crisis that the more comfortable and convenient technology makes our lives, the more vulnerable we become to the constraints of civilization and the resulting emotional conflicts that arise. Indeed, the paradox of modern technology is that the "easier" and "safer" life becomes, the more we become susceptible to "stress" and "uncertainty." Why should this be the case? In one regard, the simplest Heideggerian response is that "care" still prevails in one form or another, and however its structure is instantiated historically, culturally, and personally, the self is still beset by worry and has its existence "to be." Freud, on the other hand, points to the various phobias, neuroses, and psychoses that threaten the self in the absence of the environmental struggle of brute survival, which has all but vanished with civilization's reliance on technology. Yet despite many differences, Freud's and Heidegger's inquiries converge when we observe that the frailty and finitude of human existence—what the former describes as the clash between *eros* and *thanatos*—are always ready to intrude where the walls of technological defenses appear most impenetrable.[34]

Kierkegaard addressed the phenomena of anxiety and despair almost fifty years before Freud examined their pernicious effects on the human psyche. We cannot simply jump from the plane of philosophy to that of psychology, however. And in acknowledging this limit, we observe a curious development in the history of being which, ironically, casts light on the rise of psychoanalysis as a way of treating the maladies of the self, for the question that psychoanalysis never asks is "why self?" to begin with, regardless of how we characterize its condition of relative health or illness. And the answer is that the forgottenness of being culminates in a metaphysics of subjectivity, which brings to the foreground a concern for the "interiority" of the self as the personal space of the impersonal Cartesian *cogito*. The subjectivity of "inwardness" in Kierkegaard's sense proves to be the metaphysical precursor to the introspective study of the conflicts of the human psyche. And hence, the phenomenology task of re-asking *die Seinsfrage*, as a historical possibility within the history of being, must begin with an existential analysis of everyday Dasein. In the conclusion to the Kant book, Heidegger characterizes this point of departure as a "critique of the subjectivity of the human subject."[35] As if to encourage members of the medical profession to transpose their focus of thinking, Heidegger interjects an appeal to the importance of studying Kant during one of the seminars he conducted in collaboration with Medard Boss (1963):

> Yes—the young people. You cannot talk about colors to the blind. But perhaps one can open their eyes. The precondition for this is that these people glance out beyond their profession and practice and that for once they open themselves and let themselves into something entirely different.
>
> Therefore, I propose we read my little treatise [on] "Kant's Thesis about Being" [1961] together, i.e., some passages of it. . . . It does not do any harm for physicians to have something about Kant in their libraries too.[36]

Kant's thinking becomes relevant for physicians! Well, at least insofar as he revived the importance of human finitude, and thereby provided a clue to addressing the being of the self. Given this orientation to human finitude, Heidegger, like Freud, reexamines the human capacity for selfhood. But phenomenology, unlike psychoanalysis, achieves the critical distance to relocate the self's origin within the expanse of openness, and hence according to the dynamics of its relation to being (rather than in isolation). In this way, Heidegger transposes Freud's project. Accordingly, the conflicts that Freud addresses can still be considered "real." But they indicate the larger crisis of the human subject's struggle within the clutches of technology, as it is "abandoned" to the "ontical" craving for security, the desire for fulfillment and self-realization, and the array of emotional distress accompanying this abandonment.

The abandonment of being also pertains to human existence. Since the self is a being, being's abandonment of beings also puts the self in jeopardy through a contracting of the ontological openness. Through this contraction, the self becomes fixated on its own needs, desires, interests, and security. Recalling Heidegger's reverence for the ancients, the Greek experience of the self's fixation as a result of a contracted openness lies in the myth of Narcissus. We might say that this character epitomizes a modern trend to emphasize the I, which forms the presupposition for addressing either the "mental" health or illness of the self. Fueled by this study of psychic interiority, a new narrative arises that chronicles the plight of the self as caught in the struggle between health and illness, of fulfillment and despair. One hundred years ago, the individual's personal story line did not include reports of child abuse and failed parenting. But just as the metaphysics of subjectivity is a disguise for Dasein's capacity for self-questioning, the psychoanalytic movement also indicates, if only by counterexample, a deeper problem about the self's entanglement in a technological setting, where the traditional bonds of family, friendship, and intimacy have been broken.

We can describe the plight of the self as thrust forth on the waves of a struggle for power, almost a condition of "fatelessness," since any victory of defeat is momentary and without deeper meaning.

> This struggle is of necessity planetary and as such undecidable in its being because it has nothing to decide, since it remains excluded from all differentiation, from the difference (of being and beings), and thus from truth. Through its own force it is driven out in what is without destiny: in the abandonment of being.[37]

Put in terms that can encapsulate the narrative psychoanalysis, the self is "abandoned" to its own whims of self-indulgence, and care is reduced to a triadic concentration on money, sex, and power. The individual then becomes subject to the twists of circumstance and "fortune"—and thereby to failure, disappointment, and despair—since the self-aggrandizement of the will corresponds to an abandonment of any ties to ancestry and family, and hence entails a pervasive uprootedness. Because the fortune that is sought is so fickle, and desire to ascend to the "top" of society so great, stress becomes the prevalent symptom of a deeper anxiety and distress that speak to the unsettling condition of modern technology. Psychoanalysts from Freud to Jung thereby become particularly influential, because they identify symptoms of this deeper anxiety and distress. According to Heidegger, anxiety and distress are dispositions that reveal the pervasive uprooting of human existence. And then the question arises as to whether the therapeutic practices of psychoanalysis can reach the heart of the crisis of the self, as well as alleviate many of its painful symptoms, without yielding to the same instrumental mechanisms that are endemic to technology.

The basic difficulty with psychoanalysis is that it holds onto vestiges of a Cartesian view of the self, the interiority of the self where ego-consciousness meets with influences from the unconscious. But there is another side to this emphasis on interiority. Implicitly, the appeal to the unconsciousness also implies a view of the self that is not reducible to ego-consciousness and may involve an array of psychosomatic responses. Thus rationality and cognition are not capacities that exclusively define the self. Presupposed in the psychoanalytic appeal to the unconscious is a critique of the Cartesian, rationalistic, substantialist view of the self, as Michael Langlais demonstrates.[38] William Richardson points to the "onto-conscious" self to distinguish the wider scope of self-concern that may conceal aspects—feelings and emotions—from the periphery of human consciousness.[39] Conversely, whatever these layers of concealment may be, they presuppose the ecstatic character of the self as a tension between concealment and unconcealment. Hence, whatever "inner"-oriented issues the self may have, their significance cannot be abstracted from the self-interpretation of the possibilities that the self has as being-in-the-world.

The case in point is the phenomenon of anxiety. Kierkegaard made that issue prominent when he defined anxiety as an unsettling state that arises from the awakening of the self to a tension between the infinite and the finite. Anxiety thus corresponds to freedom, and, in a positive way, liberates the self from its bondage to despair and points to its capacity for choice and potential to be "educated in the school of possibility."[40] Heidegger also emphasizes this dimension of anxiety but details as well its ontological character as a component of disclosedness. He thereby stands in stark contrast to the psychoanalytic schools, which emphasize anxiety more as a negative form of interior mood and less as an aspect of our already finding ourselves thrown into a situation, of our being-in-the-world. Though the psychoanalytic schools seek their inspiration from Kierkegaard, it was Kierkegaard's teacher, Schelling, as Heidegger recognizes, who brought the concern for anxiety to the foreground.[41] According to Schelling, anxiety is a primordial life experience that places the self on the case of undecidability and decision, and thereby exacts of it heroic responses. In retrieving Schelling's idealism, Heidegger defines anxiety as a grounding-attunement which interposes the self into the tension of unconcealing/concealing, a struggle in which the self becomes a tragic figure willing to risk life and death.

As Heidegger states in his 1936 lectures on Schelling: "Life-anxiety is a basic metaphysical necessity. It is the presupposition of human greatness. Without that, what would a hero be: either a ruffian or a comedian?"[42] Perhaps in this statement as much as any other, Heidegger emphasizes the positive side of anxiety, which sharply diverges from its character as a symptom to which psychoanalysts appeal in diagnosing the pathology of a given patient. Two questions immediately come to mind: (1) Are these the same phenomena that phenomenology and psychoanalysis are describing? (2) Have we entered into a culture which, with its search for a cure in the form of pills, seeks to eliminate uncomfortable experiences, even if these, from another perspective, can be construed as part of the "difficulty of factical life"?[43] Beginning with the second question, we must answer yes. As Scott Peck emphasizes, we exist in a culture that places the desire for instant gratification ahead of the importance of suffering as a component of human growth. "What makes life difficult is that the process of confronting and solving problems is a painful one. . . . We attempt to skirt around problems rather than meet them head on. We attempt to get out of them rather than suffer through them."[44] Thus moods such as anxiety tend to be viewed negatively, and therapist and patient view the experience more symptomatically than as an indicator of human being's basic life situation. That being said, the answer to the first question is in part no, for the psychoanalyst views anxiety as a derivative response or "symptom" to a larger psychic problem, where the phenomenologist views it as a definitive in its own right or originary. A phenomenological approach to the psychic phenomenon of anxiety, however, could still distinguish between an anxiety that invites an openness (e.g., including to emotions) and an overwhelming uncertainty (about life, emotions) eliciting defenses that drive the individual away from openness and into a posture of seeking security. In the latter case, Medard Boss, who was both an acquaintance of Heidegger's and a proponent of his hermeneutic phenomenology, makes this distinction in an effort to convey to patients the importance of confronting anxiety as a prelude to being released into the richness of life's possibilities.[45]

In regard to the phenomenon of guilt, we find another divergence between phenomenological and psychoanalytic approaches to addressing the crisis of the human situation. Freud's way of construing guilt as a constellation of unconscious fears and recriminations—remaining, for the most part, repressed—has some basis in the individual's experience of his or her daily problems. The fact that guilt may have some ancestral origin as the internalization of an authority figure—whether projected personally on a parent or impersonally on a deity—adds credibility to the universal character of that experience. Moreover, the pangs of guilt also elicit a vague sense of anxiety about the state of one's existence as such. Once again, however, the phenomenologist interprets this anxiety positively rather than negatively, indicating the importance of the self-affirmation of finitude rather than simply the discomfort of being bound by the repression of emotions. For Heidegger, the overlap between guilt and anxiety lies in the way that the former phenomenon reawakens the individual to limitations stemming from his or her thrownness into a situation. Anxiety then arises as the self's awakening to its inability to impart complete mastery over its existence, and hence to the accompanying discomfort of having to choose between mutually exclusive alternatives (e.g., a mother's or father's need to work versus spending more time with the children).

Despite obvious differences, Heidegger's and Freud's analyses of the phenomenon of guilt are not necessarily incompatible. Heidegger, however, provides the missing thread between them, insofar as he makes explicit the link between the experience and the corresponding structure of care vis-à-vis facticity/thrownness. While Freud assumes the universality of guilt given its ancestral, mythic roots, Heidegger shows how human being's experience of it—-whether interpreted positively or negatively—stems from the essential constitution of Dasein itself as being-in-the-world. Accordingly, guilt can appear as a pervasive psychological conflict, because the self's encounter with it speaks to the finitude of existence and to its corresponding experience of the pathos of the human condition. The basic difference lies in the way that for Heidegger Dasein's being-guilty challenges it to accept its limitations and thereby serves as an occasion for openness. For Freud, on the other hand, guilt suggests a kind of "closure" associated with the "return of the repressed," the unconscious influences that continue to have an adverse effect on one's behavior. However, the confrontation with one's guilt, by making the influence of guilt evident, can equally have a "liberating" effect by allowing the individual to exercise a greater degree of choice over his or her future. In other words, openness provides the presupposition for the therapeutic practice having the liberating effects that it does, the success of the treatment, which is ongoing insofar as its stage is Dasein's way of temporalizing as coming toward itself from the future, returning from the past, and arriving in the present.

The "liberated" self, then, recovers the "can be" of existence and thereby can pursue its own possibilities rather than those defined by the "they." In heeding its own capacity for guilt, the authentic self resists the tendency toward falling. Conversely, many of the problems that psychoanalysis addresses arise with the intensification of falling, as the self's identify retreats into the "they," and who it becomes dispenses among many conflicting concerns. As the locus for the instantiation of Dasein's thrownness, the body also provides the focal point, as it were, for the self's experiencing the complexity of symptoms marking the fragmentation of its identity. Corresponding to an uncontrollable "anxiousness" would be physical responses such as "nervousness," and, in the worst-case scenario, "tremors." These uncomfortable sensations, however, are not just neurological occurrences paralleling a psychic implosion or disintegration. On the contrary, the body is the "wherein" or worldliness of the so-called dissociation of the personality. The more fragmented the self's identity (personality) is, the more detached it becomes from its rootedness in its situation, including its relation to others. The ecstasy of "outsidedness" recedes, as it were, to the point that one becomes vulnerable to the exaggerated and chaotic occurrence of feelings, which the fragmented self experiences as idiosyncratic and "subjective." Unable to cope with this chaos, the individual seeks to regain the loosest connection (with the world and others), albeit in an inverted way of "externalizing" and "projecting" these feelings "outward." Paranoia and fits of hysteria arise, suggesting not only the self's psychic fragmentation from within but, in terms of extreme nervousness and trembling, distinguishing the individual's detachment from his or her body and the facticity of his or her circumstances.

The psychological conflicts and physical symptoms are not disparate phenomena. On the contrary, the dissociation of the personality points back to a derivative mode of the self's worldliness, an extension of its extreme falling. Indeed, the theoretical tendency in psychoanalysis to separate the psychic from the physical harbors the vestige of Cartesian dualism, insofar as Freud begins from an unquestioned assumption of human nature divided into "inside" and "outside." As a result of this assumption, the psychotherapeutic field becomes polarized into medical fields that prescribe medication to treat physical symptoms, and analytic fields that propose a path of self-discovery to restore a sense of personal identity. Of course, these approaches are not mutually exclusive, insofar as psychiatrists may dabble in both areas. But a tension nevertheless arises between the physical and the spiritual, which fuels the tendency toward the compartmentalization specialization of the field of psychology itself. And the final linchpin in this fragmentation of the psychological field is the way in which the mode of revealing enacted in technology encourages such compartmentalizing of regions of beings, of the physical and mental and their subdivisions. And psychosomatically, the human self, as a being, gets pulled in these conflicting directions. The symptoms of the body are treated "objectively" according to medical professionals trained in the method of the physical sciences, and the conflicts of personality are treated "subjectively" according to "doctors of the soul" trained in a new method of "analysis." But in either case the extreme poles of subjectivity and objectivity betray a technological element of calculation and representation, mistakenly approaching the human entity as an independent substance divorced from the dynamic of its relation to being. As Heidegger emphasizes in the *Zollikon Seminars*, an appreciation of the psychosomatic origin of certain illnesses presupposes the relation between soma and psyche and, ultimately, the character of embodiment. "Without a sufficient characterization of the phenomenon of the body, one would not be able to state the nature of psychosomatics, whether and how it could be constructed as a unitary science, and how the distinction between *psyche* and *soma* must generally be viewed."[46]

As an intellectual exercise, psychoanalytic theory has stimulated great interest and probing discussions. Freud's and Jung's encounter with religious themes has even spawned a completely new academic discipline, the psychology of religion. Yet as a practice that is successful in helping people with their problems, psychoanalysis, as Woody Allen quips in various movies, leaves a lot to be desired. Implicitly, Heidegger may have an explanation for this lack of success when he states: "Psychoanalysis glimpses from Dasein only the mode of fallenness and its urge. It posits this constitution as authentically human and objectifies [the human being] with his 'drives' [*Triebhaftigkeit*]."[47] Put another way, psychoanalysis treats the symptoms, on the one hand, and then objectifies the individual (e.g., paranoid) around a cluster of problems and conflicts, on the other hand. But the factical return into the situational dimension of thrownness and the corollary emphasis on the "can be" of the possible remain overlooked as the key to the individual's own interpretation of his or her life predicament. In a technological realm where immediate results are the standard of success, psychoanalysis can appear outdated, if not obsolete. But the pegging of "lack of success" may have an even more problematic alternative, insofar as the criticism is advanced in the name of a completely different concept of the self based on calculative thinking. According to the methodology of the physical sciences, the self reappears as something objective whose reality can be bent to conform to various calculative and behavioral models. If a radical transformation of the personality is too far-fetched, then perhaps behavioral modification, buttressed by the use of medications, will provide the quick fix. Stanley Kubrick's *Clockwork Orange* provides an extreme example of technology run amuck, which treats people as cogs in a machine, and their unruly behavior must be altered for the good of society as a whole. The operative diagnosis of an individual as "dysfunctional" speaks volumes about the kind of technological descriptions that society, or the "they," uses to label people with psychological problems.

Cybernetics becomes the new discipline which, in the name of technology, shapes the concept of humanity for all of the other disciplines. As Heidegger states in "The End of Philosophy and the Task of Thinking":

> Philosophy turns into the empirical science of man, of all of what can become the experiential object of his technology for man, the technology by which he establishes himself in the world by working on it in the manifold modes of making and shaping. All of this happens everywhere on the basis and according to the criterion of the scientific discovery of the individual areas of beings.
>
> No prophecy is necessary to recognize that the sciences now establishing themselves will soon be determined and guided by the new fundamental science which is called cybernetics.
>
> This science corresponds to the determination of man as an acting social being. For is the theory of the steering of the possible planning and arrangement of human labor. Cybernetics transforms language into an exchange of news. The arts become regulated-regulating instruments of information.[48]

In retrospect, what stands out in the preceding quotation is Heidegger's understatement about the fact that no foresight of "prophecy" is required to recognize the unfolding of technology. Ironically, when Heidegger composed this essay in 1969, along with "The Question Concerning Technology" in 1950, he foresaw with a clarity unlike any other philosopher the development of calculative, cybernetic models whose most important progeny became the personal computer in the 1980s and the Internet in the 1990s. Who would have foreseen the global reach of the power of the personal computer which, aided by the Internet, connects everyone from everywhere?

Be that as it may, the human being becomes understandable in terms of calculative models, that is, according to an analogy formed between its brain and the calculous of the computer. Probably Heidegger did not foresee this link as explicitly, at least not in the way that the study of artificial intelligence, or cognitive science, becomes a privileged part of the curriculum in philosophy departments throughout the United States. But despite his lack of foresight into this specific development, Heidegger did recognize that Descartes's vision of rationality as the standard of intelligence—in the name of an ontological dichotomy between mind and body—prefigures the modern proliferation of cybernetics as the key to defining the human essence. Indeed, Descartes's test for establishing the existence of other minds, according to analogy with the operation of the "I think," that is, *cogito*, cogitation, and calculation, harbors the irony that today it would be unable to distinguish human intelligence from artificial intelligence. Even more foreboding is the creation of "artificial" examples of human beings, or so-called "cyborgs," whose circuitry and intelligence are so advanced as to grant them a degree of "independence." But are they "human" at all, or does the dispossession of any "bodiliness," or connection to "incarnality," seem to discount any such humanity (to the cyborg), who, despite its intelligence, may still lack the quality of being "human, all too human?" And in what may this too-human humanity consist if not in the exposure of the flesh through the cycle of natality and mortality, the going under of its sacrifice (Nietzsche) for future generations? Indeed, on many levels, the cyborg may be indistinguishable from human beings, but, if anything, it is its perfectability, its lack of the "all too" dimension—the refusal of frailty—that casts doubt on its humanity.

The allusion to Nietzsche's locution may have more importance than what we may have originally thought, if only because of the implicit reference to the priority of human finitude. Indeed, we might try to distinguish the characteristics that human beings possess, that a cyborg lacks, in order to suggest a line of demarcation between them. But this attempt would be folly, because it would be just another form of "anthropologism" or "essentialism," which falls back into the trap of metaphysics. We could argue about human being's distinct capacity to speak, keeping in mind, however, that language speaks first of all, and that we do so only by corresponding to it. We could point to the distinctive capability that human beings have to confront the inevitability of death and anticipate that possibility from beginning to end. And perhaps this strategy would be more to the point. We could emphasize Dasein's participation in truth, yet it is not so much in addressing the positive side of this issue that strides can be taken. On the contrary, the more salient point lies in human being's affiliation with negativity, all of those activities that correspond to its affinity for the other side of truth, with concealment, dissimulation, and self-interested pursuit arising thereby (e.g., "lying," "cheating"). Perhaps Heidegger summarizes this matter best in his 1929–1930 lectures:

> Is the essence of man higher than the essence of the animal? All this is questionable even as a question. . . . In any case this comparison between man and animal, characterized in terms of world-formation and poverty in world, respectively, allows no evaluative ranking or assessment with respect to completeness or incompleteness, quite irrespective of the fact that such evaluative ranking is factically premature and unsuitable here. For we immediately find ourselves in the greatest perplexity over the question concerning greater or lesser completeness in each case with respect to the accessibility of beings, as soon as we compare the discriminatory capacity of a falcon's eye with that of the human eye or the canine sense of smell with our own, for example. However ready we are to rank man as a higher being with respect to the animal, such an assessment is deeply questionable, especially when we consider that man can sink lower than any animal. No animal can become depraved in the same way as man.[49]

Conversely, perhaps it is not in what we can do "better" than the cyborg (e.g., demonstrating innovation and creativity) that sets us apart, but rather what we can do "worst" in terms of dementedness and desecration.

Aided now by the mechanisms of technology, we cannot discount our own capacity for self-destruction. This potential can be more overt in that with science's unleashing the power of the atom, we can engage all life on the earth through a nuclear holocaust. Even if that outcome is not intentional, an accidental discharging of nuclear weapons, as dramatized in Kubrick's movie, *Dr. Strangelove*, illustrates even more profoundly the illusion in our belief that we can master technology. The illusion, however, fuels humanity's self-destructive impulses, or at least magnifies them. Indeed, those impulses become greatest when humanity identifies with the *hubris* of technology, and, ironically, seeks under the auspices of self-aggrandizement an escape from the inevitability of death itself. The more technology extinguishes the self's individuality in confronting death, the more, collectively, human beings as a "species" become vulnerable to a self-destructive tendency, for example, through the desolation of the environment. As Heidegger states in *Contributions*:

> The *darkening* and what is ownmost to *instinct*: preservation of the self and the *priority of the "species,"* which does not know any "individual" as self-related [*selbstisches*]. . . .

> The numbing and life's falling-back [stem] from within the incipient enopening. . . .
>
> Why does earth keep silent in this destruction? Because earth is not allowed the strife with a world, because earth is not allowed the truth of be-ing. . . .
>
> Must nature be surrendered and abandoned to machination?[50]

The designation of human being as a species is part of the impersonalization that occurs through technology. Arising alongside the psychoanalytic revival of the myth of Narcissus is the technological emphasis on humanity itself, whether conceived biologically (Darwinism), sociologically, or anthropologically. Just as the rise of natural science in the nineteenth century coincided with materialistic philosophical systems (e.g., Marxism), so presently evolutionary biology reconstructs humanity as a material being that is created by chance causes of genetic mutation and natural selection.

Freud employed mythic images of the conflict between *eros* and *thanatos* to describe the precarious condition of civilization as teetering on the abyss of destruction. But at least he still recalled mythic images that transmitted the wisdom of tradition, thereby acquiring the historical self-understanding requisite to criticize contemporary culture. While psychoanalysis retains this curious tie to the ancients, the other disciplines that interweave a "theory" of "man" may not be so fortunate. As Heidegger states in"Science and Reflection," "*science is the theory of the real.*"[51] That is, science seeks to bring a region of beings within the scope of a preset model of representation, a "picture frame," as it were. Among these, we cannot overlook the theory whose prominence stands out among all others at the beginning of the twenty-first century, namely, evolutionary biology. The limitation of this science of man, or its character as a theoretical framework, becomes evident in the evolutionary emphasis on the animal origin of the human *species*. The individuality of the individual becomes secondary to the survival of the species and the transmission of the most advantageous traits relative to the environment.

Heidegger was certainly not a proponent of evolutionary biology, which for him smacked of the kind of "biologism" that he associated with Spengler and other such "theorists."[52] "It is not by accident that Darwinism emphasized the concept of self-preservation, which in this sense grew out of an economic perspective upon man. For this reason, the concept is misleading in many respects and one which has also given rise to misleading questions within biology, as the whole phenomenon of Darwinism shows."[53] Fueled by practical applications in genetics, the genome project, on the one hand, and the possibility of cloning, on the other hand, evolutionary biology now competes with other theories, not to mention with religion systems such as Christian fundamentalism, to provide a more "realistic" view of humanity as a member of the animal kingdom. Yet despite its startling realism, evolutionary theory labors under more than one "anomaly," if not downright paradox. How can a "selective" bias in favor of the survival of the human species simultaneously include a potential for self-destruction? Put another way, how can a tendency toward self-destructiveness be inherited by a species as a trait whose importance has presumably been selected through a million years of evolution as beneficial for survival? As Richard Dawkins points out, a gene implying a predilection for suicide and self-destructiveness would be difficult to explain. Such a gene would conflict with the law of evolution and reproduction, since the possibility for its transmission and inheritance to future generations would hang in the balance.[54] The proper response to this anomaly, however, is not to denounce evolutionary biology, as a "creationist" might do, but instead to distinguish its *theoretical* presuppositions and measure its limitations accordingly.

Evolutionary biology is also a "theory of the real." We discover the limitations of its theoretical framework when we recognize that the evolutionist's account of "man" is first and foremost a narrative about origins. But the question of origins pertains only to a being who has the capacity to place itself in question, and this self-questioning capacity forms the presupposition for the inquiry that evolutionary biology undertakes. As the etymology of the word suggests, "archeo-logical" interests—including the kind of questions that evolutionists pose—are precisely those whose significance hinges on the awareness provided by temporality. Indeed, only a release into the ecstasy of time can ignite the spark of wonder—the inquisitiveness and corresponding grounding attunement—concerning what lies at the root of these origins. Only given this wonder, "whose place would be to hover, like a dove, between heaven and earth,"[55] can there be a "pause" within the flux of life that allows us to be mired in a controversy in the first place over our biological, "apely" ancestors. Indeed, the manner of placing myself in question, and the questioning of the question, must already be enacted in order for there to be any ancillary concern about human origins. That is, for Heidegger, the question of being defines the essence of human being (and not the reverse), in such a way as to root our potential to be in its finitude. This methodological shift or dislocation of the customary way of giving priority to empirical data may seem odd to many. What Heidegger suggests, however, is that there is a more primeval datum, the *factical* undertaking of inquiry, the capacity for which *already* is assumed, regardless of whether we posit any empirical steps of genesis—evolutionary or otherwise—to explain the origin of the species we call "rational animal," or "homo sapiens," or even "featherless biped." Heidegger begins from the radical and decisive fact that "there is being," and, concomitantly, "there is temporality," but given this zero point, the explanation of how we got "here" requires piecing together a "story" (e.g., the fossil record) whose chronology implies an outcome (e.g., sentient beings) without which the "narrative" of human origins could never be told or have any audience.

The possibility that human origins can be reduced to "genes" boasts a new materialism of the twenty-first century. But genetics can also by reinterpreted as an indication of human facticity, that we are always "born" into some situation or another; and in the end, we may have little control over the specific ways in which these genetic traits are expressed, or the phenotype, as distinguishing marks of factical dispersion, of embodiment as such. The possibility of differentiation and diversity is the hallmark of genetics, whose end sexual reproduction serves. Sexual difference is the thread of common ancestry, expressed genetically as the crossing over of chromosomes of the double helix—as mentioned at the beginning of chapter 2—present throughout nature. The diversity of nature is predicated upon this difference, and the complexity of its life-forms that have evolved upon the earth suggests a narrative of evolution whose grammar still hinges on this basic rule of differentiation. Indeed, despite whichever model we wish to root human being in its embodiment, the potential for its self-articulation and interpretation still hinges upon a corresponding form of grammar that originates the vestige of intelligibility. In its embodiment, Freudian "man" as moved by the desire of *eros* or Darwinian "man" as beset by natural demands to transmit genes to future offspring must still bow to the most elemental of all forms of thrownness, or the language that enables us to mediate our desires and pass down a "sir" or family name to our progeny.

In *On the Way to Language*, Heidegger points to a decisive moment in which the launching of the Sputnik satellite (1957) signals the ultimate uprootedness of human being's leaving the *earth*; he depicts the Russian satellite as a "'thing' that races around in a worldless 'world'—space."[56] Though space travel today is a long way off from the colonization of other planets, Heidegger indirectly suggests that technological advancements and discoveries continue to challenge the traditional concepts by which we examine what it means to be human. Indeed, he emphasizes the dual character of technology as both a blessing and a curse, as endemic of the fact that concealment overshadows the possibility of unconcealment. And that concealing, as perpetrated through digital technology, which Heidegger did not fully anticipate, includes a displacing of lived-spaced and a disembodiment of the lived-body, along with a flight from earth—both figuratively and literally.

Today we applaud the instantaneous character of e-mail and ridicule the inefficiency of "snail mail." The echo of a voice that resonates in a handcrafted letter gives way to the monotone, if that, in the continuous arrival of one e-mail after another. The efficiency that is gained by digital technology—witness how much easier it was to organize the 2004 North American Heidegger

Conference with the aid of e-mail than it was to organize the 1992 conference without the advantage of this instantaneous, ubiquitous, albeit impersonal, form of communication—is offset by a loss of intimacy. Let us then take this new historical paradigm as the backdrop against which we can project Heidegger's breakthrough attempt in *Contributions* to reopen the question of human selfhood.

Revisiting the Self

Heidegger's questioning of technology goes hand in hand with a critique of the subjectivity of the subject. The will to domination and control requires the interposing of man qua subject into the center of beings; through centrality of the subject, humanity finds in its own capacity to represent beings as objects a standard for determining their value (e.g, utility, survival, and expediency). Ironically, the more encompassing this tendency toward objectification is, the more "subjectively" beings appear in terms of the fluctuating desires and needs of society. Anthropoligism and humanism then become the natural extensions of the end and completion of metaphysics. But does a critique of the subjectivity of the subject, of its interposition with the center of beings, lead to renouncing the very concept of selfhood? Or do we instead rediscover the self, as it were, as dislocated from this position of centrality? The answer would then be redefined in terms of that in relation to which appears othermost, being as such in the dynamic of its concealing-revealing, rather than through the fixity of sameness as the coincidence of its own identity. To the extent that this transformation occurs, it takes its cue from a development occurring through being itself and not just an end that the subject posits as valuable. In offering one of his most explicit observations on the "turning," Heidegger states in his "Letter" to Father Richardson, S. J.: "Man here is not the object of an anthropology whatever. Man comes into question here in the deepest and broadest, in the genuinely fundamental, perspective: man in his relation to being—sc. in the turning; be-ing (*Seyn*) and its truth in relation to man."[57]

The turning makes explicit what is already coming to pass with the existential analytic of Dasein, namely, reexamining shifting the axis of the self's identity to include its participation in disclosedness. As a being, the human self depends upon disclosedness. Hence, it is always in relation to being as unconcealment that the self can find its identity. It is as if in its search for identity, the self turns hither and thither, directionless yet in the quandary of always looking for one. Paradoxically, the more willful this search becomes, the more entangled the individual becomes in the web of falling, as the self's flight into addiction testifies. A compass of direction can only be given through the relation of reciprocity with which self stands to being. A direction is thereby granted, rather than imposed, in accordance with the *worauf*, or "whereto," of the self's emerging into openness, the ecstasy of its movement of coming into its own. The self then becomes a participant in the dynamic of emerging, coming into presence which, as Heidegger emphasizes in his 1942 lecture on Aristotle, transposes human being into its place in nature. Rather than standing apart from nature as a separate subject harboring the power to objectify, Dasein finds that its own emergence is tied to its capacity to allow the diversity of nature to manifest itself. Dasein discovers who it is, then, in the openness of letting be, and it is within this open expanse that the vectors of guidance, the "*worauf*," come to be granted, providing direction to the self's pursuits.

But how do we understand this "direction?" Obviously, the direction cannot simply be linear, which implies the goal-oriented focus of technology. One possible example comes from the entelechy of animals, in that essence becomes realized through a process of growth and maturation. But that direction forward, however, is modified by a backward movement or return into the origins when, for example, through the act of reproduction, an adult animal passes down its genes to its offspring. Human being's presencing is distinct, insofar as it makes explicit the countermovement of absencing, in which the tension of these contraries creates an openness that includes the vectors of the disclosure of the world (e.g., transcendence) as well as an affinity for the earth. And since pres-absentiality is another name for temporalizing, the self finds its direction in harmony with the rhythm that temporality enacts, as illustrated, for example, in the biblical phrase "for everything there is a season." As David Wood states: "To the extent that things bear and embody rhythms, pulses of temporal development, they form part of a manifold and stratified field in which these rhythms interact, interpenetrate, interfere with one another, become locally coordinated and so on. Fireflies come to flash synchronously at the end of an evening, while cicadas carefully space (or time) their periodicities of their emergence from hibernation so as not to overlap and compete."[58] Temporality determines the timeliness of the moment, not according to a linear model of expediency but in terms of an elliptical movement in which any advance depends upon a return to (one's) origins. Thus it is by thinking the way that such temporality governs the genesis of the self, and not the reverse, that can address the possibility of selfhood outside of the technological model of subjectivity. We first encounter this new experiment of rethinking the possibility of selfhood in *Contributions*.

When Heidegger addresses the possibility of selfhood, he does not ask what is unique about human beings that they exhibit this potential. This would be a topic for philosophical anthropology, as exhibited in Scheler's *Wertphilosophie*. As early as *Being and Time*, Heidegger subverts the Cartesian view of the self when he appeals to care as Dasein's being as the basis for reopening the question of the self. The reflexivity of certitude, as embodied in the Cartesian *cogito*, gives way to a double relation of the self, in which identity can be discovered along a circuitous path or a detour through (an encounter with) otherness. Thus identity arises only through a doubling of the self as caller and called, through the voice of conscience as a sounding board of otherness. The questioning of the self, then, must always be linked to the question of being, as this question becomes increasingly radicalized, with the turning around and transformation of the question of itself, so the point of departure for addressing the possibility of selfhood changes. And in *Contributions*, the radicalization of this point of departure becomes most abrupt when the concern for the possibility of selfhood reverts to the question of what we mean by "identity" as such.

Obviously identity can no longer be viewed according to a model of simple self-presence, of a perfect coincidence of the I with itself Because of its affiliation with being, the self must be defined by that which is first and foremost ontologically relevant, namely, the dynamic of revealing-concealing. Thus perfect transparency, in the guise of a privileged power attributed to consciousness, remains a mere chimera. On the contrary, because Dasein participates in the ontological drama of revealing-concealing, its own identity bears the hallmark of this happening. The problem of identity is thereby compounded, because as a being, Dasein is already bound by the possibility of being's withdrawal. Thus ontologically, human beings can define themselves as the subject of constant presence, as displayed in Descartes's ontology. But individually, or ontically, Dasein can misunderstand who it is as an "ego" defending its desire of security, or the image it believes it sees. Ironically, the more the self tries to isolate the characteristics that make it unique, both ontologically and ontically, the more it accomplishes the opposite result of grossly misunderstanding who it is.

And the misunderstanding consists in the fact that identity does not consist of anything identical but in how Dasein stands in proximity to being and the relationship to which it belongs thereby. In assuming a metaphysics of presence, Descartes not only misconstrues the self as an isolated ego, he also divorces the dynamic of selfhood from its bodily manifestation. Cartesian dualism thereby converts the body into a material substance, which can be defined by mechanistic and geometric principles of nature; but this dualistic vision neglects the possibility of the intertwining of the self-identity with occurrence of embodiment. In contrast, Heidegger suggests that the forgottenness of being underlies the Cartesian tendency to denigrate the body into a material substance, where materiality is in turn denigrated by its reduction to static present-at-handness. In his 1924 lectures on Aristotle, Heidegger emphasizes instead that body includes a situational dimension whereby the individual finds himself or herself within the world.[59] Because Descartes's denigration of the body is an offshoot of the metaphysics of presence, the reopening of the question of self-identity must retrieve the body as part of its strategy. Indeed, the body's recovery points back to the temporal particularity of the how-to of the self's situatedness in the world. A relational concept of the self thereby emerges, a self whose identity is not simply given (as present at hand) but must be enacted through its own dynamic of environmental and social interaction.

Identity is thereby a relation of "belonging together," in which Dasein stands toward what elicits its inquisitiveness and provokes its engagement. The belonging together is a relation that allows Dasein to be addressed by what is most completely other. Correlatively, the proportional response, as a supreme act of freedom in which Dasein ventures into the open, is that of "letting be." But what does such letting be have to do with Dasein's selfhood? Does the essence of the self, then, lie in freedom? This would be an interesting conclusion to draw, given our preceding discussions, if it could be spelled out concretely. The key to doing so lies in construing the letting be as a form of reciprocation, in which Dasein volunteers to safeguard that miraculous event into which it is admitted: "*es gibt Sein.*" The reciprocation, then, implies the ecstatic unfolding of enowning, commissioning Dasein to serve in its task of stewardship. Thus who the self is is in part defined by how it fulfills this task, so that it becomes enowned, and comes into its own, by deferring its identity with itself in favor of its devotion to what is completely other. The paradox of an identity coming into its own is that it hinges upon heightening the tension of otherness, so to be one's own is always to be willing to challenge that identity by welcoming ever new and novel encounters with otherness, including, for example, its concrete embodiment through other Dasein. Thus an exchange with other people, provided that both parties are mutually open (to the unconcealing power of the word), can be an occasion of self-discovery.

Through subverting the Cartesian *cogito*, Heidegger makes the retrieval of the self a priority. We do not overcome metaphysics by rejecting all of its seminal issues. Such issues as self and community have been improperly grounded on an inadequate ontology, in such a way that a completely new ground must first be cleared. Heidegger thereby brings the (issue) of the self in the foreground once again according to the dynamic of its reciprocity with being. But in reopening the question of the self, he cultivates a completely new landscape and topography that remove the basic dualisms of mind and body, "I" and other (minds), which have blocked access to the originary phenomena, to the "things themselves." Solipsism, the enigma of my relation to other minds, becomes a pseudo-problem that stems from the assumption of these "founded" or "derived" dualisms. It is not due to some cerebral power that Dasein can relate to others. On the contrary, it is due to its inhabitation of language, an opening forth of a world that Dasein occupies with other, that, ontologically, it acquires the capacity to be with others in a fundamental way: by hearing their voice(s). Ontologically, it is the fact of our embodiment that we harbor this ability, insofar as hearing becomes the chief way that Dasein is enowned through its inhabitation of language as, for example, when the self heeds the "voice of a friend."

Voice, which implies tonality, attunement, and hearing, thereby distinguishes an embodied form of our being-with-others. As Heidegger states in *Contributions*:

> *It is only from Da-sein that what is ownmost to a people can be grasped,* and that means at the same time knowing that the people can never be goal and purpose, and that such an opinion is only a "popular" extension of the "liberal" thought of the "I" and of the economic idea of the preservation of "life."
>
> What is ownmost to a people is, however, its "voice. This *voice* does not speak in a so-called immediate outpouring of the common, natural, unspoiled and uneducated "man." For the "man" thus called-up as witness is already very *spoiled* and no longer functions within the originary relations to beings. The *voice* of the people seldom speaks and only in the few—and can it still be made *at all* resonate?[60]

When consciousness, and its dualistic opposition to physicality, crumbles, then the possibility arises of addressing the ownedness of the self.[61] But this ownedness is not something we can simply fixate, since it can appear only through the dynamic of placing ourselves in question through the question of being/technology. But in this development Dasein is not engaged in self-questioning in order to formulate the question of being, but rather, the turning around of the question allows for a more radical interrogation of the essence of selfhood as such.

As such, the clearing of the ground to reopen the question of the self is not a "laying the foundation" or fundamental ontology, but, on the contrary, it takes the form of a departure from such grounding, that is, a "leap." To quote Heidegger:

> Inabiding in this occurrence of own-hood initially enables man to come to "himself" historically and to be *with-himself* provides above all the sufficient ground for truly taking over the "*for another.*" But coming-to-oneself is also never a priori, detached I-representation. It is rather taking over the belongingness to the truth of being, leaping into the t/here [Da]. Ownhood as ground of selfhood grounds Da-sein. But ownhood itself is in turn the steadfastness of the turning in enowning.[62]

The allusion to "steadfastness" recalls a vestige of Heidegger's attempt in *Being and Time* to re-define Dasein's identity in terms of the temporalizing enactment of "self-constancy," or the interval of the "stretching along" between the extremities of birth and death.

In emphasizing self-constancy, Heidegger seeks to overcome the conception of the self as a substance, as a form of continual presence. But that attempt is restricted in its success by the stage it occupies in the hermeneutical inquiry. At that stage, Heidegger addresses Dasein's temporality in order to make it explicit as the horizon for any understanding of being. In the turning around of the question itself, however, temporality reemerges as the dynamic of being's ecstatic openness. In this turning, time and being mutually implicate each other, in such a way that as a being Dasein is redefined through its participation in this ecstatic openness, through its preparedness to endure the tension of being's revealing-concealing and undergoes its strife. The perduring of this strife defines the steadfastness that Heidegger alludes to previously. But perduring does not only involve the passivity of suffering, since it also includes the activity of decision, of entering into the indecision of decisiveness. "Decision deals originarily with deciding or not-deciding. . . . Decision about decision (turning) [is] reflection but the opposite of that: [deciding] about the *decision*, i.e., already knowing enowning."[63] On the side of the decider, as it were, such decision is always experienced as holding forth the tension of revealing-concealing, in such a way as to elicit those possibilities that have previously been foreclosed, withheld, or kept in incubation. In this way, decision, as the occasion for the self coming into its own, prompts the decider to enter the open expanse of being, whereever new possibilities historically emerge, and to summon Dasein's engagement.

What, then, is decision making? It is the vortex of time-space, the moment where successive generations meet in the common mission of dwelling on the earth and safeguarding it for posterity. As Heidegger states in "Overcoming Metaphysics," it is one thing to exploit nature for our instrumental ends, but it is quite another "to receive the blessing of the earth and to become at home in the law of this reception."[64] He calls this law "the inviolability of the possible."[65] The self is essentially this release toward possibility, in such a way that the ecstatic overtness of exposure of the possible is equally a turning into being-at-home in that area of in-betweenness, the niche that our bodying forth makes in marking the interval between sky and earth. In this respect, the body includes its own special component of the twofold, and it is in carrying out this dynamic of differentiation, of dwelling on the earth and yet aspiring toward the beyond, that the self finds its identity by becoming at home in its incarnatedness. Within the overcoming of dualism, spiritual *practices*, such as yoga and breathing exercises, root us in our embodiment,[66] and, conversely, the more fully "incarnated" we become, the more genuinely we can honor what is sacred or *holy*.[67] When human beings dwell in the abode of the body, they respond to the kinship that they share with other embodied creatures, and thereby they become more adept in the practice of dwelling on the earth. In the *bodily exposure of earthly dwelling*, the axis of human selfhood turns around. This incarnatedness, as the seeking out of a location from which being can emerge in the singularity of its manifestness, ignites the spark of interrogation by which the questioning of the self, in its identity, can proceed in a more radical way. Inhabiting the earth, as Bruce Foltz suggests, is not merely one activity among others but instead is a meaning-engendering event, an idiom of the body.[68]

To inquire into Dasein's mode of embodiment, which Heidegger left implicit, becomes a way of advancing an inquiry to the self. This inquiry takes its guidance from the stimulus to question, which the turning in enowning provides, and a desire to keep open the question, to which our discussion of embodiment contributes. As he states in *Contributions*: "We comprehend nothing of the direction of the questioning which is enopened here if we, unawares, take the random idea of man and of 'beings as such' as our foundation, instead of putting into question at one and the same time 'man' and being (not only the being of man)—and keeping them in question."[69] Indeed, only as being opens forth so as to prompt the turning around of the question itself can a path be cleared for addressing the self beyond the restrictions of anthropologism, pragmatism, humanism, and any other "ism" for that matter. The hallmark of an "ism" is to shut off the openness of inquiry in order to define "man" according to a representational model that assumes the givenness of human nature, as already present: as a "material" being of economic need (Marxism), as a spiritual being in need of salvation (religious idealism), as an environmental being in struggle for survival (evolutionary biology and pragmatism). All of these representational characterizations of the self recede in favor of the language of the turning, which provides the momentum to overcome the metaphysics of subjectivity. Forever elusive, this language speaks through the tension of a double gesture: the ecstasy of the body and the embodiment of "ek-sistence."

If incarnatedess defines a permutation of being's manifestation, which is necessary for us to experience the "turning," then the more we can grasp the ecstatic character of human embodiment, the more decidedly we can proceed along the path of thinking. To think the turning, however, is to be drawn along the path (*Denkweg*) that the turning clears for us, and thus this endeavor becomes the foremost instance of thinking as such. We must then recognize that this path, like the dynamic of history itself, twists and bends in many ways and cannot yield a straightforward, linear direction. As Heidegger states toward the conclusion of *Being and Time*, we do not really know where the questioning of being leads until we have gone along the way.[70] And so it is not any goal that we seek to reach that proves decisive, but, on the contrary, becoming more adept in practicing the craft of thinking. As Heidegger exhorts us: "Let us learn thinking."[71]

Ironically, we best learn thinking by engaging in it, in other words, by addressing that which, through its elusiveness and withdrawal, most challenges us to think in our technological age. In an age where what is "most thought-provoking is that we are still not thinking,"[72] the incarnality of being provides an occasion to proceed along the path of thought. And the practices by which we *return to the earth*, such as ecology, then provide a *logos* to express the incarnality of being, its emergence through the conjunction of time and space (*Zeit-Raum*). For only by heeding being's incarnality can we appreciate our position as inhabitants of the earth and pay homage to the remarkable diversity of life.

Notes

Introduction

1. See Hans-Georg Gadamer, *Heidegger's Ways*, trans. John Stanley (Albany: State University of New York Press, 1994), 104–105.

2. Heidegger, *Sein und Zeit*, *Gesamtausgabe* 2 (Frankfurt am Main: Vittorio Klostermann, 1975), 151, *Being and Time*, trans. John Macquarrie and Edward Robinson (New York: Harper & Row, 1962), 143. Hereafter, references to Heidegger's *Gesamtausgabe* will be abbreviated as GA, followed by the volume number and the page of the English translation, where available (GA, p. ; tr.). For an inaugural attempt to close this gap in Heidegger's thinking, see David Michael Levin, *The Body's Recollection of Being* (London: Routledge, 1985), 7–15. Also see Levin, "The Ontological Dimension of Embodiment: Heidegger's Thinking of Being," in *The Body: Classic and Contemporary Readings*, ed. D. Welton (Oxford: Blackwell, 1999), 122–49. For a recent attempt to reexamine the problem of embodiment as an outgrowth of our being-in-the-world, see Søren Overgaard, "Heidegger and Embodiment," *Journal of the British Society for Phenomenology* 35:2 (May 2004): 116–31.

3. Heidegger, "Der Ursprung des Kuntwerkes," in *Holzwege*, GA 5 (Frankfurt am Main: Vittorio Klostermann, 1977)," 50; see also "The Origin of the Work of Art," in *Poetry Language, Thought*, trans. Albert Hoftstader (New York: Harper & Row, 1971), 38–39.

4. Heidegger, *Beiträge zur Philosophie (Vom Ereignis)*, GA 65 (Frankfurt am Main: Vittorio Klostermann, 1988), 378–89; *Contributions to Philosophy (From Enowning)*, trans. Parvis Emad and Kenneth Maly (Bloomington: Indiana University Press, 1999), 264–71.

5. Heidegger, "Time and Being," in *On Time and Being*, trans. Joan Stambaugh (New York: Harper & Row, 1972), 23.

6. See Bruce Foltz, *Inhabiting the Earth* (Atlantic Highlands, NJ: Humanities Press, 1995), 4–19. Also see Michael E. Zimmerman, *Contesting Earth's Future: Radical Ecology and Postmodernity* (Berkeley: University of California Press, 1994), 4–17.

7. Hans Jonas, *The Gnostic Religion: The Message of the Alien God and the Beginnings of Christianity*, 3rd ed. (Boston: Beacon Press, 2001), 64–65, 335–40; David Farrell Krell, *Daimon Life: Heidegger and Life-Philosophy* (Bloomington: Indiana University Press, 1992), 152.

8. GA 65, p. 278; tr. 195.

9. Heidegger, "Letter on 'Humanism,'" in *Wegmarken*, GA 9 (Frankfurt am Main: Vittorio Klostermann, 1977), 356–60; "Letter on 'Humanism,'" trans. Frank Capuzzi in *Pathmarks,* ed. William McNeill (Cambridge: Cambridge University Press, 1998), 268–71. See Miguel de Beistegui, *Thinking with Heidegger* (Bloomington: Indiana University Press, 2003), 43–44. Also see Frank Schalow, *The Renewal of the Heidegger-Kant Dialogue* (Albany: State University of New York Press, 1992), 267–69.

10. See John Llewelyn, "Prolegomena to Any Future Phenomenological Ecology," in *Eco-Phenomenology: Back to the Earth Itself,* ed. Charles S. Brown and Ted Toadvine (Albany: State University of New York Press, 2003), 65.

11. Zimmerman, *Contesting Earth's Future*, 6–7. See Zimmerman, "Heidegger's Phenomenology and Contemporary Environmentalism," in *Eco-Phenomenology*, 86–90. For a skeptical view of Heidegger as a protoecologist, see Thomas Sheehan, "Nihilism: Heidegger/ Jünger/Aristotle," in *Phenomenology: Japanese and American Perspectives*, ed. B. Hopkins (Dordrecht: Kluwer Academic, 1998), 273–317.

Chapter 1. The Materiality of the World

1. Krell, *Daimon Life*, 53.

2. See Jean-François Mattéi, "The Heideggerian Chiasmus," in *Heidegger from Metaphysics to Thought*, trans. Michael Gendre (Albany: State University of New York Press, 1995), 42–44.

3. GA 2, p. 260; tr. 240.

4. Rainer Maria Rilke, *Rilke on Love and Other Difficulties*, trans. John J. L. Mood (New York: W. W. Norton & Company, 1975), 25.

5. GA 2, pp. 58–60; tr. 68–70.

6. GA 2, pp. 576–577; tr. 487.

7. See Michael E. Zimmerman, *Heidegger's Confrontation with Modernity* (Bloomington: Indiana University Press, 1990), 166–90.

8. GA 2, pp. 107–16; tr. 110–20.

9. GA 2, pp. 110–20; tr. 167–78.

10. Herbert Marcuse, *One-Dimensional Man* (Boston: Beacon Press, 1964), 31–34.

11. Marcuse, *One-Dimensional Man*, 89.

12. Heidegger, *Zur Seinsfrage*, in *Wegmarken*, GA 9, 389–400; *On the Question of Being*, trans. William McNeill, in *Pathmarks*, 294–303. See also Zimmerman, *Heidegger's Confrontation with Modernity*, 46–57. Also see Hubert Dreyfus, "Between *Technē* and Technology," in *The Thought of Martin Heidegger*, ed. Michael E. Zimmerman, *Tulane Studies in Philosophy* 32 (1984): 27–34.

13. Karl Marx, *Capital*, vol. 1, trans. Ben Fowkes (New York: Random House, 1977), 188–92. For a contrast between Heidegger's and Marx's view of technology, and the presuppositions governing the former's critique of the latter, see Zimmerman, *Heidegger's Confrontation with Modernity*, 251–55. For a discussion of how Heidegger's distaste for economic ideologies—Marxist or capitalist—was a factor preventing him from linking (monetary) exchange with everydayness, see Frank Schalow, "Heidegger and the Question of Economics," *American Catholic Philosophical Association* vol. LXXIV, no. 2 (2000): 249–67.

14. Marx, *Capital*, 188–93.

15. GA 2; p. 190; tr. 186.

16. Heidegger, "Die Frage nach der Technik," in *Vorträge und Aufsätze*, GA 7 (Frankfurt am Main: Vittorio Klostermann, 2000), 16–36. "The Question Concerning Technology," in *The Question Concerning Technology and Other Essays*, trans. William Lovitt (New York: Harper & Row, 1977), 16–35.

17. GA 65, pp. 378–89; tr. 264–71. For an interesting analysis of the technological configuration of space as "cyberspace," as the denigration to the specificity of the "place" of human dwelling, see William Armstrong, "Cyberspace and the Relation between Being and Place," *Southwest Philosophy Review* 10:2 (July 1994): 33–47.

18. Heidegger, *Vom Wesen der Wahrheit: Zu Platons Höhlengleichnis und Theätet*, GA 34 (Frankfurt am Main: Vittorio Klostermann, 1988), 213–14; *The Essence of Truth: On Plato's Cave Allegory and Theaetetus*, trans. Ted Sadler (Continuum Press, 2002), 153 emphasis added.

19. Heidegger, "Vom Wesen und Begriff der Φύσις in Aristotle's, *Physics* B," in *Wegmarken*, GA 9, 267–79. "On the Essence and Concept of Φύσις in Aristotle's *Physics* B," trans. Thomas Sheehan, in *Pathmarks*, 191–202.

20. See Heidegger's discussion of Heraclitus Fragment 30, pertaining to the dynamics of "fire." See "Aletheia," in *Vorträge und Aufsätze*, GA 7, 282–84; "Aletheia," in *Early Greek Thinking*, trans. David. F. Krell and Frank Capuzzi (New York: Harper & Row, 1975), 117–19.

21. Heidegger, *Der Satz vom Grund*, GA 10 (Frankfurt am Main: Vittorio Klostermann, 1997), 3–4; *Principle of Reason*, trans. Reginald Lilly (Bloomington: Indiana University Press, 1991), 4.

22. Michael Heim, *The Metaphysics of Virtual Reality* (Oxford: Oxford University Press, 1993), 70.

23. Quoted from *The Great Conversations*, ed. Norman Melchert (Los Angeles, CA: Mayfield, 1999), 20.

24. See Richard Polt, *Heidegger: An Introduction* (Ithaca, NY: Cornell University Press, 1999), 171–72.

25. See Miguel de Beistegui, *Heidegger and the Political* (London: Routledge, 1998), 158. Heidegger tends to refer to money in a derogatory way to suggest a uniform standard to which everything is reduced. See Heidegger, *Was heißt Denken?*, GA

8 (Frank am Main: Vittorio Klostermann, 2002), 87–88; *What Is Called Thinking*?, trans. J. Glenn Gray (New York: Harper & Row, 1968), 82–83. For a discussion of the question of how global communications facilitate the "marketing" of products on an international scale, see Edward Johnson, "Media Ownership," in *Encyclopedia of Applied Ethics*, vol. 3 (New York: Academic Press, 1988), 145–53.

26. For a critical view of Heidegger's tendency to minimize the importance of embodiment, see Lilian Alweiss, *The World Unclaimed: A Challenge to Heidegger's Critique of Husserl* (Athens: Ohio University Press, 2003), 2, 90–94.

27. Heidegger, GA 9, p. 197; tr. 151.

28. Heidegger, *Four Seminars*, trans. Andrew Mitchell and François Raffoul (Bloomington: Indiana University Press, 2003), 31–32. See also James B. Steeves, *Imagining Bodies: Merleau-Ponty's Philosophy of Imagination* (Pittsburgh: Duquesne University Press, 2004), 138.

29. Heidegger, *Zollikon Seminars*, ed. Medard Boss, trans. Franz Mayr and Richard Askay (Evanston: Northwestern University Press, 2001), 138, 200–202.

30. GA 2, p. 56; tr. 67.

31. GA 2, pp. 168–74; tr. 163–68.

32. GA 2, pp. 169–73; tr. 164–67.

33. Abraham J. Twerski, M.D., *Addictive Thinking* (Center City, MN: Hazeldon, 1997), 16.

34. See Francis F. Seeburger's use of these Heideggerian terms in his "philosophical" treatment of addiction. See *Addiction and Responsibility* (New York: Crossroad, 1993), 6–19. Cf. GA 2, pp. 235–39; tr. 221–24. For a different approach, see Bruce Wilshire, *Wild Hunger: The Primal Roots of Modern Addiction* (Lanham, MD: Rowman & Littlefield, 2003), 12–26.

35. GA 2, pp. 237–38; tr. 223.

36. GA 2, pp. 237–38; tr. 223. See Heidegger's early discussion of care—as a form of dynamism—in his lecture course from the summer semester of 1923. See *Ontologie: Hermeneutik der Faktizität*, GA 63 (Frankfurt am Main: Vittorio Klostermann, 1988), 101–104; *Ontology—The Hermeneutics of Facticity*, trans. John van Buren (Bloomington: Indiana University Press, 1999), 78–80.

37. See John D. Caputo, *Radical Hermeneutics* (Bloomington: Indiana University Press, 1987), 3–7. Also see Lama Yeshe, *Introduction to Tantra: A Vision of Totality* (Boston: Wisdom Publications, 1987), 31–39.

38. Seeburger, *Addiction and Responsibility*, 139.

39. Heidegger, *Die Grundbegriffe der Metaphysik*, GA 29/30 (Frankfurt am Main: Vittorio Klostermann, 1983), 282–88. *The Fundamental Concepts of Metaphysics*, trans. William McNeill and Nicholas Walker (Bloomington: Indiana University Press, 1995), 192–95. As Twerski points out, "Although almost every human disease can be found among animals, there is little evidence that animals in their normal habitat develop addictive diseases" *Addictive Thinking*, 113.

40. GA 2, pp. 140–41; tr. 139.

41. Heidegger, *Zollikon Seminars*, 80–81, emphasis.

42. Michael E. Zimmerman, "Ontical Craving versus Ontological Desire," in *From Phenomenology to Thought, Errancy, and Desire: Essays in Honor of William J. Richardson*, S.J., ed. Babette E. Babich (Dordrecht: Kluwer Academic Publishers, 1995), 503, emphasis added. See also Yeshe, *Introduction to Tantra*, 35–36. "Feeling somehow incomplete, insecure and unfulfilled, we look outside ourselves for something or someone whereas ordinarily the pleasure that comes from contact with desirable objects *narrows* our attention and leads to a restrictive obsession for more and better pleasure."

43. GA 2, pp. 259–60; tr. 240.

44. Zimmerman, "Ontical Craving versus Ontological Desire," 501.

45. Seeburger, *Addiction and Responsibility*, 84–86.

46. GA 2, pp. 259–60; tr. 240.

47. Heidegger, "Anmerkungen zu Karl Jaspers 'Psychologie der Weltanschauungen,'" in *Wegmarken*, GA 9, 26–29. Also see "Comments on Karl Jaspers's *Psychology of Worldviews (1919–1921)*," in *Pathmarks*, ed., William McNeill (Cambridge: Cambridge University Press, 1998), 22–25.

48. Seeburger, *Addiction and Responsibility*, 139.

49. John van Buren, *The Young Heidegger* (Bloomington: Indiana University Press, 1994), 157 ff; Theodore Kisiel, *The Genesis of Heidegger's Being and Time* (Berkeley: University of California Press, 1993), 149 ff.

50. Franco Volpi, "*Being and Time: A 'Translation' of Nichomachean Ethics?*", trans. John Protevi, in *Reading Heidegger from the Start*, ed. Theodore Kisiel and John van Buren (Albany: State University of New York Press, 1994), 195–211.

51 . See Benjamin Crowe, "Resoluteness in Middle Voice," *Philosophy Today* 42:2 (Fall 2001): 225–41.

52. GA 9, pp. 27–30; tr. 22–25.

53. Ernest Becker, *The Denial of Death* (New York: Free Press, 1973), 11–24. Seeburger suggests that addiction entails "missing the mark" in the search for the "infinite." See *Addiction and Responsibility*, 113–19. I would agree, but with the qualification that the "infinite" be taken as a target that has not yet been understood in relation to "meaning" that we experience by first confronting our finitude.

54. GA 2, pp. 402–403; tr. 351.

55. Franz Rosenzweig, *The Star of Redemption*, trans. William W. Hallow (Notre Dame, IN: Notre Dame Press, 1962), 288.

56. GA 65, pp. 112–14; tr. 79.

57. GA 2, pp. 347–48; tr. 306.

58. Seeburger, *Addiction and Responsibility*, 184.

59. GA 2, pp. 483–89; tr. 416–17.

60. Seeburger, *Addiction and Responsibility*, 129.

61. GA 2, p. 379; tr. 331.

62. Twerski points out that a key to overcoming addiction is the shift in attitude from "shame" to "guilt," if we understand the latter as acquiring a sense of responsibility. See *Addictive Thinking*, 68–69. See also Frank Schalow, "Guilt and the Unconscious," *Review of Existential Psychology and Psychiatry*, vol. 22, nos. 1, 2, 3 (1994): 69–83. For a practical application of Heidegger's "*Dasein's* Analytic," see Ludwig Binswanger, "The Existential Analysis School of Thought," trans. Ernst Angel, in *Existence: A New Dimensions in Psychiatry and Psychology*, ed. Rollo May (New York: Basic Books, 1958), 195–201. I wish to thank Professor Edward Johnson for providing me with this reference.

63. E. Levinas, *Collected Philosophical Papers*, trans. A. Lingus (The Hague, the Netherlands: Martinus Nijhoff, 1987), 52–53.

64. See Frank Schalow, *Imagination and Existence* (Lanham, MD: University Press of America, 1986), 166–71.

65. Heidegger, *Metaphysische Anfangsgründe der Logik im Ausgang von Leibniz*, GA 26 (Frankfurt am Main: Vittorio Klostermann, 1978), 172–72; *The Metaphysical Foundations of Logic*, trans. Michael Heim (Bloomington: Indiana University Press, 1984), 137.

66. GA 7, pp. 16–20; tr. 17–20.

67. Heidegger, "Überwindung der Metaphysik," in *Vorträge und Aufsätze*, GA 7, 70; "Overcoming Metaphysics," in *The End of Philosophy*, trans. Joan Stambaugh (New York: Harper & Row, 1973), 87.

68. GA 7, p. 70; tr. 87, emphasis in original.

69. Zimmerman, "Ontical Craving versus Ontological Desire," 501.

70. GA 7, pp. 25–30; tr. 26–30.

71. Heidegger, "Wissenschaft und Besinnung," in *Vorträge und Aufsätze*, GA 7, 63–64; "Science and Reflection," in *The Question Concerning Technology and Other Essays*, 180.

72. See Levin, *The Body's Recollection of Being*, 62–67.

Chapter 2. The Erotic, Sexuality, and Diversity

1. Jacques Derrida, "*Geschlecht*: Sexual Difference and Ontological Difference," in *Feminist Interpretations of Martin Heidegger*, ed. Nancy J. Holland and Patricia Huntington (University Park: Pennsylvania State University Press, 2001), 53–72.

2. GA 31, pp. 129–30; tr. 90.

3. Heidegger, *Zollikon Seminars*, 80.

4. Krell, *Daimon Life*, 50.

5. Jonas, *The Gnostic Religion*, 64–65, 335–40.

6. Jean-Paul Sartre, *Being and Nothingness*, trans. Hazel Barnes (New York: The Philosophical Library, 1956), 383.

7. Michel Foucault, *The History of Sexuality. Vol. 1: An Introduction*, trans. Robert Hurley (New York: Random House, 1978), 3–13.

8. GA 9; pp. 157–58 tr. 122.

9. Heidegger, *Nietzsche, Zweiter Band* (Pfullingen: Günther Neske, 1961), 243. *Nietzsche, Volume IV: Nihilism,* trans. Frank A. Capuzzi (New York: Harper & Row, 1982), 185.

10. Heidegger, *Nietzsche, Zweiter Band*, p. 207; tr. 153, emphasis in original.

11. Heidegger, *Einleitung in die Philosophie*, GA 27 (Frankfurt am Main: Vittorio Klostermann, 1996), 146–47.

12. GA 27, pp. 146–47.

13. GA 26, p. 199; tr. 157.

14. GA 26, pp. 172–73; tr. 137.

15. Medard Boss, "Forward" to *Meaning and Content of Sexual Perversions: A Daseinanalytic Approach to the Psychopathology of the Phenomenon of Love*, trans. Liese Lewis Abell (New York: Grune & Stratton, 1949), x–xi. I am grateful to Professor Edward Johnson for providing me with this reference.

16. Boss, *Meaning and Content of Sexual Perversions*, 145–46.

17. GA 24, p. 187; tr. 132, emphasis in original.

18. Heidegger, *Nietzsche, Der Wille Zur Macht als Kunst*, GA 43 (Frankfurt am Main: Vittorio Klostermann, 1985), 126. Translation provided by Kenneth Maly. See also Frank Schalow, "The *Gesamtausgabe* Nietzsche: An Exercise in Translation and Thought," *Heidegger Studies* 9 (1993): 150.

19. Heidegger, *Zollikon Seminars*, 85–87.

20. "Der Ursprung des Kuntwerkes," GA 5, 35; "The Origin of the Work of Art," 47–48.

21. Merleau-Ponty, *The Phenomenology of Perception*, 154–73. See also Michel Haar, "Late Merleau-Ponty's Proximity to and Distance from Heidegger," *Journal of the British Society for Phenomenology* 30:1 (January 1999): 18–34.

22. See Frank Schalow, "The Hermeneutical Design of Heidegger's Analysis of Guilt," *Southern Journal of Philosophy* 23:3 (Fall 1985): 361–76.

23. Ibid., 370–75.

24. GA 27, pp. 123–26; I am grateful to Lawrence Hatab for providing me with this reference.

25. Heidegger, *Zollikon Seminars*, 139.

26. Heidegger, *Zollikon Seminars*, 87. See also Kevin Aho and Charles Guignon, "A Missed Opportunity: A Dialogue on the Body between Heidegger and Merleau-Ponty," in *Proceedings of the 38th Annual North American Heidegger Conference*, ed. Frank Schalow and François Raffoul.

27. Benedict de Spinoza, *Ethics*, trans. R. H. M. Elwes, in *The Rationalists* (New York: Anchor Books, 1974), 321.

28. Historically, as Foucault points out, marriage has emerged as an institution in which women have been viewed as the "property" of men. See Michel Foucault, *The History of Sexuality. Vol II: The Use of Pleasure*, trans. Robert Hurley (New York: Random House, 1985), 145–47.

29. See Schalow, *The Renewal of the Heidegger-Kant Dialogue*, 107–12.

30. Max Scheler, *Man's Place in Nature* (Boston: Beacon Press, 1961), 38, 47–50.

31. Giorgio Agamben, *Potentialities*, ed. and trans. Daniel Heller-Roazen (Stanford, CA: Stanford University Press, 1999), 204. Also see Frank Schalow, "Heidegger, Martin," *Sex from Plato to Paglia: A Philosophical Encyclopedia*, ed. Alan Soble (Westport, CT: Greenwood Press, 2005), 435–39.

32. Heidegger, "Phänomenologie und Theologie," in *Wegmarken*, GA 9, 48–49; "Phenomenology and Theology," trans. James G. Hart and John C. Maraldo, in *Pathmarks*, 51–52.

33. Nietzsche, *On the Genealogy of Morals*, 107.

34. Frederick Elliston, "In Defense of Promiscuity," in *Philosophical Perspectives on Sex and Love*, ed. Robert M. Stewart (Oxford: Oxford University Press, 1995), 146–58.

35. GA 2, p. 378; tr. 331.

36. M. C. Dillon, "Sex, Time, and Love: Erotic Temporality," in *Sex, Love, and Friendship: Studies of the Society for the Philosophy of Sex and Love 1977–1992*, ed. Alan Soble (Amsterdam and Atlanta, GA: Editions Rodopi, 1993), 316–25.

37. Heidegger, *Zollikon Seminars*, 190.

38. Spinoza, *Ethics,* 310–11.

39. Heidegger, *What Is Philosophy?*, trans. Jean Wilde and William Kluback (New Haven, CT: Twayne Publishers, 1958), 45, 47.

40. Heidegger, GA 2, pp. 353–54; tr. 308. See Nietzsche, *Thus Spoke Zarathustra*, in *The Portable Nietzsche*, 183–86.

41. Rilke, *Letters to a Young Poet*, trans. M. D. Herter Norton (New York: W. W. Norton & Company, 1962), 59.

42. Merleau-Ponty, *Phenomenology of Perception*, 137–47.

43. Goethe, *The Sorrows of Young Werther*, in *The Sorrows of Young Werther and Novella*, trans. Elizabeth Mayer and Louise Bogan (New York: Random House, 1971), 161–67.

44. Merleau-Ponty, *Phenomenology of Perception*, 166–71. See Wayne Froman, "Merleau-Ponty's 1959 Heidegger Lectures: The Task of Thinking and the Possibility of Philosophy Today," *Chiasmi International* 5 (2003): 17–29.

45. Merleau-Ponty, *Phenomenology of Perception*, 179.

46. GA 2, pp. 146–47; tr. 144.

47. See Jennifer Gosetti, "Figures of the Feminine in Heidegger's Theory of Poetic Language," in *Feminist Interpretations of Heidegger*, 206.

48. GA 65, p. 394; tr. 277.

49. Gabriel Marcel, *Homo Viator*, trans. Emma Craufurd (New York: Harper & Row, 1951), 135–54.

50. For an explanation of temporality as the presupposition for monogamy, see Vincent C. Punzo, "Morality and Human Sexuality," in *Social Ethics*, ed. Thomas A. Mappes and Jane S. Zembaty (New York: McGraw Hill, 2002), 168–69.

51. GA 31, pp. 263–64; tr. 180.

52. GA 26, p. 247; tr. 192.

53. Rilke, *Letters to a Young Poet*, 54.

54. Richard Wasserstrom, "Is Adultery Immoral?," in *Morality and Moral Controversies*, ed. John Anthur (Englewood Cliffs, NJ: 1993), 603–610.

55. Nietzsche, *Twilight of the Idols*, 544.

56. Van Buren, *The Young Heidegger*, 227.

57. Agamben, "Potentialities," 204. See also Heidegger, *Four Seminars*, 1.

58. Rilke, *Letters to a Young Poet*, 53–54.

59. Rainer Maria Rilke, *Sonnets to Orpheus*, trans. M. D. Herter Norton (New York: W. W. Norton & Company, 1942), 53 (Sonnet 19).

60. John van Buren, "What Does It All Come To?," *Philosophy Today* 41:2 (Summer 1997): 330.

61. Julia Kristeva, "Women's Time," in *The Kristeva Reader*, ed. Kelly Oliver (New York: Columbia University Press, 1997), 349–68.

62. Luce Irigaray, *The Way of Love*, trans. Heidi Bostic (London: Continuum Press, 2002), 77–78.

63. Irigaray, *The Way of Love*, 163.

64. Patricia Huntington, "Being-in-the-Family," Proceedings of the 38th Annual North American Heidegger Conference.

65. David F. Krell, *Intimations of Mortality* (University Park: Penn State University Press, 1986), 176.

66. Herbert Marcuse, *Eros and Civilization* (New York: Random House, 1962), 208.

67. GA 2, p. 22; tr. 37.

68. Frank Schalow, "Imagination and Embodiment: The Task of Reincarnating the Self," *International Studies in Philosophy* 35:4 (2004): 201–15.

69. Hegel, *Phenomenology of Spirit*, 443.

70. Paul Ricoeur, "The Hermeneutics of Symbol and Philosophical Reflection," trans. Denis Savage, in *The Philosophy of Paul Ricoeur*, ed. Charles E. Reagan and David Stewart (Boston: Beacon Press, 1978), 43.

71. Eugene O'Neill, *Desire under the Elms*, in *Three Plays* (New York: Random House, 1952), 45–58.

72. See Seeburger, *Addiction and Responsibility*, 54.

73. GA 34, pp. 204–16; tr. 147–55.

74. See Zimmerman, "Ontical Craving versus Ontological Desire," 501.

75. Sartre, *Being and Nothingness*, 471–95.

76. GA 34, p. 236; tr. 169, emphasis in original. As Heidegger states in the Kant book "human being, as finite, can only 'have' its body in a transcendental sense [i.e., through transcendence]." GA 3, 172; tr. 121.

77. Rilke, *Letters to a Young Poet*, 35.

78. Nietzsche, *The Gay Science*, trans. Walter Kaufmann (New York: Random House, 1974), 274.

79. Zimmerman, "Ontical Craving versus Ontological Desire," 501.

80. Lawrence Hatab, 37th Annual North American Heidegger Conference. See also Schalow, "Imagination and Embodiment," 209.

81. GA 3, pp. 153–56; tr. 107–109.

82. John Sallis, *Double Truth* (Albany: State University of New York Press, 1995), 122.

83. Schalow, "Imagination and Embodiment," 209–10.

84. GA 3, pp. 153–56; tr. 107–10.

85. Schalow, *The Renewal of the Heidegger-Kant Dialogue*, 174–76.

86. Heidegger, *Einfürhung in die Metaphysik*, GA 40 (Frankfurt am Main: Vittorio Klostermann, 1983), 158.

87. Helen Longino, "Pornography, Oppression, and Freedom: A Closer Look," in *Morality and Moral Controversies*, 436–42.

88. Alan Soble, *Pornography, Sex, and Feminism* (New York: Prometheus Books, 2002), 7–15.

89. GA 65, pp. 303–305; tr. 214–15.

90. GA 65, p. 312; tr 219, emphasis in original.

CHAPTER 3. *ETHOS*, EMBODIMENT, AND FUTURE GENERATIONS

1. Kant, *Foundation for the Metaphysics of Morals*, trans. Lewis White Beck (Indianapolis: Bobbs Merrill Company, 1959), 9.

2. See Schalow, *The Renewal of the Heidegger-Kant Dialogue*, 267–304.

3. GA 31, p. 296; tr. 200–201.

4. GA 26, p. 199; tr. 157.

5. GA 65, pp. 112–16; tr. 79–80.

6. Heidegger, *Prolegomena zur Geschichte des Zeitbegriffs*, GA 20 (Frankfurt am Main: Vittorio Klostermann, 1979), 174–77. *History of the Concept of Time*, trans. Theodore Kisiel (Bloomington: Indiana University Press, 1985), 126–28.

7. For an ethical turn in the direction of desire, see E. Levinas, *Collected Philosophical Papers*, trans. Alphonso Lingus (The Hague, the Netherlands: Martinus Nijhoff, 1987), 56–57. Also see Carol Gilligan, *In a Different Voice* (Cambridge, MA: Harvard University Press, 1982), 122–31 and Arne J. Vetlesen, *Perception, Empathy, and Judgment: An Inquiry into the Preconditions of Moral Performance* (University Park: Pennsylvania State University Press, 1994), 82–97; Lawrence Hatab, *Ethics and Finitude* (Lanham, MD: Roman & Littlefield, 2000), 7–22; Joanna Hodge, *Heidegger and Ethics* (London: Routledge, 1995), 35–42.

8. GA 24, pp. 190–94; tr. 135–37. GA 2, p. 360; tr. 316.

9. Kant, *Foundation for the Metaphysics of Morals*, 14–17, 17n-18n.

10. GA 24, p. 189; tr. 133.

11. GA 65, pp. 91–92; tr. 63.

12. GA 3, pp. 158–59; tr. 111.

13. See Heidegger, *Grundfragen der Philosophie: Ausgewählte "Probleme" der "Logik,"* GA 45 (Frankfurt am Main: Vittorio Klostermann, 1984), 151; *Basic Questions of Philosophy: Selected "Problems" of "Logic,"* trans. Richard Rojcewicz and André Schuwer (Bloomington: Indiana University Press, 1994), 130.

14. GA 45, pp. 151–53; tr. 131–32.

15. GA 45, p. 153; tr. 132.

16. Heidegger, *Parmenides*, GA 54 (Frankfurt am Main: Vittorio Klostermann, 1982), 118–19; *Parmenides*, trans. André Schuwer and Richard Rojcewicz (Bloomington: Indiana University Press, 1992), 80.

17. GA 65, pp. 371–79; tr. 259–64.

18. GA 45, pp. 152–53; tr. 131–32.

19. Aristotle, *Nichomachean Ethics*, trans. Terence Irwin (Indianapolis: Hackett, 1985), 170–71 (book 6, ch. 13, 1142b).

20. GA 45, pp. 150–51; tr. 131.

21. GA 65, p. 98; tr. 67.

22. Hans-Georg Gadamer, *Heidegger's Ways*, trans. John Stanley (Albany: State University of New York Press, 1994), 32. Also see Charles M. Sherover, "The Temporality of the Common Good," *Review of Metaphysics* 38 (1984): 475–86; William McNeill, *The Glance of the Eye* (Albany: State University of New York Press, 1999), 127–34.

23. GA 2, p. 360; tr. 316.

24. GA 3, pp. 158–59; tr. 111.

25. GA 31, p. 296; tr. 200–201.

26. Françoise Dastur, "The Call of Conscience," trans. David Allison and Emily Lee, in *Heidegger and Practical Philosophy*, 93.

27. Heidegger, *Grundbegriffe der aristotelischen Philosophie*, GA 18 (Frankfurt am Main: Vittorio Klostermann, 2002), 109–13.

28. See Heidegger, *Grundbegriffe der antiken Philosophie*, GA 22 (Frankfurt am Main: Vittorio Klostermann, 1993), 311–13.

29. Franco Volpi, "*Being and Time*: A 'Translation' of the *Nicomachean Ethics*," trans. John Protevi, in *Reading Heidegger from the Start*, ed. Theodore Kisiel and John van Buren (Albany: State University of New York Press, 1994), 210. Also see Walter Brogan, "The Place of Aristotle in the Development of Heidegger's Phenomenology," in *Reading Heidegger from the Start*, 219.

30. Kant, *The Doctrine of Virtue*, trans. Mary J. Gregor (New York: Harper & Row, 1962), 60–62, 103.

31. Van Buren, *The Young Heidegger*, 229.

32. GA 26, pp. 172–74; tr. 136–38.

33. GA 9, pp. 33–34; tr. 30–31.

34. GA 65, p. 379 ; tr. 265.

35. Charles M. Sherover, *From Kant and Royce to Heidegger* (Washington, DC: The Catholic University of America Press, 2003), 177.

36. François Raffoul, "Heidegger and the Origins of Responsibility," in *Heidegger and Practical Philosophy*, 218.

37. GA 10, p. 5; tr. 6.

38. GA 2, p. 502; tr. 426.

39. GA 9, p. 175; tr. 135.

40. Aristotle, *Nicomachean Ethics*, 256 (book 9, ch. 9, 1169a20).

41. See Frank Schalow, "Language and the Tragic Side of Ethics," *International Studies in Philosophy*, vol. XXVII, no. 2 (1995): 49–64. See also Dennis J. Schmidt, *On*

Germans and Other Greeks: Tragedy and Ethical Life (Bloomington: Indiana University Press, 2001), 90–115.

42. GA 9, p. 165; tr. 122. Also see John Sallis, *Double Truth* (Albany: State University of New York Press, 1995), 166–70.

43. GA 9, pp. 174–75; tr. 134.

44. See Robert Bernasconi, "On Heidegger's Other Sins of Omission," in *Heidegger*, ed. John D. Caputo, *American Catholic Philosophical Quarterly*, vol. LXIL, no. 2 (Spring 1995): 333–49. Also see E. Levinas, *Time and the Other*, trans. Richard A Cohen (Pittsburgh: Duquesne University Press, 1987), 87, 93, 109. As Levinas states: "The offense done to the other by being's 'good conscience' is already an offense done to the widow, the orphan" (p. 109).

45. Charles E. Scott, *The Question of Ethics* (Bloomington: Indiana University Press, 1990), 1–12.

46. Krell, *Daimon Life*, 33.

47. Heidegger, *Vom Wesen der Sprache*, GA 85 (Frankfurt am Main: Vittorio Klostermann, 1999), 164–65. *On the Essence of Language*, trans. Wanda Torres Gregory and Yvonne Unna (Albany: State University of New York Press, 2004), 139–40.

48. GA 85, pp. 164–65, 172–73; tr. 139–40; 144–45.

49. GA 3, p. 160; tr. 129, emphasis.

50. Hannah Arendt, *The Human Condition* (Chicago: University of Chicago Press, 1958), 176–77. For a different perspective on ethics and embodiment, see John Russon, "Embodiment and Responsibility: Merleau-Ponty and the Ontology of Nature," *Man and World* 27 (1994): 301–302.

51. GA 27, pp. 123–26.

52 GA 2, p. 291; tr. 262.

53. Heidegger, *Zollikon Seminars*, 140.

54. GA 9, p. 313; tr. 239

55. GA 7, p. 35; tr. 34.

56. Heidegger, *Four Seminars*, 51.

57. GA 85, p. 67; tr. 58.

58. See Michel Haar, *The Song of the Earth*, trans. Reginald Lilly (Bloomington: Indiana University Press, 1993), 7–15.

59. GA 9, p. 175n; tr. 135n. See also George Kovacs, "The Leap (*Der Sprung*) for Being in Heidegger's *Beiträge zur Philosopher (Vom Ereignis)*," *Man and World* 25 (1992): 131.

CHAPTER 4. OF EARTH AND ANIMALS

1. Nietzsche, *The Gay Science*, 181.

2. Nietzsche, *Thus Spoke Zarathustra*, 125, emphasis in original. For a discussion of Nietzsche as an environmentalist, see Max Hallman, "Nietzsche's Environmental Ethics," *Environmental Ethics* 13:2 (Winter 1991): 99–125. For a later discussion that counterposes Nietzsche's concept of will to power with his interest in preserving the earth, see Martin Drenthen, "Nietzsche and the Paradox of Environmental Ethics," *New Nietzsche Studies* 5:1–2 (Spring–Summer 2002): 12–25.

3. Heidegger, "The End of Philosophy and the Task of Thinking," 57.

4. Gadamer, *Heidegger's Ways*, 99, emphasis in original.

5. Max Scheler, *Man's Place in Nature* (Boston: Beacon Press, 1961), 83.

6. Michael E. Zimmerman, "Heidegger's Phenomenology and Contemporary Environmentalism," in *Eco-Phenomenology*, 83.

7. Gadamer, *Heidegger's Ways*, 104.

8. GA 3, p. 29; tr. 20–21.

9. Nietzsche, *Thus Spoke Zarathustra*, 238.

10. Zimmerman, *Contesting Earth's Future*, 7–14.

11. GA 65, p. 320; tr. 225.

12. Heidegger, *Four Seminars*, 61, emphasis in original.

13. Zimmerman, *Contesting Earth's Future*, 104–22.

14. Tom Regan, *The Thee Generation* (Philadelphia: Temple University Press, 1991), 3–6.

15. GA 2, pp. 511–12; tr. 435.

16. GA 4, pp. 34–35; tr. 54.

17. GA 10, pp. 3–4; tr. 4.

18. Caputo, *Radical Hermeneutics*, 187–92.

19. GA 3, p. 229; tr. 160.

20. GA 9, p. 397; tr. 300.

21. GA 29–30, pp. 384–85; tr. 264.

22. GA 9, p. 297; tr. 227.

23. Scheler, *Man's Place in Nature*, 39, 47–50. See also Schalow, *The Renewal of the Heidegger-Kant Dialogue*, 107–15.

24. Peter Singer, "All Animals Are Equal," in *Morality and Moral Controversies*, 227–35.

25. GA 9, p. 324 ; tr. 247.

26. GA 54, p. 118; tr. 80.

27. Heidegger, "Das Ding," in *Vorträge und Aufsätze*, GA 7, 180; "The Thing," in *Poetry, Language, Thought*," 178.

28. Rilke, *Sonnets to Orpheus*, 39.

29. J. Baird Callicott, "Animal Liberation: A Triangular Affair," in *Morality and Moral Controversies*, 237–52.

30. Regan, *The Thee Generation*, 3–6, 22.

31. See Mark Sagoff's critique of Peter Singer's thesis of "equal consideration," "Animal Liberation and Environmental Ethics: Bad Marriage, Quick Divorce," in *Law Journal* 22:2: 297–98.

32. See Simon Glendinning, "Heidegger and the Question of Animality," *International Journal of Philosophical Studies* 4:1 (March 1996): 75–82. Also see Zimmerman, "Ontical Craving Versus Ontological Desire," 501–23. Though initially Zimmerman emphasized the ecological implications of Heidegger's thought, over time he became more skeptical about the import of hermeneutical phenomenology for deep ecology.

33. George S. Cave, "Animals, Heidegger, and the Right to Life," *Environmental Ethics* 4:3 (Fall 1982): 249–54. See also Robert Frodeman's review of Bruce Foltz's book *Inhabiting the Earth: Heidegger, Environmental Ethics, and the Metaphysics of Nature*, *Environmental Ethics*, 19:2 (1997), 217–19.

34. See Schalow, *Language and Deed*, 201–203.

35. Zimmerman, *Contesting Earth's Future*, 15–25.

36. GA 9, pp. 255–68; tr. 196–205. Also see John van Buren, "Critical Environmental Hermeneutics," in *Environmental Ethics* 17 (Fall 1995): 259–75.

37. "Bauen Wohnen Denken," in *Wegmarken*, GA 7, 156. "Building Dwelling Thinking," in *Poetry, Language, Thought*, 152. Heidegger writes: "*Accordingly, spaces receive their being from locations not from 'space.'*" Cave's description of how a cat becomes upset with the rearrangement of furniture in the house provides a good example of how spatiality in the Heideggerian sense determines the concerned involvement of animals. Though Cave restricts his analysis to the early Heidegger, his point is well taken. See "Animals, Heidegger, and the Right to Life," 253. See Alejandro Valega, *Heidegger and the Issue of Space* (University Park: Pennsylvania State University Press, 2003), 22–31.

38. See Krell, *Daimon Life: Heidegger and Life-Philosophy*, 44–50.

39. Zimmerman, "Ontical Craving versus Ontological Desire," 501–23.

40. GA 29–30, pp. 257–61; tr. 373–80.

41. GA 29–30, pp. 346–50; tr. 238–40.

42. GA 42, p. 255; tr. 148.

43. Heidegger, *Discourse on Thinking*, trans. John Anderson and E. Hans Freund (New York: Harper & Row, 1966), 588–61.

44. GA 12, pp. 26–30; tr. 205–207. Also see Foltz, *Inhabiting the Earth*, 4–17.

45. Zimmerman, *Heidegger's Confrontation with Modernity*, 145 ff.

46. Carl Cohen, "The Case for the Use of Animals in Biomedical Research," in *Intervention and Reflection*, 5th edition, ed. Ronald Munson (Los Angeles: Wadsworth, 1996), 405–12.

47. Singer, "All Animals are Equal," 227–35. For a similar argument from a Heideggerian perspective, see Cave, "Animals, Heidegger, and the Right to Life," 249–54. This essay was written, of course, prior to the publication of Heidegger's *Die Grundbegriffe der Metaphysik.*

48. Hans Jonas, *The Phenomenon of Life* (New York: Harper & Row, 1966), 284.

49. Hannah Arendt, *Lectures on Kant's Political Philosophy*, ed. Ronald Biener (Chicago: University of Chicago Press, 1982), 27.

50. Glendinning, "Heidegger and the Question of Animality," 75–82.

51. GA 12, pp. 9–14; tr. 188–92.

52. GA 12, pp. 27–30; tr. 206–207.

53. John Llewelyn, *The Middle-Voice of Ecological Conscience* (New York: St. Martin's Press, 1991), 9–25.

54. John Llewelyn, "Prolegomena to Any Future Phenomenological Ecology," in *Eco-Phenomenology*, 70.

55. GA 7, p. 87; tr. 109, emphasis added.

56. Christian Diehm, "Natural Disasters," in *Eco-Phenomenology*, 177.

57. GA 9, pp. 188–89; tr. 144–45.

58. Ken Wilber, *Sex, Ecology, Spirituality* (Boston: Shambala Press, 1995), 23–42.

59. For an interesting discussion of how animals communicate, see Tim Friend, *Animal Talk* (New York: Free Press, 2003), 7–22.

Chapter 5. The Body Politic

1. GA 4, p. 47; tr. 63.

2. Sallis, *Double Truth*, 210.

3. Heidegger, *Zollikon Seminars*, 266, translation modified.

4. GA 9, p. 189; tr. 145.

5. GA 2, pp. 272–73; tr. 249.

6. GA 31, p. 209; tr. 144.

7. GA 2, pp. 257–58; tr. 238–39.

8. GA 2, p. 258; tr. 239.

9. GA 2, pp. 163–64; tr. 158–59.

10. GA 42, p. 276; tr. 159.

11. GA 31, p. 271; tr. 185.

12. GA 26, p. 192; tr. 152, emphasis in original.

13. GA 9, pp. 160–62; tr. 123–24.

14. GA 3, p. 198; tr. 139.

15. Raffoul, *Heidegger and the Subject*, 21–25.

16. See Frank Schalow, "Why Evil? Heidegger, Schelling, and the Tragic View of Being," *Idealistic Studies* 25:1 (Winter 1995): 52–67.

17. GA 9, p. 197; tr. 151.

18. GA 31, pp. 302–303; tr. 205, emphasis in original.

19. GA 31, p. 135; tr. 93, emphasis in original.

20. GA 24, p. 17; tr. 12.

21. Kant, *Foundation for the Metaphysics of Morals*, 66–67.

22. GA 31, p. 134; tr. 93, emphasis in original.

23. Heidegger, "Time and Being," 4–12.

24. GA 8, pp. 98–113; tr. 94–110.

25. Nietzsche, *Thus Spoke Zarathustra*, 252–53.

26. Nietzsche, *Thus Spoke Zarathustra*, 211, 251.

27. Nietzsche, *Ecce Homo*, trans. Walter Kaufmann, in *On the Genealogy of Morals and Ecce Homo* (New York: Random House, 1969), 258.

28. GA 2, pp. 511–12; tr. 435.

29. GA 2, pp. 511–12; tr. 435, emphasis in original.

30. GA 12, p. 91; tr. 9–10.

31. Friedrich-Wilhelm Herrmann, "Besinnung als seinsgeschichtliches Denken," *Heidegger Studies* 16 (2002): 52–53.

32. GA 31, p. 130; tr. 129, emphasis in original.

33. GA 9, p. 423; tr. 320.

34. Sallis, "Free Thinking," 12.

35. GA 9, p. 364; tr. 276.

36. GA 42, p. 263; tr. 152.

37. Schelling, *Of Human Freedom*, 51.

38. Sallis, "Free Thinking," 9.

39. Kant, *Critique of Judgment*, 129. See Jean-François Lyotard, "Reflection on Kant's Aesthetics," trans. Charles T. Wolfe, *Graduate Faculty Philosophy Journal* 16:2 (1993): 375–411.

40. GA 65, p. 312; tr. 219, emphasis in original.

41. Zimmerman, *Heidegger's Confrontation with Modernity*, 107, 264.

42. GA 7, p. 79; tr. 102.

43. GA 18, p. 46.

44. GA 18, pp. 127–34.

45. See Schalow, "Imagination and Embodiment," 212.

46. See Werner Marx, *Is There a Measure on the Earth?*, trans. Tom Nenon and Reginald Lilly (Chicago: University of Chicago Press, 1987), 21–35.

47. GA 18, pp. 104–106, tr.

48. Kant, *Critique of Judgment*, 74–76. See also Arendt, *Lectures on Kant's Political Philosophy*, trans. Ronald Beiner (Chicago: University of Chicago Press, 1982), 10–15. For an interesting discussion of this topic, see Dean C. Hammer, "Incommensurable Phrases and Narrative Discourse: Lyotard and Arendt on the Possibility of Politics," *Philosophy Today* 41:4 (Winter 1997): 475–90.

49. GA 31, p. 292; tr. 198, emphasis in original.

50. See Schalow, *The Renewal of the Heidegger-Kant Dialogue*, 356–70.

51. Schmidt, *On Germans and Other Greeks*, 87–95.

52. Levinas, *Philosophical Papers*, 52–59.

53. John D. Caputo, "Sorge and Kardia: The Hermeneutics of Factical Life and the Categories of the Heart," in *Reading Heidegger from the Start*, 327–43.

54. See Scott, *The Question of Ethics*, 141–54.

55. Nietzsche, *The Genealogy of Morals*, 72–81.

56. Kierkgaard, *Works of Love*, in *A Kierkegaard Anthology* (Princeton: Princeton University Press, 1946), 301–23.

57. Nietzsche, *The Antichrist*, 612–13.

58. Schelling, *Of Human Freedom*, 51. Also see GA 42, p. 262; tr. 151.

59. GA 42, p. 277; tr. 160.

60. Schelling, *Of Human Freedom*, 50.

61. GA 9, p. 175; tr. 135.

62. See Schalow, *Language and Deed*, 143.

63. GA 2, pp. 511–12; tr. 437.

64. GA 42, p. 272; tr. 160.

65. James Risser, *Hermeneutics and the Voice of the Other* (Albany: State University of New York Press, 1997), 138.

66. Sherover, *Are We in Time?*, 204.

67. See Frank Schalow: "At the Crossroads of Freedom: Ethics without Values," in *A Companion to Heidegger's Introduction to Metaphysics*, 250–62.

68. Ibid., 250–53.

69. Robert Bernasconi, "Preface," in *Race*, ed. Robert Bernasconi (New York: Blackwell, 2001), x–xii.

70. Arendt, *Lectures on Kant's Political Philosophy*, 10–15.

71. Arendt, *The Life of the Mind*, vol. 2, 257.

72. Heidegger, *Zollikon Seminars*, 201.

73. Kant, *Critique of Pure Reason*, A 739, B 767.

74. Paul Tillich, "Heidegger and Jaspers," in *Heidegger and Jaspers*, ed. Alan M. Olson (Philadelphia: Temple University Press, 1994), 25. For further discussion of this point, see Frank Schalow, *Language and Deed* (Amsterdam and Atlanta: Editions Rodopi, 1998), 79.

75. GA 31, p. 264; tr. 181.

76. GA 65, pp. 412–17; tr. 289–93. See also Schalow, *Heidegger and the Quest for the Sacred*, pp. 131–62.

77. See Zimmerman, *Heidegger's Confrontation with Modernity*, 126–33.

78. Gregory S. Paul, "The Great Scandal: Christianity's Role in the Rise of the Nazis," *Free Inquiry* 23:4 (October–November 2003): 20–28.

Chapter 6. The Return to the Earth and the Idiom of the Body

1. Heidegger, "The End of Philosophy and the Task of Thinking," 57. See Levin, *The Body's Recollection of Being*, 123–41.

2. Heidegger, "Einleitung zu 'Was ist Metaphysik?'", in *Wegmarken*, GA 9, 376. See also "Introduction to 'What Is Metaphysics?'", in *Pathmarks*, 285.

3. Heidegger, *Four Seminars*, 60–61.

4. GA 2, pp. 51–52; tr. 64.

5. GA 45, p. 153; tr. 132.

6. See Frank Schalow, "At the Interface of Destiny and Freedom: The New Interface of History in Heidegger's 1936 Schelling-Lectures," *Clio* 28:1 (Fall 1998): 53–69.

7. GA 2, pp. 51–52; tr. 62–63, emphasis in original.

8. Heidegger, "My Way to Phenomenology," in *On Time and Being*, 82.

9. GA 9, p. 328; tr. 250.

10. GA 5, p. 64; tr. 76.

11. Richard Polt, *Heidegger: An Introduction*, 121–37.

12. GA 4, p. 33; tr. 51.

13. GA 4, pp. 35–36; tr. 54.

14. GA 9, pp. 410–11; tr. 310–11.

15. GA 7, p. 35; tr. 34, emphasis in original.

16. Heidegger, "The Turning," 36–49.

17. Albert Camus, *The Plague*, trans. Stuart Gilbert (New York: Random House, 1972), 235–47.

18. See Zimmerman, *Contesting the Earth's Future*, 58, 83.

19. Heidegger, "The Turning," 41.

20. GA 7, p. 88; tr. 110.

21. Zimmerman, *Contesting the Earth's Future*, 336, 372.

22. Heidegger, "The Turning," 41, emphasis in original.

23. Heidegger, "The Turning, 41.

24. GA 65, pp. 250–52; tr. 177.

25. GA 65, pp. 407–409; tr. 287. For an excellent discussion of the "turning," see Parvis Emad, "On 'Being': The Last Part of *Contributions to Philosophy (From Enowning)*," in *Companion to Heidegger's Contributions to Philosophy*, ed. Charles E. Scott et al. (Bloomington: Indiana University Press, 2001), 230–32.

26. McNeill, *The Glance of the Eye*, 187.

27. Heidegger, *Zollikon Seminars*, 81.

28. GA 7, p. 88; tr. 110.

29. Aldous Huxley, *Brave New World* (New York: Harper & Row, 1932), 159–63.

30. GA 12, p. 27; tr. 205.

31. Heidegger, "The Turning," 43–44.

32. GA 7, p. 88; tr. 110.

33. GA 12, p. 27; tr. 205. See Parvis Emad, "Heidegger on Pain: Focusing on a Recurring Theme in His Thought," *Zeitschrift für Philosophische Forschung* 36 (July–September 1982), 354–55.

34. Sigmund Freud, *Civilization and Its Discontents*, trans. James Strachey (New York: W. W. Norton & Company, 1961), 185.

35. GA 3, p. 205; tr. 144.

36. Heidegger, *Zollikon Seminars*, 267.

37. GA 7, p. 79; tr. 102.

38. Michael Langlais, *A Heideggerian Critique of C. G. Jung's Concept of the Self* (Doctoral dissertation, Union Institute, Cincinnati, OH, 2003), 4–12.

39. William J. Richardson, S. J., "The Place of the Unconscious in Heidegger," in *Heidegger and Psychology*, ed. Keith Hoeller (Atlantic Highlands, NJ: Humanities Press, Inc., 1988), 177–78.

40. Søren Kierkegaard, *The Concept of Dread*, trans. Walter Lowrie (Princeton, NJ: Princeton University Press, 1957), 140, 142.

41. See Gadamer, *Heidegger's Ways*, 163–64.

42. GA 42, p. 263; tr. 152.

43. Caputo, *Radical Hermeneutics*, 4–9.

44. M. Scott Peck, *The Road Less Traveled* (New York: Simon & Schuster, 1978), 16.

45. Medard Boss, *Psychoanalysis and Daseinanalysis*, trans. Ludwig Lefebre (New York: Basic Books, 1963), 22–44.

46. Heidegger, *Zollikon Seminars*, 93.

47. Heidegger, *Zollikon Seminars*, 174.

48. Heidegger, "The End of Philosophy and the Task of Thinking," 57–58.

49. GA 29–30, pp. 286–87; tr. 194.

50. GA 65, pp. 278–79; tr. 195, emphasis added.

51. GA 7, p. 40; tr. 157.

52. See Michael E. Zimmerman, "The Ontological Decline of the West," in *A Companion to Heidegger's Introduction to Metaphysics*, 200–202.

53. GA 29–30, p. 377; tr. 259.

54. Richard Dawkins, *The Selfish Gene* (Oxford: Oxford University Press, 1978), 185.

55. Sallis, *Double Truth*, 210.

56. GA 12, p. 158; tr. 6.

57. Heidegger, "Preface" to William J. Richardson's *From Phenomenology through Thought* (Bronx, NY: Fordham University Press, 2003), xx.

58. David Wood, "What Is Eco-Phenomenology?," in *Eco-Phenomenology*, 216.

59. GA 18, pp. 27–28.

60. GA 65, p. 318; tr. 224, emphasis in original.

61. GA 65, p. 318–22; tr. 224–25.

62. GA 65, p. 320; tr. 225, emphasis in original.

63. GA 65, p. 102; tr. 70, emphasis in original.

64. GA 7, p. 87; tr. 109.

65. GA 7, p. 87; tr. 109.

66. Heidegger, *Heralkit*, GA 55 (Frankfurt am Main: Vittorio Klostermann, 1979), 311 ff. See Michael E. Zimmerman, "Heidegger and Heraclitus on Spiritual Practice," *Philosophy Today* 28 (1983): 89.

67. See Schalow, *Heidegger and the Quest for the Sacred*, 138–39.

68. Foltz, *Inhabiting the Earth*, 23–35.

69. GA 65, p. 318; tr. 224.

70. GA 2, pp. 576–77; tr. 487.

71. GA 8, p 92; tr. 87.

72. GA 8, p. 6; tr. 6.

Index